TOWARD MORE SUSTAINABLE METAPHORS
OF WRITING PROGRAM ADMINISTRATION

TOWARD MORE SUSTAINABLE METAPHORS OF WRITING PROGRAM ADMINISTRATION

EDITED BY
LYDIA WILKES, LILIAN W. MINA,
AND PATTI POBLETE

UTAH STATE UNIVERSITY PRESS
Logan

© 2023 by University Press of Colorado

Published by Utah State University Press
An imprint of University Press of Colorado
1624 Market Street, Suite 226
PMB 39883
Denver, Colorado 80202-1559

All rights reserved

 The University Press of Colorado is a proud member of the Association of University Presses.

The University Press of Colorado is a cooperative publishing enterprise supported, in part, by Adams State University, Colorado State University, Fort Lewis College, Metropolitan State University of Denver, University of Alaska Fairbanks, University of Colorado, University of Denver, University of Northern Colorado, University of Wyoming, Utah State University, and Western Colorado University.

ISBN: 978-1-64642-305-7 (paperback)
ISBN: 978-1-64642-306-4 (ebook)
https://doi.org/10.7330/9781646423064

Library of Congress Cataloging-in-Publication Data

Names: Wilkes, Lydia, editor. | Mina, Lilian W., editor. | Poblete, Patti, editor.
Title: Toward more sustainable metaphors of writing program administration / edited by Lydia Wilkes, Lilian W. Mina, and Patti Poblete.
Description: Logan : Utah State University Press, [2023] | Includes bibliographical references and index.
Identifiers: LCCN 2022040212 (print) | LCCN 2022040213 (ebook) | ISBN 9781646423057 (paperback) | ISBN 9781646423064 (epub)
Subjects: LCSH: Writing centers—Administration. | English language—Rhetoric—Study and teaching (Higher) | Academic writing—Study and teaching (Higher) | College administrators—Vocational guidance. | Metaphor. | Sustainability.
Classification: LCC PE1404 .T688 2023 (print) | LCC PE1404 (ebook) | DDC 808/.0420711—dc23/eng/20220920
LC record available at https://lccn.loc.gov/2022040212
LC ebook record available at https://lccn.loc.gov/2022040213

Cover illustration from wallpaperflare.com

CONTENTS

Preface
 Lydia Wilkes, Lilian W. Mina, and Patti Poblete   vii

Introduction: Sustaining Our Programs, Sustaining Ourselves
 Lydia Wilkes, Lilian W. Mina, and Patti Poblete   3

SECTION I: ORGANIC RELATIONSHIPS

1. From Putting Out Fires to Managing Fires: Lessons for WPAs from Indigenous Fire Managers
 Lydia Wilkes   19

2. Seeing the Forest and the Trees: A Rhizomatic Metaphor for Writing Program Administration
 Jacob Babb   35

3. Light and the Quantum Physics of WPA Work
 Andrew Hollinger and Manny Piña   49

4. Grounding WPA Work: A Phenomenology of Program Development as a Liminal WPA
 Ryan J. Dippre   66

SECTION II: INSTITUTIONAL LANDSCAPES

5. The WPA as Labor Activist
 John Belk   83

6. Learning, Representing, and Endorsing the Landscape: WPA as Cartographer
 Katherine Daily O'Meara   97

7. Approaching WPA Labor with *Ahimsa*: Mapping Emotional Geographies through Sustainable Leadership
 Christy I. Wenger   123

8. Representing the Basement
   Alexis Teagarden   145

9. Interlocking Circles
   Cynthia D. Mwenja   157

SECTION III: PERFORMANCE CRAFTS

10. The Affordances and Risks of Artisanal Production as a Metaphor for Writing Program Administration
    Robyn Tasaka   177

11. "Building the Plane as We Fly It": Revising Our Thinking about Our First-Year Experience Program
    Rona Kaufman and Scott Rogers   199

12. I'm Just Playin': Directing Writing Programs as Improv
    Kim Gunter   215

Afterword: Sustaining What for Why?
Douglas Hesse   235

Index   243
List of Contributors   251

PREFACE

Lydia Wilkes, Lilian W. Mina, and Patti Poblete

Toward More Sustainable Metaphors was composed, reviewed, and revised prior to summer 2020, when the murders of Breonna Taylor, George Floyd, Ahmaud Arbery, and too many more people of color focused public and scholarly attention with renewed intensity on the deadliness of anti-Black racism and white supremacy in the US. To say that much has happened—and that much scholarship has been published—that affects WPAs, teachers of writing, and writing students; the CWPA as an organization; and the collective endeavor of writing instruction in the US between then and the moment you access this book is to understate the frenetic pace of events. Reflecting the cultural moments of 2018 and 2019, when the initial call for proposals circulated, authors contributed and revised their chapters, and the collection was reviewed, this collection does not focus explicitly on antiracism or the roles that metaphors play in sustaining, challenging, or dismantling racist structures within US education via writing program administration or writing instruction. Although antiracism and white supremacy were certainly important topics at the time, located primarily in conversations about racist judgments of language via assessment, they registered more as one set of topics among many than as *the* set of topics undergirding the systems and structures that sustain white supremacy in the spaces that we, all of us, occupy. The fact that white supremacy, and antiracist action to recognize and eliminate it, did not register as urgent in the time this collection came to fruition reveals yet again how pervasively the white racial habitus conditions scholarship within rhetoric, composition, and writing studies. We hope that readers imagine more sustainable metaphors of writing program administration in concert with antiracist scholarship.

With deep gratitude we thank the many people who made this collection possible. We thank the authors for their insightful contributions. We thank the WPAs who have gone before us and created pathways along which we have traveled to reach a point where this collection became possible to envision. We thank Rachael Levay at Utah State University Press for her enthusiasm about this collection from the beginning and for shepherding it through the publication process with great encouragement and kindness. We thank the two anonymous peer reviewers for their helpful suggestions, which have improved the collection.

This collection emerged from many generative spaces at the Council of Writing Program Administrators conference, first and foremost the WPA Workshop. We thank our workshop leaders and cohorts for inspiring this collection; you keep us hopeful about sustaining our WPA work through times of strife. CWPA was also an important site for circulating information about this collection. Susan Miller-Cochran's 2018 plenary address provided a kairotic moment for circulating the CFP and generating interest in the collection, and we thank her for her leadership and support for this collection from its beginnings.

We hope that the ideas in this collection inspire current and future WPAs to continue to do the challenging, rewarding work of writing program administration in ways that sustain people first.

TOWARD MORE SUSTAINABLE METAPHORS OF WRITING PROGRAM ADMINISTRATION

Introduction
SUSTAINING OUR PROGRAMS, SUSTAINING OURSELVES

Lydia Wilkes, Lilian W. Mina, and Patti Poblete

Writing program administrators (WPAs) have been using metaphors habitually to understand WPA work since the founding of the Council of Writing Program Administrators (CWPA) and the *WPA: Writing Program Administration* journal (hereafter *WPA* journal) in the 1970s. As Stephanie Roach (2019) notes in the *WPA* at Forty issue, "metaphor is a productive entry point into how WPAs understand and explain WPA identity. In naming our job as another job, we present . . . [an] argument about who we are" (15). Metaphors comparing WPA work to other occupations appeared often in the journal's first twenty years and helped WPAs establish, maintain, or shift identity, typically in solidarity with labor unions and workers' movements. By the time Diana George's collection *Kitchen Cooks, Plate Twirlers and Troubadours* appeared in 1999, lived experience as a site of knowledge-making also informed WPA metaphors, and authors discussed persistent problems like burnout and the continuous push of austerity, of doing more with less. Twenty years later, WPAs continue to define ourselves and our roles with the trope of metaphor as the scope and types of WPA work have expanded (e.g., Adams Wooten, Babb, and Ray 2018; Baker et al. 2005; Charlton et al. 2011; Enos and Borrowman 2008; Ratcliffe and Rickly 2010; Roach 2019).

Metaphors of writing program administration often feature a single person juggling, shepherding, plate-twirling, firefighting, or otherwise taking sole, shared-but-dysfunctional, or shared-and-functional responsibility for negotiating among different stakeholders' urgent, often contradictory demands (George 1999). Not only is this work exhausting and unsustainable (Hesse 2013), it evinces both the performative aspects at any given moment of becoming a WPA (Ratcliffe and Rickly 2010; see Hollinger and Piña, this volume, and Gunter, this volume) and what Donna Strickland (2011) calls the "managerial unconscious" of composition (3). Pervasive among composition scholars and WPAs who uncritically identify management with capitalism, the managerial unconscious describes a "default stance" of "traditional humanist intellectuals" who tend to "distrust management as, at best, nonintellectual and, at worst, soul-murdering" (2011, 10). With this default stance informing much WPA practice, as Tony Scott and Nancy Welch note, composition has not yet "developed understanding of how labor conditions shape pedagogy, scholarship, and the production of literacy and students' writing" (2016, 6), making the field "vulnerable to new entrepreneurial schemes" masquerading as "innovative" pedagogy (7). We WPAs need metaphors that resist inhumane labor conditions, metaphors like Robyn Tasaka's artisan (this volume) and John Belk's labor activist (this volume). While juggling and plate-twirling refer to performing arts on television talk shows and shepherding and cat-herding suggest pastoral and domestic settings, all of these metaphors index managerial activity—performative and frenetic activity, but no less managerial for being so.

Occupational metaphors mingle with managerial metaphors and mix with metaphors related to other WPA identities and roles. These identities and functions have accreted over the years to include "development" and "advocacy" roles (Hesse 2015, 134). Like Peace Corps Volunteers, WPAs perform (professional) development "to better teaching and learning by bringing advanced practices to classroom villages" while, like missionaries, WPAs also spread the good word about composition studies (we note deeply troubling resonances with ongoing settler colonialism). As advocates, WPAs focus on "resources, working conditions, and expectations," keenly aware of their effects on learning (2015, 134). An activist identity and role can be added to this list: an activist WPA works to shift institutional narratives through collective construction of knowledge and values (Adler-Kassner 2008). This accretion of WPA identities and roles has led to "more work . . . [and] different kinds" of it (Hesse 2015, 134), and to the emergence of more metaphors to describe the new work, identities, and roles.

This collection further expands the possibilities for understanding WPA identities and work by offering metaphors that help sustain our programs and ourselves through composition's (and higher education's) many crises. Whether these crises are within the bounds of human control, such as casualized labor or white supremacy, or beyond it, such as a pandemic or natural disaster, metaphors that generate more sustainable ways of being, doing, and becoming WPAs (Charlton et al. 2011; Hollinger and Piña, this volume) help us respond intentionally to crises as they (re)erupt. This collection originated as a response to ongoing crises of austerity and racism in writing programs highlighted in CWPA plenary addresses by Nancy Welch and Tony Scott in 2018 and Asao Inoue in 2016. Inspired by the CWPA Workshop's activity on metaphors, this collection focuses on the generative affordances of metaphorical thinking as authors ponder, propose, and research more sustainable metaphors. Sustainability of various kinds has interested composition scholars for decades and was featured as the theme of the 2015 CWPA conference. This collection combines these threads to generate new perspectives and lenses on WPA identities and work that help us navigate amid systemic anti-Black racism (Baker-Bell 2020; Inoue 2016; Perryman-Clark and Craig 2019), bullying (Elder and Davila 2019), and hierarchical microaggressions (Brewer and di Gennaro 2018), to name only a few challenges. We hope WPAs in all stages of their careers find the chapters in this collection generative as we are called to constantly adapt to shifting circumstances.

Since identities and roles interrelate, we are also suggesting a sustainability role for WPAs, a role WPAs perform when they advocate for conditions that sustain programs over time and attend to the health of all inhabitants in a program's ecosystem. We suggest this role hesitantly, wary of adding yet more work and another kind of it, all while sharing Seth Kahn's (2015) skepticism about the term "sustainability." As Kahn argued in his 2015 CWPA plenary, the word smacks of empty institutional initiatives that do more to sustain a dysfunctional, exploitative, toxic status quo than to attend to the health and well-being of all. More work of another, possibly dubious kind in a time when everyone is overworked seems decidedly unsustainable as an ask or a practice. Still, as Jonathan Alexander, Karen Lunsford, and Carl Whithaus (2020) note, "an analysis of the dominant metaphors of a given field of study might yield generative ways of understanding—and perhaps revisioning—a field's theoretical preoccupations and dispositions, primary objects of study, and orientations toward those objects" (106). As WPAs ourselves, we came to experience the challenges Kahn identified and critiqued. We also wanted to change the narrative surrounding our and other WPAs' work by charting new sustainable metaphors that may inspire WPAs and WPA scholars to "revision" WPA identities, work, landscapes, relationships, and performances.

Whenever a WPA plans for their professional future or their program's future—particularly a future for their program when they are no longer the WPA—that WPA enacts a sustainability-oriented identity and performs a sustainability role.[1] In short, many WPAs may already perform a sustainability role; more sustainable metaphors afford opportunities to deliberately build more sustainable identities. Thus we argue that creating, studying, and reflecting on more sustainable metaphors not only helps us reconsider our WPA work but also shapes our approaches and attitudes toward that work and how we experience both the short- and long-term significance and position of this work.

And yet, as Jacob Babb asks in his chapter, "is WPA work actually sustainable?" Drawing on data from the National Census of Writing, Babb observes that, although "some WPAs . . . have served for more than twenty years, the norm seems to be that most WPAs do not stay in their positions beyond five years." Rhizomatic networks cultivated by WPAs during this relatively short period of time tend to move with them and the work of cultivating a new rhizomatic network (or reestablishing one that has fallen out of use) lies with the new WPA. Further, as the beginning of *Writing Program Architecture* shows, external forces like the decades-old trend of state budget cuts to higher education can unmake successful programs, such as Shevaun Watson's first-year writing program at the University of Wisconsin–Eau Claire, in the wake of "draconian" budget cuts by the governor (White-Farnham and Finer 2017, 3). Similar blows have been dealt to state funding of higher education in Alabama, Arizona, Colorado, Georgia, Hawai'i, and almost every other state since 2008, resulting in cut programs, dismissed faculty, and soaring tuition (Mitchell, Leachman, and Saenz 2019). And that was before the pandemic worsened these trends and institutions began to dismiss faculty in greater numbers.

Certainly, these funding models are not sustainable; certainly, the increased casualization of academic labor is not sustainable; certainly, the racism endemic to white writing programs is not sustainable. So, as Elizabeth Boquet asked during her 2015 CWPA plenary, "what remains and what sustains" for WPAs? "Who and what," Boquet asked, "sustains us across time in doing the work our institutions call on us to do . . . [and] what remains of us—any of us, all of us—when we are gone, whether on a temporary or permanent leave-taking[?]" (95). To Boquet's questions we add: what practices, attitudes, frameworks, and heuristics sustain a WPA and program in a time when crisis rhetoric informs discursive and material conditions in higher education? What is a more sustainable metaphor? What role(s) might metaphors play for WPA work derived from a more ecological or sustainable orientation toward the world and its embodied inhabitants, given current conditions? The rest of this introduction answers these questions. But first: do WPAs even need more metaphors?

METAPHORS . . . AGAIN?

Far more than any other trope, metaphors dominate WPA identity talk. Stephanie Roach (2019) writes that "it is the nature of metaphor to help us understand something (or part of something) we don't fully understand via something else we more certainly do understand" (14) which gives metaphors "the power to show us something about the WPA position, capture something of how WPAs feel in that position, and imply something about our relationships to WPA work" (15). As anyone who has attended the CWPA Workshop can attest, metaphors both frame our work and reveal values and guiding principles that can be shared and applied in our programs. Moreover, the metaphors we use to describe our work carry not only our observations but their implications (Burke as cited in Alexander, Lunsford, and Whithaus 2020). As such, metaphors can be crucially important to the kind of "intentional" writing program administration advocated by Susan Miller-Cochran in her 2018 CWPA plenary address. This collection argues that WPAs need more sustainable metaphors for the "conflicted, liminal space" we occupy (Miller-Cochran 2018, 107). One such metaphor is Miller-Cochran's rocking chair, which affords listening, compassion, and a way to "lead a writing program without losing your soul," a metaphor that represents both perception and action, or observation and implication in Burke's terms. But Miller-Cochran's rocking chair is an exception, not the rule, in WPAs' talk of metaphors. Like Colin Charlton and colleagues in *GenAdmin: Theorizing WPA Identities in the Twenty-First Century*, we also find ourselves unsatisfied with the "metaphors that permeate our discipline" (2011, 127). We too "want to counter WPA narratives as 'war stories' and 'cautionary tales' with something more productive" (2011, 127), as Courtney Adams Wooten, Jacob Babb, and Brian Ray have done with travel as a guiding metaphor for WPA transitions. Hence this collection calls WPAs to (re)consider the metaphors that have been shaping and influencing our administrative work along critical, generative, and sustainable lines.

This collection also considers the risks of metaphor as a trope. Metaphors can "inadvertently mask differences" and thereby sustain a toxic status quo of inequitable power relations (Ratcliffe 2005, 92). In *Performing Feminism and Administration in Rhetoric and Composition*, Krista Ratcliffe and Rebecca Rickly prefer oxymoron to metaphor for feminist administrators, because oxymoron affords "the ability to keep two conflicting ideas in one's head at the same time and to engage that conflict as a springboard for productive feminist action" (ix). While metaphors are a central trope in this collection, oxymoron's sibling paradox also emerges as a theme (see, in this volume, Belk; Gunter; Hollinger and Piña). When considered critically, a metaphor's power to erase difference diminishes, though it still remains to some extent and can reify structures of oppression. To take a recent example, in "Administering while Black" Carmen Kynard relates her experiences of being treated by white faculty, staff, and students as "the help," experiences she organizes using the figure of the mammy. Crucially, the racist mammy stereotype is "more than just a metaphor" for her story "but an actual social mechanism that attempts to reproduce a certain kind of labor for black women" that, particularly when Black women are administrators, "brings the academy's antiblackness into stunning view" (2019, 37). Metaphors help us name oppressions, just as they help us name identities and roles, yet when we name oppressions we must be very careful to resist them, as Kynard does, not reify them. Because metaphors are so powerful, they must be handled and adopted with care as WPAs explore new or unexpected ways of thinking about WPA identities and roles afforded by metaphors.

WHY SUSTAINABILITY?

Sustainability is not a new idea in composition (see, e.g., Owens 2001). Is sustainability any more than the least we can do? Is it a sufficiently radical solution to a set of wicked problems? Kahn (2015) argues that the "sustainability trope" attempts to correct for environmental activism, as activism is too radical for corporatized capitalism: "Sustainability sounds more reasonable, more technocratic, than environmentalism and is, therefore, both more palatable and more vulnerable to cooptation" (113). While suspicious of the sustainability trope, Kahn nonetheless asserts that "thinking ecologically and sustainably can help us decide at moments like this [when labor is made casual] what layers of context are how important and to whom" (116). Kahn advocates for an expanded frame of sustainability that "makes room for an activist impulse" toward the health of an ecosystem (117), capturing the sort of sustainability that inspired the compilation of this collection:

> A concept of sustainability that focuses on life-sustaining inter-relations among all the members of an ecosystem is better. A concept of sustainability that isn't framed as defending the status quo from imminent destruction, or heaven forbid as resource management, is better. Ecology in our field is often another metaphor for *system*, one that evokes nature and dynamism and adaptability, but I want to push that one step further. Not only are the people who work with us in our programs and on our

campuses part of complex systems (and understand I mean that very inclusively: students, administrators, staff, all of us), but they're people (and so are we) whose lives and livelihoods often depend on the health of the environment. And it's really easy to lose sight of how connected we are within that environment. (115)

The more sustainable metaphors in this collection foreground connection, dynamism, adaptability, and negotiation with people across the complex local context of any campus to knit together those "life-sustaining inter-relations among all the members of an ecosystem." While only a few authors in this collection explicitly engage environmental ecologies, all consider relations in social and institutional ecologies.

This version of sustainability that works toward the health and well-being of all in an ecosystem implies work toward social justice (as a component of health and well-being). A key aspect of social justice is accountability, particularly the accountability of those with more privilege and power to those with less privilege and power. Sustainability and accountability can go hand in hand, as Kathleen J. Ryan shows in her application of ecological thinking to feminist writing program administration. She asserts that "ecological knowers are situated, embodied, interconnected persons whose recognition of the limits of perspectives positions them to be accountable for what they know and do because they are cognizant of the politics of location and relation" (2012, 78). Each chapter in this collection, whether it issues from an ecological orientation or not, embodies Ryan's ecological knowers, who are accountable to the complex systems in which they reside, survive, and, hopefully, thrive. These ecological knowers must be accountable to systemic racism within writing programs because WPA work "is always and already race work" (Perryman-Clark and Craig 2019, 9)—a fact that is often overlooked or quietly ignored because the "white racial habitus" thrives on invisibility (Inoue 2016, 146). The work toward sustainability and accountability is difficult and constant, yet, if we are invested in the health and well-being of all, it must be done, and done with care and compassion. Metaphors help us envision this work and guide its enactment. We hope that this collection inspires new thinking and feeling among WPAs everywhere so that all of us might work together toward our mutual flourishing.

MORE SUSTAINABLE METAPHORS OF WRITING PROGRAM ADMINISTRATION

We have organized this collection into three sections—Organic Relationships, Institutional Landscapes, and Performance Crafts—that showcase the relational, spatial, and performative aspects of contributors' more sustainable metaphors. We note that chapters speak to each other across sections and that a chapter in one section may also emphasize something named in another section, such as a relational metaphor that includes a heavy dose of performance or a spatial metaphor that also relies on relationships.

The Organic Relationships section begins with Lydia Wilkes's revision of the firefighter metaphor in chapter 1, "Revising the Firefighter Metaphor toward Sustainability: Lessons from Indigenous Fire Managers." Wilkes asserts that the commonly used phrase "putting out a fire" rests on a settler-colonial model of firefighting that obscures the many roles, both literal and figurative, played by fire. From a different set of assumptions about the values of land and education, she revises the firefighter into a fire manager, affording a responsive stance for WPAs toward many kinds of fire, some of which need to burn for new growth to occur. Wilkes examines the fire manager metaphor at different scales to suggest one more sustainable way of living with metaphorical fires in WPA work. In a similarly ecological vein, Jacob Babb offers a rhizomatic metaphor in "Seeing the Forest and the Trees: A Rhizomatic Metaphor for Writing Program Administration," in which "WPAs are trees, dwelling in forests of varying sizes," connected by an underground root system. Like tree roots, WPAs are always weaving "the complex web of relationships that [they] depend on to do their work," and this ecological perspective "remind[s] us that our work is far less solitary than it often feels." Cultivating and maintaining rhizomatic relationships with faculty, administrators, students, and the WPA community provides a WPA with the sustenance necessary to make WPA work more sustainable.

In "Light and the Quantum Physics of WPA Work," Andrew Hollinger and Manny Piña offer light "as a metaphor to frame, focus, and understand the work of a WPA." Drawing concepts like indeterminacy, emergence, and complementarity from quantum physics, Hollinger and Piña show that a WPA can never be determined in advance of a situated moment, because WPAs, like light, emerge differently depending on material intra-actions. Playing with light's paradoxical duality as *both* a particle *and* a wave (a configuration that is not possible in classical physics), the authors present their chapter in an unconventional way that performs their argument about duality and indeterminate, emergent, locally contextualized WPA identities. From fire to trees to light, Ryan Dippre considers the ground on which all rests. In "Grounding WPA Work: A Phenomenology of Program Development as a Liminal WPA," Dippre highlights how his jWPA (junior Writing Program Administrator) decisions were grounded in "the local needs and concerns of students, teachers, and the program," and how he "ground up" observational and interview data to inform his grounded writing program administration. Describing his experience as marked by uncertainty, trust, and mediation as he occupied liminal space as a jWPA, Dippre asserts that his "grounded" metaphor and the practices associated with it have sustained his working life as a liminal WPA.

The second section, Institutional Landscapes, highlights relationships within institutional contexts through spatial metaphors. John Belk's chapter "The WPA as Labor Activist" opens this section with "the literal labor activist . . . as a metaphor that encompasses the WPA's paradoxical orientations toward bureaucracy, management, curriculum, and personnel." Belk traces the foundational principles of American labor—radical collectivity, anti-exploitation, and diversity—as "roots [that] might serve as new key principles" for WPAs. These principles inform a heuristic for facing "the complex and often 'unwinnable' decisions of writing program administration," which he then applies to his work as a jWPA labor activist bound by sometimes contradictory principles and pragmatism.

Chapters 6 and 7 offer mapping practices for WPAs. Katherine Daily O'Meara forwards a metaphor of WPAs as cartographers in her chapter, "Learning, Representing, and Endorsing the Landscape: WPA as Cartographer." O'Meara's metaphor is fitting for WPAs because they always need to "plan for the futures of their programs, teachers, and students" using institutional maps that constantly change. Presenting two mapmaking scenarios from her career as a gWPA (graduate Writing Program Administrator) and jWPA, O'Meara discusses how her choice of metaphor facilitates the understanding of "the complex landscape of a writing program and other institutional writing spaces" and ultimately the development of better work relationships. Christy I. Wenger also employs mapping in her chapter, "Approaching WPA Labor with *Ahimsa*: Mapping Emotional Geographies through Sustainable Leadership." Ahimsa is "a skill of mindfulness" comprising a nonviolent way of being mindful or attentive from moment to moment in a nonjudgmental manner. Pointing to the often "unexamined and automatic emotional labor" WPAs perform, Wenger suggests ahimsa as a way to "identify the emotional geographies of their programs in order to create sustainable spaces that invite ongoing self-reflection."

Wenger's emotional geographies resonate with Alexis Teagarden's reclamation of the basement as a more sustainable space than the venerated Ivory Tower in her chapter, "Representing the Basement." Though the basement has been figured as a an undesirable space in both scholarship and popular culture, Teagarden rejects calls to move out of the basement or scrub it from WPA metaphors and instead suggests that "we embrace the idea of the basement as an inherently sustainable, inclusive space." Embracing the basement as a metaphorical space is ultimately a way for WPAs to "reimagine their program's place in the academy, a space that can help minimize traditional ills of isolation and hierarchy while also promoting the values of community and sustainability." Along similar lines, Cynthia D. Mwenja's chapter, "Interlocking Circles," closes the Institutional Landscapes section with a metaphor drawn from a student practice on her campus of using "circle metaphors to govern their group relationships and dynamics": one closed circle representing the strength of unity and one open circle welcoming newcomers. Circles provide a proactive, responsive space for mitigating conflict among a WPA's many stakeholders. Mwenja invites WPAs to consider themselves in overlapping and interconnected circles with their stakeholders, asserting that "interlocking circles of support" can "enhance our work in practical and sustainable ways."

The final section, Performance Crafts, emphasizes the performative, artisanal nature of WPA work. Robyn Tasaka, a tutor coordinator in a writing center, explores the affordances and risks of an artisanal production metaphor for tutor and instructor labor, training, and advertising. Drawing on Michael Pollan's work, Tasaka positions artisanal production as a sustainable alternative to exploitative mass production in higher education. Tasaka argues that, though this metaphor carries some risks, it affords the sort of self-definition necessary for smaller centers and institutions to distinguish themselves from their larger counterparts. Turning more explicitly to performance in their chapter, "'Building the Plane as We Fly It': Revising Our Thinking about Our First-Year Experience Program," Rona Kaufman and Scott Rogers reflect on their associate provost's use of the titular metaphor "in moments of structural upheaval or policy change." The metaphor does considerable work for the authors by "reveal[ing] the improvisational nature of our work" within curricular and campus constraints and exposing "the limitations and the risks of our work" even as it also resounds with hope. The thrill and urgency of continually building the plane as they fly it is ultimately a matter of perseverance for the authors because their "institutional lives depend on it." Continuing the theme of improvisation, Kim Gunter advocates for improvisational comedy as a parallel for WPA work in "I'm Just Playin': Directing Writing Programs as Improv." Although improv may appear chaotic, as Gunter notes, its success hinges on rules shared by other performers and on an improv WPA's internalization of those rules, willingness to play along, and repertoire of past performances. She emphasizes an embodied metic outlook of being present in the now rather than being cowed by precedent. Gunter suggests that the more experience WPAs gain through quick improvisation on the basis of their extensive knowledge of WPA literature and lore, the more effective they will be in their institutions.

Douglas Hesse's afterword, "Sustaining What for Why?," closes the collection by questioning the impetus to sustain WPA positions, work, and identities, and writing programs themselves. As WPA roles have evolved over the past forty years from a relatively accidental role in the 1970s to one sought intentionally by graduate students for the past decade or longer, Hesse worries that the project of "sustaining the construct of program administration," as professionals and professional societies are wont to do, may overtake the goal of "sustaining writers and writing." As he traces the energies, challenges, and metaphorical frameworks that have animated WPAs' livelihoods over the years, Hesse observes that WPAs would do well to follow Robyn Tasaka's lead in this collection and consider WPAs as artisans who rely on craft to produce unique artifacts. Beyond the artisanal metaphor, Hesse argues, lies that of WPA as writer of programs who drafts, revises, decides, collaborates, shares, and much more. Ultimately, Hesse concludes, "sustainability matters because writing matters, because citizens and societies benefit from writing done well and suffer from writing done poorly," and metaphors like those in this book can help WPAs continually strive toward the end of sustaining writers and writing.

NOTE

1. Two collections on WAC/WID (writing across the curriculum / writing in the disciplines) programs and WPA work emphasize program sustainability (Cox, Galin, and Melzer 2018; Reiff, Bawarshi, Ballif, and Weisser 2015) but do not focus on sustainable metaphors or administrative identities.

REFERENCES

Adams Wooten, Courtney, Jacob Babb, and Brian Ray. 2018. *WPAs in Transition: Navigating Educational Leadership Positions*. Logan: Utah State University Press.

Adler-Kassner, Linda. 2008. *The Activist WPA: Changing Stories about Writing and Writers*. Logan: Utah State University Press.

Alexander, Jonathan, Karen Lunsford, and Carl Whithaus. 2020. "Toward Wayfinding: A Metaphor for Understanding Writing Experiences." *Written Communication* 37 (1): 104–31.

Baker, Anthony, Karen Bishop, Suellynn Duffey, Jeanne Gunner, Rich Miller, and Shelley Reid. 2005. "The Progress of Generations." *WPA: Writing Program Administration* 29 (1–2): 31–57.

Baker-Bell, April. 2020. *Linguistic Justice: Black Language, Literacy, Identity, and Pedagogy.* New York: Routledge.

Boquet, Elizabeth. 2015. "What Remains and What Sustains: Companions in Mission, Colleagues in Action, WPAs for Life." *WPA: Writing Program Administration* 39 (1): 94–108.

Brewer, Meaghan, and Kristen di Gennaro. 2018. "Naming What We Feel: Hierarchical Microaggressions and the Relationship between Composition and English Studies." *Composition Studies* 46 (2): 15–34.

Charlton, Colin, Jonikka Charlton, Tarez Samra Graban, Kathleen J. Ryan, and Amy Ferdinandt Stolley, eds. 2011. *GenAdmin: Theorizing WPA Identities in the Twenty-First Century.* Anderson, SC: Parlor Press.

Cox, Michelle, Jeffrey R. Galin, and Dan Melzer. 2018. *Sustainable WAC: A Whole Systems Approach to Launching and Developing Writing across the Curriculum Programs.* Urbana, IL: NCTE.

Elder, Cristyn L., and Bethany Davila, eds. 2019. *Defining, Locating, and Addressing Bullying in the WPA Workplace.* Logan: Utah State University Press.

Enos, Theresa, and Shane Borrowman. 2008. *The Promise and Perils of Writing Program Administration.* Lauer Series in Rhetoric and Composition. West Lafayette, IN: Parlor Press.

George, Diana, ed. 1999. *Kitchen Cooks, Plate Twirlers and Troubadours: Writing Program Administrators Tell Their Stories.* Portsmouth, NH: Heinemann-Boynton/Cook.

Hesse, Douglas. 2013. "What Is a Personal Life?" In *A Rhetoric for Writing Program Administrators*, edited by Rita Malenczyk, 407–14. Anderson, SC: Parlor Press.

Hesse, Douglas D. 2015. "The WPA as Worker: What Would John Ruskin Say? What Would my Dad?" *WPA: Writing Program Administration* 38 (2): 129–40.

Inoue, Asao B. 2016. "Racism in Writing Programs and the CWPA." *WPA: Writing Program Administration* 40 (1): 134–54.

Kahn, Seth. 2015. "Towards an Ecology of Sustainable Labor in Writing Programs (and Other Places)." *WPA: Writing Program Administration* 39 (1): 109–21.

Kynard, Carmen. 2019. "Administering while Black: Black Women's Labor in the Academy and the 'Position of the Unthought.'" In Perryman-Clark and Craig, 28–50.

Miller-Cochran, Susan. 2018. "Innovation through Intentional Administration: Or, How to Lead a Writing Program without Losing Your Soul." *WPA: Writing Program Administration* 42 (1): 107–22.

Mitchell, Michael, Michael Leachman, and Matt Saenz. 2019. "State Higher Education Funding Cuts Have Pushed Costs to Students, Worsened Inequality." *Center on Budget and Policy Priorities*, October 24, 2019. https://www.cbpp.org/research/state-budget-and-tax/state-higher-education-funding-cuts-have-pushed-costs-to-students.

Owens, Derek. 2001. *Composition and Sustainability: Teaching for a Threatened Generation.* Urbana, IL: NCTE.

Perryman-Clark, Staci M., and Collin Lamont Craig. 2019. *Black Perspectives in Writing Program Administration: From the Margins to the Center.* Studies in Writing and Rhetoric. Urbana, IL: NCTE.

Ratcliffe, Krista. 2005. *Rhetorical Listening: Identification, Gender, Whiteness.* Carbondale: Southern Illinois University Press.

Ratcliffe, Krista, and Rebecca Rickly. 2010. "Introduction. Actions Un/becoming a Feminist Administrator: Troubled Intersections of Feminist Principles and Administrative Practices." In *Performing Feminism and Administration in Rhetoric and Composition*, edited by Krista Ratcliffe and Rebecca Rickly, vii–xv. Cresskill, NJ: Hampton Press.

Reiff, Mary Jo, Anis Bawarshi, Michelle Ballif, and Christian Weisser. 2015. *Ecologies of Writing Programs: Program Profiles in Context.* Anderson, SC: Parlor Press.

Roach, Stephanie. 2019. "Tools of the Trade: Occupational Metaphors in the First Decade of WPA." *WPA: Writing Program Administration* 42 (3): 12–19.

Ryan, Kathleen J. 2012. "Thinking Ecologically: Rhetorical Ecological Feminist Agency and Writing Program Administration." *WPA: Writing Program Administration* 36 (1): 74–93.

Scott, Tony, and Nancy Welch. 2016. "Introduction: Composition in the Age of Austerity." In *Composition in the Age of Austerity*, edited by Nancy Welch and Tony Scott, 3–17. Logan: Utah State University Press.

Strickland, Donna. 2011. *The Managerial Unconscious in the History of Composition Studies*. Studies in Writing and Rhetoric. Carbondale: Southern Illinois University Press.

Welch, Nancy. 2018. "'Everyone Should Have a Plan': A Neoliberal Primer for Writing Program Directors." *WPA: Writing Program Administration* 41 (2): 104–12.

White-Farnham, Jamie, and Bryna Siegel Finer. 2017. *Writing Program Architecture: Thirty Cases for Reference and Research*. Logan: Utah State University Press.

SECTION I

Organic Relationships

1
FROM PUTTING OUT FIRES TO MANAGING FIRES
Lessons for WPAs from Indigenous Fire Managers

Lydia Wilkes

I keep a map of a forest fire on my office wall to remind myself that, however often I say I'm putting out a fire, that fire is metaphorical.[1] As a member of GenAdmin (Charlton et al. 2011) still rather new to the annual fire season in the western United States, I remain intrigued by parallels and disjunctions between fighting physical fires and writing program administrators' talk of metaphorical firefighting. Metaphorical firefighting invoked by WPAs typically refers to solving urgent, unexpected problems so quickly that reaction, not response, characterizes the manner of addressing them. Such circumstances include issues related to racist policies for placing students and assessing their writing, sudden changes in enrollment or funding, shenanigans from the institutional powers that be, "managerial creep" and "state encroachment" on curriculum (Malek and Micciche 2017, 90), and a plethora of other problems. This kind of metaphorical firefighting resonates with residential firefighting: the house is on fire, so there is a rush to protect valuables, douse the flames, and minimize loss of life and property. "Putting out fires" suggests multiple metaphorical fires flaring up discreetly here and there more than it suggests interconnected fires. Perhaps that's one reason putting them out seems like an endless, sometimes lonesome, always frantic task.

A metaphor of residential firefighting assumes a settler-colonialist perspective of land as a commodity. Such a perspective extends to the education that occurs on the land, as the two are intimately connected.[2] This settler-colonialist perspective of land and education as commodities narrows the scope and context of our professional endeavors to our collective peril. Austerity measures in higher education that stem from the ongoing commodification of education as a private rather than public good continue to our collective peril (Welch and Scott 2016). Global warming—accelerated so rapidly by fossil fuel extraction and use in the past thirty years that a significant global temperature increase is not only unstoppable but will happen within the next few decades—continues to our collective peril (Wallace-Wells 2019). In short, both higher education and the planet itself are burning and will continue to burn for the foreseeable future. Both will look different in coming decades because fire does more than just destroy: it also transforms and creates.

WPAs who find themselves "putting out fires" need a revised, more sustainable metaphor of firefighting, one that issues from an Indigenous, ecological, decolonial understanding of land and human responsibilities toward land, a perspective that informs educational practices and institutions built upon land. Rather than viewing land and education from a Western perspective as private property or a commodity, Indigenous peoples—particularly the American Indian peoples emphasized in this chapter[3]—view land as a gift that entails a responsibility and generates a reciprocal relationship (Kimmerer 2013), a relational accountability we have to all our kin (Riley-Mukavetz 2020; Wilson 2008). I advocate for a shift from a settler-colonialist view of land and education as commodities to be controlled, including by diligent firefighters, to an Indigenous, decolonial view of land and education as existing in and for themselves in complex, reciprocal relationships that obligate humans to care for (and manage care for) specific human and nonhuman others. Like metaphorical trees in a metaphorical forest (Babb, this volume), WPAs as metaphorical firefighters are always nestled in complex networks of interrelated beings.

In revising the firefighter metaphor to a fire manager metaphor based on an Indigenous perspective of land and, by extension, education, I seek to bend WPA reactions to metaphorical fires toward critical management grounded in a few lessons from Indigenous fire managers. First, fire has transformative powers that land and institutions built on land need as part of periodic renewal (Lewis and Anderson 2002; Kimmerer 2013). Serious, in some cases existential, threats to first-year writing posed by precollege credit options, chronic and accelerating underfunding of higher education in many states, and other systemic problems require sustainability-minded administrators to consider these threats as part of an ecologically adaptive cycle (Ratliff 2019) in which fires, both physical and metaphorical, play a crucial transformative role. Second, humans who have forgotten fire's creative capacities must learn to live with fires, physically on an ever-warming planet (Tidwell 2014; Wallace-Wells 2019) and metaphorically in ever-tightening economic conditions in which, to take only one example, states have increasing economic interests in incentivizing or mandating precollege credit options like dual enrollment (Hansen and Farris 2010; Malek and Micciche 2017). A key lesson for living with fire is that some fires should be allowed to burn in order to clear new ground as part of a sustainable, adaptive process (Tidwell 2014; Kimmerer 2013). Finally, the fire manager metaphor—in contrast to the firefighter metaphor—means WPAs must make decisions at an ecological scale with an orientation toward both land and relational accountability (Riley-Mukavetz 2020; Wilson 2008) about which sparks to nurture, which brushfires to suppress or ignore, how to manage massive fires that threaten the most valuable or vulnerable aspects of a program, and what to expect and do after the earth has been scorched or when a flame kindled and nurtured is suddenly snuffed out. Intentional, principled response, not quick reaction, characterizes a fire manager's role in relation to fire.

After revising the firefighter metaphor to a fire manager metaphor, this chapter elucidates metaphorical fire management at a few different scales: national, state, and personal. It concludes by considering fire's decolonial and antiracist possibilities.

FROM FIREFIGHTER TO FIRE MANAGER: THE RISKS AND BENEFITS OF REVISING A METAPHOR

Metaphors have considerable capacity to reveal unexpected similarities and conceal or erase important differences (Ratcliffe 2005). The firefighter metaphor belongs to a class of first-responder and military-adjacent metaphors that buttress "the service image (if not the hero image) of the WPA" who "operate[s] on a regular basis in . . . crisis mode" (Charlton et al. 2011, 126). Fundamentally unsustainable, this metaphor of crisis response nonetheless remains quite popular, as do metaphors of war (Charlton et al. 2011, 127), which suggests an embattled, exhausted, and as I discuss later, burnt-out WPA. Are yet more metaphors worth the effort of revision when metaphors carry, along with the benefits of fresh insight, the considerable risk of reinforcing an oppressive status quo (Ratcliffe 2005)?

When metaphors are used carefully, with attention to important differences, the risk is worth it. To attend to some important differences, I must note that WPA work is not a matter of immediate life or death; the stakes and scope of WPA work and firefighting are hardly comparable. Further, as I, a white woman, revise a metaphor rooted in settler colonialism on the basis of Indigenous orientations toward land and fire management, I risk appropriating rich cultural traditions that white people have appropriated repeatedly in service of an oppressive status quo. An anthropologist, comparing social theories to drugs, humorously captures this risk: "Decolonialism is peyote. If you're not Indigenous or being guided by an Indigenous person, there's a high chance you're doing it wrong and are going to trip over your own ass and look like an idiot" (Argo 2019). Though Newe (Northern Shoshoni) elder Drusilla Gould, one of the first people to write the oral Newe language down (Gould and Loether 2002), guides me in Newe language and culture, very young children raised in traditional homes apprehend far more than I do. But it's worth the risk of tripping and looking ridiculous on the path to decolonial action within higher education, particularly if tripping leads one to pay closer attention to the land we all traverse.

It's also worth the risk of staying with metaphors. In addition to their longevity and popularity among WPAs, they reveal values and guiding principles. In her 2018 CWPA plenary, Susan Miller-Cochran notes that "starting with metaphors can help us dig beneath the surface to understand what our own guiding principles are," which is "the key to intentional administration and to navigating the conflicts that we inevitably experience" (111). Miller-Cochran connects her metaphor of a rocking chair to one of her guiding principles of administration, "to act with compassion" by listening in order to understand and perceive new possibilities. Pushing back on the sense of crisis and urgency that prompts the use of the firefighter metaphor, she argues that "being intentional in administration means being proactive, rather than just reactive" (116). Joyce Malek and Laura Micciche describe a similarly reactive stance as they relate a failure to get state policy makers in Ohio to hear their expert advice about precollege credit. They write: "State-mandated changes not only put us in a reactive stance, continually off-balance as we respond to crisis, but the changes also have the potential to threaten our faculty's livelihood" (2017, 89), something also at stake in Miller-Cochran's program at the University of Arizona and the program I administer at a midsize doctoral-granting university in the mountain West. I contend that the firefighter metaphor is most commonly used in the "off-balance," "just reactive" sense of trying to avert a crisis or minimize the damage. It needs revision.

FIRE MANAGER VALUES FROM AN AMERICAN INDIAN ORIENTATION TO LAND

A fire manager metaphor shares affinities with WPA work framed as location-specific and contextual (e.g., Ratcliffe and Rickly 2010), as well as with ecological and sustainable approaches to writing and WAC program administration (Cox, Galin, and Melzer 2018; Reiff et al. 2015; Ryan 2012). What's new here is an Indigenous, decolonial orientation to land rooted in relational accountability to land and people (Kimmerer 2013; Riley-Mukavetz 2020; Wilson 2008). In *Research Is Ceremony*, Shawn Wilson offers "one view of an Indigenous research paradigm" in which "relationships do not merely shape reality, they *are* reality" and "accountability to relationships" is the "shared aspect of an Indigenous axiology and methodology" (2008, 7). Drawing on Wilson, Andrea Riley-Mukavetz writes in *College Composition and Communication*, "I am going to encourage you, dear reader, to develop a rich, deep, and reciprocal relationship to the land you dwell on and the Indigenous people of that land—to carry those histories, cultures, and teachings with you in your writing, research, teaching, and everyday practice" (2020, 548). And, I would add, administration.

The fire manager metaphor rests on American Indian knowledge, values, and assumptions as part of an attempt to revive, metaphorically at least, the sustainable land-management practices that shaped the land over millennia of human action in relation to land (Lewis and Anderson 2002). A decolonial perspective of land based on Indigenous beliefs and practices offers lessons for WPAs that stem from an abiding sense of mutual responsibility. Robin Wall Kimmerer, who is Citizen Potawatomi (Aninshinaabe) and a botanist, provides a perspective on land held more or less in common across American Indian nations: "In the settler mind, land was property, real estate, capital, or natural resources. But to our people, it was everything: identity, the connection to our ancestors, the home of our nonhuman kinfolk, our pharmacy, our library, the source of all that sustained us. Our lands were where our responsibility to the world was enacted, sacred ground. It belonged to itself; it was a gift, not a commodity, so it could never be bought or sold" (2013, 17). Roxane Dunbar-Ortiz makes a similar point in *An Indigenous Peoples' History of the United States*: "Everything in US history is about the land—who oversaw and cultivated it, fished its waters, maintained its wildlife; who invaded and stole it; how it became a commodity ('real estate') broken into pieces to be bought and sold on the market" (2014, 1). For people who believe that land belongs to itself, that "[t]he world is constantly creating itself because everything is alive and making choices that determine the future" (Deloria Jr. 1999, 46), theft and desecration of land amounts to theft and desecration of world. But the people are still here, still asserting political and rhetorical sovereignty, still keeping traditional ways, and still attuning to all of the inhabitants of the world as they attempt to carry on traditions of sustainable land management.

This American Indian perspective of land situates humans as responsible for caring for land so as to enable the mutual flourishing of land and all its inhabitants—the original version of sustainability. As Kimmerer writes, "We are bound in a covenant of reciprocity, a pact of mutual responsibility to sustain those who sustain us" (382). Responsibility, care, and reciprocity are values of land from an American Indian perspective that govern the careful, respectful management of land with fire. Responsibility, care, and reciprocity resonate with values of ecological feminist administration (Ryan 2012), an approach to WPA work that I build upon as I discuss the affordances of metaphorical fire for metaphorical fire managers.

DIFFERENT AFFORDANCES OF METAPHORICAL FIRE

Fire as Threat

In addition to emphasizing relationality, care, and responsibility, an Indigenous perspective of land reorients firefighting and firefighters ecologically and affords metaphorical valences of fire that are not typically emphasized in contemporary Western culture. That is, contemporary Western culture tends to fear fire's destructive capacity and hence focus on fire as a devastator of land, human-built structures, and lives, both human and nonhuman (Kimmerer 2013). When WPAs refer to "putting out fires," we figure fire as destructive, a threat to be snuffed out immediately. For decades in the twentieth century, the US Forest Service mismanaged wildland fires in just this way by preventing them or rushing to put them all out as quickly as possible (Tidwell 2014), the same reactive but not responsive or intentional stance indexed by the phrase "putting out fires." Tanzania's government is making a similar mistake in their fire management by ignoring traditional Masaai burning practices (Butz 2009). The US has seen the results of mismanagement for the past few decades: larger, more frequent fires that, thanks to global warming, burn earlier, longer, and more intensely (Wallace-Wells 2019). Tanzania appears to be on the same path (Butz 2009). And, though the Amazon rainforest lost "a swath of jungle nearly the size of Lebanon" to wildfire in 2019, the rainforest may be threatened more by Brazil's agribusiness-friendly decision to relax protections that prevent aggressive deforestation (Sandy 2019). The continued pursuit of environmental destruction via resource exploitation only hastens global warming and results in hotter fires that burn longer. Fire is indeed a threat, and humans exacerbate it with colonialist and extractive capitalist practices. But fire is more than *just* a threat.

Governing agencies and many people worldwide have forgotten that humans lived with fire for much of our species' existence in "fire-adapted landscapes" that "evolved to burn" (Kaplan, Yi, and Sadof 2018). This forgetting stems in part from a settler-colonialist perspective of land as property to be bought and sold or a resource to be exploited: fire is a threat when land is a commodity, but when land belongs to itself, fire is much more than just a threat. Fire is needed to renew ecosystems adapted to it as part of an adaptive cycle.

Fire as Transformative Creation

Indigenous peoples across the planet learned long ago to live with fire and use fire responsively and responsibly to manage land. While I focus on American Indian fire management in this chapter, other Indigenous peoples—for example the Pemon in Venezuela (Sletto 2009), the Masaai in Tanzania (Butz 2009), and the Wik in Australia (Perry et al. 2018)—have used fire in similar ways to manage savannah, woodland, and open forest ecosystems (Butz 2009). Kimmerer's Citizen Potawatomi people "learned to set fires that were small and in just the right place and time so that they helped rather than hurt. The people set these fires on purpose, to take care of the land—to help the blueberries grow, or to make meadows for deer" (2013, 362). Her people's name means "People of the Fire": for her people, fire is "an amazing gift to carry in your pocket and a serious responsibility to be used well" (361). Kimmerer observes, "In modern times the public thinks fire is only destructive, but they've forgotten, or simply never knew, how people used fire as a creative force" (363).

The notion that fire can be a creative force may seem downright heretical to anyone steeped in putting out fires. To be clear, some metaphorical fires should be suppressed. For example, WPAs should fight the metaphorical fire of white-supremacist language standards and assessments that manufacture failure for "those historically most likely to suffer 'failures' in writing classrooms: students of color, multilingual students, and working class students" (Inoue 2014, 330). But WPAs also need to choose wisely which fires to fight—to the degree that WPAs get to choose—for we cannot fight them all and some we should consider fueling.

NATIONAL FIRES: AUSTERITY AND DUAL ENROLLMENT

The ecological principles behind Indigenous fire management, such as ecological resilience, have gained traction in response to Nancy Welch and Tony Scott's work on austerity, the national fire that is perhaps most existentially threatening to higher education's health. In a 2019 special issue of *Pedagogy* devoted to resilience in the age of austerity, Clancy Ratliff examines the resilience of the first-year composition requirement. She draws on ecological resilience as "the capacity of a system to withstand disturbance while still retaining its fundamental structure, function, and internal feedbacks" (285). This notion is based on "the simple premise that change is inevitable and that attempts to resist change or control it in any strict sense are doomed to failure" (285). An "adaptive cycle" emerges in which "resilience is built, maintained, threatened (and destroyed), and rebuilt" (285). Ratliff maps these four phases on to the history of first-year composition, arguing that "the adaptive cycle schema offers us a new narrative of the history of required FYC" that has "some explanatory power" (286), though of course neither she nor I means to suggest wholly literal equivalences.

After outlining the phases of building and maintaining FYW as a required course, Ratliff writes: "If . . . a resilient program needs strong faculty with the requisite job security and academic freedom to grow as teachers and researchers . . . then our system of required FYC is losing resilience" (288). She continues: "The question now becomes what to do if we are, in fact, truly in the midst of the release phase, which would destroy the FYC ecosystem as we know it and force reorganization" (289). Ratliff turns to the threats of dual enrollment and public disinvestment in higher education in Louisiana, which I also see as large wildfires burning across the US higher education landscape, fires fanned by frames of accountability, efficiency, and entrepreneurship keyed to economic growth in state and federal attempts to reform education (Welch and Scott 2016).

Ratliff is far from the first composition scholar to envision the end of the first-year composition requirement (see, e.g., Connors 1996; Crowley 1998). But unlike those in the abolitionist camp, Ratliff takes a reformist—or perhaps adaptive—position and offers "possibilities for adapting college writing to the present changes in higher education" (295), possibilities such as "tak[ing] ownership of dual-enrollment programs," "align[ing] with campus student success initiatives," "tak[ing] translanguaging seriously," and "pursu[ing] writing beyond the first year," among others (295–98). This reorganization of college writing ecosystems may happen alongside the destruction of the FYW requirement as it has existed since the nineteenth century, Ratliff suggests. "[I]f FYC is to remain a resilient student learning experience," she concludes, we must improve working conditions for the majority of contingent faculty who teach the course, and "we must redouble our efforts to share our knowledge as much as possible, with policy makers and with teachers and students at all levels" (299). As a WPA in Idaho, a state with a small human population distributed unevenly across a large landmass, I have witnessed as a latecomer some of the benefits of "relentless engagement with state educational policy reform" (Estrem, Shepherd, and Duman 2014, 88)—attempts to direct the flames of reform where they are most needed. Yet I have also witnessed metaphorical fires too massive to contain and glimpsed the human cost of containment efforts.

MANAGING THE FIRES OF STATE EDUCATIONAL REFORM

A fire manager approach to dual enrollment views it as emplaced in one or more feedback loops in an ecosystem in which disruption and change are inevitable aspects of an adaptive cycle that also includes human intervention. In Idaho, dual enrollment interacts not just with FYW at the handful of two- and four-year colleges and universities in southern Idaho but also with the English masters programs at Boise State University and Idaho State University, and Idaho State University's English PhD program, which together supply the lion's share of composition teachers in secondary and postsecondary environments across a large region with a geographically dispersed population. By dint of state incentives for precollege credit, degree-holders from these two universities' graduate English programs find themselves teaching the same students in a high school setting who would have, under different circumstances, taken first-year writing at a local college or university (if they went on to pursue higher education). When students with precollege credit do matriculate, they struggle to meet the demands of writing in a college context, suggesting a need for a vertical writing curriculum of some kind—a niche WAC/WID has attempted to fill for decades. So it goes in many states (Ratliff 2019). In Idaho, a history of collaboration across the small number (less than ten) of public postsecondary institutions enabled WPAs to channel a potentially destructive fire—state-standardized writing placement—to a creative path based on expert knowledge. The coalition-building espoused by Malek and Micciche (2017) in response to Ohio's WPAs' inability to get a hearing from state policy makers already exists across two- and four-year colleges and universities in Idaho, and to a lesser extent with high school teachers (Idaho ENACT 2016). Of course, coalition-building is easier in a less populous state like Idaho, which has a single K–16 school board.

Thanks to provocations from the State Board of Education, Idaho's WPAs do not work in isolation, just as fire managers never work alone:

fire managers collaborate with one or more teams of experts to make decisions. WPAs and English department chairs in Idaho have been meeting annually and collaborating across institutions since 2000, after the state ignored local context and standardized placement in 1999. Heidi Estrem, Dawn Shepherd, and Lloyd Duman (2014) note that "the regular gatherings also provided a forum to discuss other issues as they arose, from the rapid increase in dual-credit programs in the early 2000s to the sharing of course outcomes in first-year writing" and much more (95). The group relentlessly engaged with state educational policy via genres familiar to that audience, such as the white paper. Through its persistence, a multiple-measures placement system was developed at Boise State "that encourages student reflection and draws on faculty expertise" (Estrem, Shepherd, and Sturman 2018, 56), and it is now in use or in development at all but one of Idaho's public postsecondary institutions. Through collaboration Idaho's WPAs kept the inner fires of motivation burning long enough to enact change to writing placement based on disciplinary expertise. This victory is certainly not the norm; many other fires must be fought continuously. And not even collaboration can prevent the cost of continuous fire management: burnout.

PERSONAL FIRES AND BURNOUT

Burnout: a fire metaphor referring to an inner fire that has consumed all its fuel and died. For Kimmerer's Citizen Potawatomi people, the inner fire is a type of Sacred Fire, "the symbol of life and spirit," which people "must tend every day" because it is the "hardest one to take care of" (364). This creative inner fire of life and spirit can burn out if it is misused, just as fire can destroy the land it is meant to preserve if it is not carefully tended. Unlike exhaustion, which "means going to the point where you can't go any further," "burnout means reaching that point and pushing yourself to keep going, whether for days or weeks or years" (Petersen 2019). "You feel burnout," writes psychoanalyst and burnout expert Josh Cohen (2016), "when you've exhausted all your internal resources, yet cannot free yourself of the nervous compulsion to go on regardless," resulting in "chronic indecision," among other symptoms. The reactive, off-balance stance of the firefighter metaphor can feel like chronic indecision.

Burnout has been posited recently as a generational condition, but it was first identified in the 1970s (Petersen 2019) and has afflicted WPAs at least since that time. Mary Pinard (1999) lists the "plate-twirling . . . anxiety" of her first year as WPA and its inevitable result: "[n]aked power.

Power games. Broken promises. Funding cuts. Professional denigration. Slippery slopes. Fickle review standards. ESL, WIC, WAC, RAC, WC, PC. Burn out" (60). In the idiom of this chapter, Pinard had too many fires to fight by herself in the late 1990s. The trends she notes have only intensified since then. Carrie Leverenz, writing a decade later, notes the "urge to 'do more'" felt by feminist administrators for whom the phrase refers to the uphill battle of making institutional change in line with social justice (2010, 4). Doug Hesse (2013a) observes that rhetoric and composition has "collectively jacked up expectations for individual agency, success, and status, in ways difficult for all aspirants to achieve or the profession to sustain," particularly "when faculty now enter rhetoric and composition more by design and desire than by default" (18), as Hesse, Pinard, and many others did in the 1980s and 1990s. For new(er) faculty, attempts to live up to outsized disciplinary expectations while receiving less and less institutional support can only result in frustration, exhaustion, attrition, and for those who stay, eventual burnout.

WPAs may be especially prone to burnout because "[a] good deal of [WPA] work is intellectually stimulating and immediately rewarding. We feel important doing it, and we are" (Hesse 2013b, 409). But like other aspects of academic labor, "program development and leadership is inexhaustible. Unless one assumes simply a managerial, caretaking role, there is always something to be made bigger or better" (409). The impulse to make something bigger or better resonates with the broader capitalist desire for unchecked economic growth that, like densely growing trees in a forest where fire is absent, is no more sustainable than the "jacked up expectations" now ubiquitous in rhetoric, composition, and writing studies. Further, the purportedly independent agent responding to these expectations is constricted by austerity. For example, contingent faculty, who are more likely to be people of color and white women, face "pressure to perform the self as a 'good investment,'" a "'neutral,' competitive, masculine subject who can acclimate, compete, and win within established power structures" (Stenberg 2016, 191). A good fighter of certain fires for the institution's economic ends—perhaps rewarded as firefighter of the month—is not a manager of fire who takes on the responsibility to balance fire's creative and destructive capabilities from a decolonial perspective of land. That said, WPAs are not always (or even often) in a position to choose a fire manager approach because of these expectations about the performance of self, among many other constraints. Further, controlled burns managed by WPAs may be perceived as fires to be snuffed out by firefighters within an institution who want to protect the status quo. Sometimes WPAs are forced into the position of fighting fires, of being reactive, when we'd much prefer to be intentional. This conflict between a WPA's commitments and the realities of WPA work can be a source of burnout. When this happens, fire manager WPAs can turn to a community of WPA kin for support and to discuss the conflict at hand.

FIRE'S DECOLONIAL AND ANTIRACIST POSSIBILITIES

Given that we must learn to live with both physical and metaphorical fires, WPAs leading writing programs and writing centers amid firestorms would do well to center this perspective of land. Such work is difficult to do, though, because this perspective is far removed from the more familiar settler-colonialist perspective in which many powerful actors are heavily invested. For example, land-grant universities, often championed for opening access to higher education, act on land as though it were a commodity and written alphabetic literacy in Standard Edited American Academic English the coin of the realm, to the exclusion of land-based literacies so long cultivated by land's human caretakers (Rìos 2015), to note only one excluded literacy. As long as these values persist, those committed to doing decolonial and antiracist work in writing programs and writing centers will have to struggle mightily, just as their predecessors in the fight for justice have done. Thinking metaphorically with and through fire's transformative powers offers an important perspective on resisting and redressing racial and colonial oppression.

Some fires should be set to clear a path for new growth. The aspects of required FYW that perpetuate inequality, inequity, and injustice should burn. These aspects include assessments that value standardized English but not students' home languages or languaging practices; reliance on part-time, undercompensated labor to teach writing to the point of burnout; the overproduction of PhDs in spite of a scorched-earth academic employment landscape; and much more. To stay with the first, in his 2019 Chair's Address at CCCC, Asao Inoue advocated for destroying white language supremacy that constantly reinforces the racist status quo (2019, 353). Addressing his colleagues of color, Inoue said, "I hope I offer you fuel, words of charcoal and fire to go back to your schools and institutions and make things burn—melt the steel bars of racism and White language supremacy in your places" (2019, 356). Burning white language supremacy clears land for a different kind of flourishing: a flourishing of multitudinous languaging practices.

To manage fire, rather than just fight it, is to take on a responsibility for balancing its creative and destructive capabilities—as much as humans and WPAs can, given the limitations of our roles in the world—so as to enable mutual flourishing. This sustainable metaphor suggests a radically different way of living and acting that is more equitable in practice than current settler-colonialist, racist, capitalist ways of living and acting allow for, predicated as they are on exploitation and inequity. WPAs as critically and sustainability-minded fire managers might lose some things and people we care about to fires beyond our capacity to manage; in these cases, we mourn. We must also prescribe controlled burns to clear invasive, toxic aspects of a racist, sexist, homophobic, transphobic, capitalist status quo; these burns require careful monitoring. We must nurture sparks of equity and justice. We must advocate for rematriating the land to the traditional caretakers, the local tribes, because decolonization is not a metaphor (Tuck and Yang 2012).[4] We can and should listen and observe carefully so we might recognize possibilities for relational accountability emerging across the land and support each other's endeavors to turn possibilities into more equitable and just realities.

NOTES

1. The map, which shows the 2018 Sharps Fire near Hailey, Idaho, was given to me by a fire manager who had just finished three days of near-nonstop work directing night crews. Though he was exhausted and had finally reached an air-conditioned place to sleep, he talked with my friend and me for an hour about how intergovernmental agencies make decisions regarding wildfire containment, answering our questions about the maps he brought for the host (who was neither of us). He and all the hotshots, smoke jumpers, helicopter pilots, dozer operators, and myriad other personnel who work day and night to contain wildfires in the western US deserve more thanks than language can convey for undertaking this hazardous work. And people who are incarcerated who are tapped to fight fires by the State of California, for example, deserve far better treatment than they receive as they support fire crews who are far better compensated for their hazardous work.

2. Higher education, like all US institutions, was built on settler colonialism's "ideology of white supremacy," the "widespread practice of African slavery," and a "policy of genocide and land theft" (Dunbar-Ortiz 2014, 2). Indeed, land-grant universities were part of a larger colonial strategy to settle Indian country with non-Indian people in the nineteenth century so that, once settlers outnumbered Indians, a bid for statehood could be made in western territories (140–41). In stark contrast, traditional education in American Indian cultures occurs quite literally on land: people sit on the ground to tell stories, always connected with the earth. Land and nonhuman inhabitants existed before humans in American Indian traditions and are regarded as wiser, older beings who have much to teach those humans capable of taking a lesson. Robin Kimmerer writes, "in Native ways of knowing . . . humans are often referred to as 'the younger brother [sic] of Creation'" because "humans have the least experience with how to live and thus the most to learn—we must look to our teachers among the other species for guidance. Their wisdom is apparent in the way that they live. They teach us by example" (2013, 9).

3. Following the most common scholarly practice, I use "Indigenous" and "American Indian" interchangeably, though "Indigenous" is the broader category. I have preferred "American Indian" to "Native American" because of the former's resonance with the American Indian Movement. As Dunbar-Ortiz notes, "Indigenous individuals and peoples in North America on the whole do not consider 'Indian' a slur," but "all citizens of Native nations much prefer that their nations' names in their own language be used, such as Diné (Navajo), Haudenosaunee (Iroquois), Tsalagi (Cherokee), and Anishinaabe (Ojibway, Chippewa)" (2014, xiii–xix).

4. I am grateful to Cana Uluak Itchuaqiyaq (Iñupiaq) for the term *rematriation*, which I use in lieu of *repatriation* to recognize and remind that land in Indigenous cultures is not only figured as female but regarded literally as our mother. "We walk on our mother," says Newe elder Drusilla Gould. Like decolonization (Tuck and Yang 2012), rematriation is not a metaphor.

REFERENCES

Argo, Hilary. 2019. "Marxism Is Amphetamines, Biopolitics Is Cocaine: Social Science Theories as Drugs." *Raving Anthropology*, October 22, 2019. https://hilaryagro.word press.com/2019/10/22/marxism-is-amphetamines-biopolitics-is-cocaine-social-science -theories-as-drugs/.

Butz, Ramona J. 2009. "Traditional Fire Management: Historical Fire Regimes and Land Use Change in Pastoral East Africa." *International Journal of Wildland Fire* 18 (4): 442–50.

Charlton, Colin, Jonikka Charlton, Tarez Samra Graban, Kathleen J. Ryan, and Amy Ferdinandt Stolley, eds. 2011. *GenAdmin: Theorizing WPA Identities in the Twenty-First Century*. Anderson, SC: Parlor Press.

Cohen, Josh. 2016. "Minds Turned to Ash." *1843 Magazine (The Economist)*, June 29, 2016. Updated October 12, 2017. https://www.1843magazine.com/features/minds-turned-to -ash.

Connors, Robert J. 1996. "The Abolition Debate in Composition: A Short History." In *Composition in the Twenty-First Century: Crisis and Change*, edited by Lynn Z. Bloom, Donald A. Daiker, and Edward M. White, 47–63. Carbondale: Southern Illinois University Press.

Cox, Michelle, Jeffrey R. Galin, and Dan Melzer. 2018. *Sustainable WAC: A Whole Systems Approach to Launching and Developing Writing Across the Curriculum Programs*. Urbana, IL: NCTE.

Crowley, Sharon. 1998. *Composition in the University: Historical and Polemical Essays*. Pittsburgh, PA: University of Pittsburgh Press.

Deloria, Vine, Jr. 1999. *Spirit and Reason: The Vine Deloria, Jr., Reader*. Golden, CO: Fulcrum.

Dunbar-Ortiz, Roxanne. 2014. *An Indigenous Peoples' History of the United States*. Boston, MA: Beacon Press.

Estrem, Heidi, Dawn Shepherd, and Lloyd Duman. 2014. "Relentless Engagement with State Educational Policy Reform: Collaborating to Change the Writing Placement Conversation." *WPA: Writing Program Administration* 38 (1): 88–128.

Estrem, Heidi, Dawn Shepherd, and Samantha Sturman. 2018. "Reclaiming Writing Placement." *WPA: Writing Program Administration* 42 (1): 56–71.

Gould, Drusilla, and Christopher Loether. 2002. *An Introduction to the Shoshoni Language: Dammen Daigwape*. Salt Lake City: University of Utah Press.

Hansen, Kristine, and Christine R. Farris. 2010. *College Credit for Writing in High School: The "Taking Care" of Business*. Urbana, IL: NCTE.

Hesse, Doug. 2013a. "Sustainable Expectations?" *College Composition and Communication* 65 (1): 16–18.

Hesse, Douglas. 2013b. "What Is a Personal Life?" In *A Rhetoric for Writing Program Administrators*, edited by Rita Malenczyk, 407–14. Anderson, SC: Parlor Press.

Idaho ENACT. 2016. First-Year Writing Across Idaho. https://sites.google.com/a/boise state.edu/fywacrossidaho/idaho-enacts.

Inoue, Asao. 2014. "A Theory of Failure in US Writing Assessments." *Research in the Teaching of English* 48 (3): 330–52.

Inoue, Asao B. 2019. "2019 CCCC Chair's Address: How Do We Language so People Stop Killing Each Other, or What Do We Do about White Language Supremacy?" *College Composition and Communication* 71 (2): 352–69.

Kaplan, Sarah, Joy Yi, and Karly Domb Sadof. 2018. "Caught in the Inferno: How the Camp Fire Overwhelmed Paradise." *Washington Post*, November 12, 2018. https://www.washingtonpost.com/graphics/2018/national/amp-stories/how-the-camp-fire-overwhelmed-paradise/.

Kimmerer, Robin. 2013. *Braiding Sweetgrass: Indigenous Wisdom, Scientific Knowledge, and the Teachings of Plants.* New York: Milkweed Editions.

Leverenz, Carrie. 2010. "What's Ethics Got to Do with It? Feminist Ethics and Administrative Work in Rhetoric and Composition." In *Performing Feminism and Administration in Rhetoric and Composition*, edited by Krista Ratcliffe and Rebecca Rickly, 3–18. Cresskill, NJ: Hampton Press.

Lewis, Henry T., and M. Kat Anderson. 2002. Introduction to *Forgotten Fires: Native Americans and the Transient Wilderness* by Omer C. Stewart, 3–16. Norman: University of Oklahoma Press.

Malek, Joyce, and Laura R. Micciche. 2017. "A Model of Efficiency: Pre-College Credit and the State Apparatus." *WPA: Writing Program Administration* 40 (2): 77–97.

Miller-Cochran, Susan. 2018. "Innovation through Intentional Administration: Or, How to Lead a Writing Program without Losing Your Soul." *WPA: Writing Program Administration* 42 (1): 107–22.

Perry, Justin J., Melissa Sinclair, Horace Wikmunea, Sidney Wolmby, David Martin, and Bruce Martin. 2018. "The Divergence of Traditional Aboriginal and Contemporary Fire Management Practices on Wik Traditional Lands, Cape York Peninsula, Northern Australia." *Ecological Management & Restoration* 19 (1): 24–31.

Petersen, Anne Helen. 2019. "How Millennials Became the Burnout Generation." *BuzzFeed News*, January 5, 2019. https://www.buzzfeednews.com/article/annehelenpetersen/millennials-burnout-generation-debt-work.

Pinard, Mary. 1999. "Surviving the Honeymoon: Bliss and Anxiety in a WPA's First Year, or Appreciating the Plate Twirler's Art." In *Kitchen Cooks, Plate Twirlers and Troubadours: Writing Program Administrators Tell Their Stories*, edited by Diana George, 56–62. Portsmouth, NH: Boynton/Cook.

Ratcliffe, Krista. 2005. *Rhetorical Listening: Identification, Gender, Whiteness.* Carbondale: Southern Illinois University Press.

Ratcliffe, Krista, and Rebecca Rickly. 2010. "Introduction. Actions Un/Becoming a Feminist Administrator: Troubled Intersections of Feminist Principles and Administrative Practices." In *Performing Feminism and Administration in Rhetoric and Composition*, edited by Krista Ratcliffe and Rebecca Rickly, vii–xv. Cresskill, NJ: Hampton Press.

Ratliff, Clancy. 2019. "The Adaptive Cycle: Resilience in the History of First-Year Composition." *Pedagogy: Critical Approaches to Teaching Literature, Language, Composition, and Culture* 19 (2): 283–300.

Reiff, Mary Jo, Anis Bawarshi, Michelle Ballif, and Christian Weisser. 2015. *Ecologies of Writing Programs: Program Profiles in Context.* Anderson, SC: Parlor Press.

Riley-Mukavetz, Andrea. 2020. "Developing a Relational Scholarly Practice: Snakes, Dreams, and Grandmothers." *College Composition and Communication* 71 (4): 545–65.

Ríos, Gabriela Raquel. 2015. "Cultivating Land-Based Literacies and Rhetorics." *Literacy in Composition Studies* 3 (1): 60–70.

Ryan, Kathleen J. 2012. "Thinking Ecologically: Rhetorical Ecological Feminist Agency and Writing Program Administration." *WPA: Writing Program Administration* 36 (1): 74–93.

Sandy, Matt. 2019. "'The Amazon Is Completely Lawless': The Rainforest after Bolsonaro's First Year." *New York Times*, December 5, 2019. https://www.nytimes.com/2019/12/05/world/americas/amazon-fires-bolsonaro-photos.html.

Sletto, Bjørn. 2009. "'Indigenous People Don't Have Boundaries': Reborderings, Fire Management, and Productions of Authenticities in Indigenous Landscapes." *Cultural Geographies* 16: 253–77.

Stenberg, Shari. 2016. "Beyond Marketability: Locating Teacher Agency in the Neoliberal University." In Welch and Scott 2016, 191–204.

Tidwell, Tom. 2014. "Learning to Live with Fire." Forest Service, US Department of Agriculture. https://www.fs.fed.us/speeches/learning-live-fire.

Tuck, Eve, and K. Wayne Yang. 2012. "Decolonization Is Not a Metaphor." *Decolonization: Indigeneity, Education & Society* 1 (1): 1–40.

Wallace-Wells, David. 2019. *The Uninhabitable Earth: Life after Warming*. New York: Tim Duggan Books.

Welch, Nancy, and Tony Scott. 2016. *Composition in the Age of Austerity*. Logan: Utah State University Press.

Wilson, Shawn. 2008. *Research Is Ceremony: Indigenous Research Methods*. Black Point, Nova Scotia: Fernwood Publishing.

2
SEEING THE FOREST AND THE TREES
A Rhizomatic Metaphor for Writing Program Administration

Jacob Babb

> *"I think for a job to be sustainable, it has to be intellectually stimulating, which means that we're doing new stuff. And it's hard to do new stuff if nobody trusts you and you don't have good relationships with people."*
>
> —John

WPAs have generated numerous metaphors in an effort to depict the kinds of work we do. In her review of occupational metaphors used in the first ten years of *WPA: Writing Program Administration*, Stephanie Roach (2019) asserts, "In naming our job as another job, we present a point of view and argument about who we are" (15). Diana George's influential collection *Kitchen Cooks, Plate Twirlers and Troubadours* (1999) shares many of these metaphors, marking an important effort for WPAs to explore the boundaries of their personal and professional lives. However, many of the metaphors WPAs have created emphasize the negative, exhausting aspects of the work, making WPA work out to be tedious and reactive and presenting WPAs as particularly prone to overwork and burnout. While all of these negative connotations can certainly be aspects of WPA work, we benefit from taking care in selecting the terministic screens that we use to present our work to our disciplinary and institutional colleagues, our students, and ourselves as we make arguments about who we are. As Charlton and their coauthors (2011) write, the "metaphors that permeate our discipline are unsatisfying to us. We want to counter WPA narratives as 'war stories' and 'cautionary tales' with something more productive" (127).

With Charlton and colleagues' charge to counter such narratives and the call of this collection's editors to develop metaphors for sustainable WPA work in mind, I offer a rhizomatic, ecological metaphor: WPAs are trees, dwelling in forests of varying sizes. This chapter highlights the rhizomatic nature of WPA work through a combination of analysis of data from the National Census of Writing (2017) and case studies of five WPAs at different kinds of institutions. The case studies, based on interviews with those WPAs, will map the connections they depend on to do their work. The chapter demonstrates how being mindful of these connections can make WPA work more sustainable, rewarding, and visible. As John notes in the epigraph,[1] WPAs must cultivate relationships built on trust to enable them to do their work.

Although the responsibilities of WPAs are just as varied as the kinds of programs they administer, the kinds of work WPAs do often center on behind-the-scenes labor to make sure that programs run as smoothly as possible. Indeed, much of our labor is invisible when done well, even if that efficient invisibility creates problems by making it difficult for people in our departments and institutions to recognize our labor's value. Melissa Ianetta (2015) argues, "Too much of my day and my achievements are unseen or diminished when I try to render them in the categories my colleagues embrace" (148). As academics who exist in the blurry space of teachers, administrators, and scholars, WPAs have long felt compelled to argue for and defend the value of their work.

As a self-identified member of GenAdmin—someone who specifically trained to be a writing program administrator and who considers WPA work an integral part of my scholarly identity—I know how important it is to make my work visible, and I am compelled by this collection's call to develop more sustainable metaphors for WPA work to acknowledge just how exhausting such demonstrative work can be. At the heart of the need to make our work visible is the implicit acknowledgment that academics are valued on an individual basis. When I filed my annual reports or submitted my tenure and promotion dossier, I was making claims about the work *I* do. But as leaders of their programs, WPAs must think in the plural: WPAs must consider our work in terms of what *we* (WPAs, writing teachers, and departmental and institutional colleagues) do rather than what *I* do. The work of WPAs is fundamentally relational.

I would like to use this chapter as an invitation to consider the complex web of relationships that WPAs depend on to do their work and to make that relationship-based work just as visible as we are expected to make our individual labor. WPAs are members of a complex ecological system of writing professionals, students, administrators, and staff members who comprise our institutions. Kathleen J. Ryan (2012) urges us to "theorize writing program administration more fully in terms of place and ecology to create new understandings of how they function epistemologically and rhetorically for WPAs" (75). She argues that thinking about how our place and ecology function supports our agency as WPAs as well as "the entire enterprise as students, teachers, and colleagues develop a sense of connection and commitment to one another, the program, and the campus community and environment" (92). My proposed metaphor can help us to enact such an ecological perspective, reminding us that our work is far less solitary than it often feels.

I posit that WPA work is most sustainable when we are mindful of our connections to those we work with and for—to see the roots that are often invisible in our daily work. WPAs can do nothing in isolation. Our impact is based on our rhizomatic relationships in our institutions and beyond. What power we have as WPAs comes from our capacity to build on our relationships, the roots that we slowly intertwine in and beyond our institutions. These roots connect us to the broader forest in which we live, and we need to see those roots clearly and frequently to sustain our work.

BUT FIRST, IS WPA WORK ACTUALLY SUSTAINABLE?

Before examining the case studies and the insights they offered on the relationships WPAs cultivate, I question whether WPA work is sustainable for individuals over long periods of time. According to the National Census of Writing, the vast majority of WPAs do not maintain their roles for more than ten years, with most serving in those roles for five years or fewer. Based on questions from both the Two-Year Institutional Survey and the Four-Year Institutional Survey, the majority of WPA respondents had occupied their positions for one to five years, with the second-largest group of respondents occupying their positions for six to ten years. These results remain consistent across different kinds of WPA work, including directing programs in writing across the curriculum, writing in the disciplines, and basic writing.[2] See table 2.1, which displays the census results for how many years respondents had directed or administered first-year writing programs and writing centers at two- and four-year institutions.

These numbers demonstrate a sharp decline following five years. At two-year institutions, 61.11 percent of FYW directors have occupied the role for one to five years, which decreases to 12.96 percent during the sixth to tenth years, while the 47.66 percent of writing center directors (WCDs) serving from one to five years decreases to 22.42 percent between the sixth and tenth years. The four-year data follows a similar trend. While there are certainly exceptions, as demonstrated by the survey results showing some WPAs who have served for more than twenty

Table 2.1. Comparison of number of years respondents held positions directing first-year writing programs and writing centers at two- and four-year institutions

	FYW at Two-Year Institutions (n=108)	FYW at Four-Year Institutions (n=388)	WC at Two-Year Institutions (n=107)	WC at Four-Year Institutions (n=394)
< 1 year	10	42	13	45
	9.25%	10.82%	12.14%	11.42%
1–5 years	66	194	51	164
	61.11%	50%	47.66%	41.62%
6–10 years	14	96	24	95
	12.96%	24.74%	22.42%	24.11%
11–15 years	8	37	11	46
	7.4%	9.53%	10.28%	11.67%
16–20 years	8	18	5	28
	7.4%	4.63%	4.67%	7.1%
20+ years	4	13	4	28
	3.7%	3.35%	3.73%	7.1%

years, the norm seems to be that most WPAs do not stay in their positions beyond five years.

The rationale for WPAs to phase out of their positions in such relatively short periods of time can be complicated, although one of the easiest explanations for WPAs transitioning out of the role is burnout. Numerous fields have conducted research on the relationship between jobs and burnout (see Crocetti et al. 2014; Fernet et al. 2010). Scholarship on burnout often focuses on teachers, whether at the K–12 or postsecondary levels (see Acheson et al. 2016; Montgomery and Rupp 2005; Santoro 2011), while other scholars focus on burnout and research (see Tregoning and Baker 2015) or burnout and emotional labor (see Erickson and Ritter 2001). Writing about burnout among nursing faculty, John R. Phillips (1984) describes a "cycle favoring burnout" that moves from enthusiasm through boredom that "dampens creativity, and lack of creativity generates boredom" (1525). Faculty lives exist in cycles based on semesters, quarters, and academic years, making it unsurprising that burnout features as a typical complicating factor of academic life.

The phenomenon of burnout among WPAs deserves more scholarly attention. In this chapter, I characterize *burnout* as a term that covers a multitude of reasons that could lead WPAs to transition out of their roles, covering the varying mental, emotional, and physical tolls that administrative work can have on individuals. During the interviews conducting in this study, several participants invoked either fear of or reaction to burnout in their responses, and their concerns undoubtedly contribute to how they approach their work. However, we must remain mindful of Amy Vidali's (2015) critique of WPA narratives that represent anxiety and depression "as caused by WPA work" and marked as "intolerable and curable" (37). Vidali asserts that such narratives leave little space for the work of disabled WPAs who contend with such conditions consistently, thus making for a "chilly climate for disability in WPA work" (37). Further, other causes than burnout, however broadly construed, could lead WPAs to choose to leave their work. Recent scholarship has drawn attention to bullying in the WPA workplace (see Elder and Davila 2019) and microaggressions in English departments (see Brewer and di Gennaro 2018). Writing about mobbing as a form of bullying in her department, Amy Heckathorn (2019) writes, "What we rarely document and discuss . . . is a situation when disciplinary disrespect is so vast and deep that action is no longer possible and we must stop our work" (165). What these scholars' work demonstrate is that the reasons WPAs leave their roles are complex and varied. While bullying and microaggression undoubtedly contribute to burnout, the field benefits from seeking more nuanced explanations than the catchall phrase *burnout* can provide.

Regardless of the reasons WPAs transition out of their positions, it is disappointing to see individuals rotate out of those roles after such a short time, given how much work most WPAs must do to cultivate rhizomatic networks on their campuses. Or rather, while in the abstract, five years does not seem like such a long time, on the individual level, five years can be a highly significant amount of time. As I write this chapter, I have occupied my WPA position for five years, all during my pretenure period, and I am soon transitioning out of the role. While I love directing the writing program at my institution, I am ready to do different kinds of work as a faculty member, and I am ready for my writing program to have another vision at the helm for a while. While it is likely that I will return to the role after a few years away—the statistics above suggest perhaps within five years, as my successor likely decides to step away from the role—my newly tenured status may lead me to some other administrative role. In either case, I would still draw on the network of relationships that I cultivated as a WPA, so I am not simply discarding the time and emotional labor that went into connecting with others; I will utilize those connections from a new position, grafting my experience to new limbs. I offer myself as an example because I think my desire to do new things in my work is reasonably typical of those who fill these roles. However, my example alone is not particularly significant. For the remainder of this chapter, I will explore how WPAs cultivate and rely on relationships within and beyond their institutions to make their work sustainable, by analyzing interviews with five WPAs.

METHOD FOR STUDYING WPAS' RHIZOMATIC RELATIONSHIPS

For this study, I decided to interview WPAs to get a sense of the kinds of ecologies they worked within and the kinds of relationships they found most important to their work. I selected participants for these interviews with the intention of capturing examples that represent a broad range of experiences, from types of institutions to the amount of time occupying those roles. My selection process for participants was, as I found appropriate to the subject of the study, based on my relationships with others in the WPA community. I contacted seven WPAs who are in different stages of their careers, from junior to senior faculty, and at different kinds of institutions to invite them to participate in the study. I invited directors of first-year writing programs, WAC/WID programs, and writing centers. Two of those invited were unable to participate in the study at that time, leaving me with five participants in the study.

Four out of five of the participants administer first-year writing programs, which seems disproportionate given the varying types of WPA positions. However, according to the National Census of Writing, 67 percent of four-year respondents and 61 percent of two-year respondents administer first-year writing programs;[3] my sample thus includes a higher-than-average percentage of first-year writing directors compared to the national data, but it is not outlandishly high. Further study would benefit from including a range of participants involved in administering different sites of writing.

The following are brief sketches of the participants' positions:

- John administers a first-year writing program at a small, public community college. He is a tenured faculty member who has directed the writing program for more than fifteen years.
- Linda administers a first-year writing program at a large, public research institution. She is a pretenure WPA in her first year in this role, although she has served as WPA at another institution.
- Sarah directs a writing center at a large, private research institution. She holds a non-tenure-track position and has directed the writing center for three years.

- Andrew administers a first-year writing program at a public regional university. He is a tenured faculty member who has directed the program for five years, and he has served as a WPA at another institution.
- Leslie administers a first-year writing program at a public comprehensive university. She is a pretenure WPA in her third year.

I developed two points of contact with each participant: a questionnaire and an interview. When a WPA agreed to participate in the study, I sent them a questionnaire that included ten questions for them to answer in writing and scheduled a video interview with them. Using the questionnaire, I sought to gather information about how participants defined the work that came with their positions and what kinds of relationships they formed with writing professionals in the programs, administrators, students, and WPAs at other institutions.

I asked participants to submit their written responses to the questionnaire at least two days before our scheduled interviews. After reading their responses, I generated codes for the kinds of patterns that emerged and developed a list of follow-up questions tailored to each participant. I sent participants their follow-up questions the day before our interviews to provide them with time to consider their responses, although I told them that they did not need to prepare responses if they lacked time or inclination.

Each interview lasted approximately thirty minutes and was conducted via video. With each participant's permission, I recorded and then coded the videos as I did the questionnaires, analyzing the data for trends and patterns. While multiple trends could be extrapolated from their responses, I have elected to focus on three areas that seem particularly illuminating regarding how the participants see their relationships to others: working with faculty and administrators, working with students, and working with the WPA community.

WORKING WITH FACULTY AND ADMINISTRATORS

Andrew, a recently tenured associate professor, notes that an unexpected effect of earning tenure was a sense of belonging to his campus. Describing a shift from a driving focus on his own work prior to tenure, he says he can be "more of a team player, quite frankly," and that "[t]his is not just where I work now, but this is my institution, and we've got a lot of work to do. I've really got some skin in the game now." Both Andrew and John have been at their institutions for several years, and both have served as WPAs for several years, with Andrew in his sixth year and John well beyond his tenth.

All of the participants emphasized the importance of establishing good relationships with instructors in their programs. John reflects on his title, writing program coordinator, as an indicator of how he should function in his program: "I started thinking more and more about that title, and *coordinator* suggests collaboration, not autocracy." Much of his role focuses on working with faculty members on curriculum development, and John finds that collaboration is crucial to his success as a WPA: "If we feel connected to the department and we feel as though we've had a voice in the curricular decisions of the department, then we're more likely to teach better." His use of the inclusive pronoun *we* points to how deeply his administrative philosophy is informed by collaboration. John also underscores the importance of being visible across the institution through committee work: "I view committee work as a way to get myself out in front of people and let them see that I care about the college and work hard. It's good for administrators to see that I'm there, because it pays dividends when it's time for me to ask for support for the writing program."

Both Linda and Sarah also describe the importance of collaboration in their positions, although more specifically with their colleagues who comprise a larger WPA team. Linda describes herself as "the center of a wheel that understands the spokes branching out of it," someone who aims to make space for a number of voices involved in running a very large writing program. As a newcomer to her institution, Linda notes both the benefits and challenges of such relationships: "It's tricky trying to figure out, is my position one where I'm trying to help everyone talk to each other and collaborate? At what point does my own vision interfere with that?" Like many WPAs, Linda is seeking a careful balance between providing direction and support. Sarah, who is a member of a larger team, finds comfort in that role: "[W]e are all pretty close and we work very collaboratively—not necessarily because we have to, but because that's just the norm."

Andrew, who has until recently been the sole compositionist at his institution, describes himself as the "catchall WPA," who has had to seek out opportunities to collaborate with others on his campus. He also expresses frustration with administrators' lack of awareness of what he does as a WPA, telling a story of being introduced by an upper administrator as the writing center director: "I have never served as the director of the writing center on my campus. I think this is an interesting symptom of a larger bureaucratic and conceptual problem." He does not feel that administrators on his campus have a good sense of what he does, and he takes it as part of his role to educate administrators about good writing practices and pedagogy, a role that he feels is challenging enough without being confused with the writing center director. The negative example he offers demonstrates how much of a difference it can make to maintain strong connections with administrators—other trees in the complex ecological system of our institutions—although his example also demonstrates that some of this work lies beyond the purview of WPAs, who cannot be the only ones who cultivate these relationships.

WORKING WITH STUDENTS

The most surprising finding of this study, perhaps, is the limited relationship that all five WPAs felt they had with undergraduates.[4] Several participants noted that they only interacted with undergraduates, at least in their capacities as WPAs, from a managerial perspective. Linda writes that her undergraduate interactions are based on requests for courses to be waived or repeated, acknowledging that "[s]adly, these interactions are not always positive because they involve difficult situations or things that undergraduates are frustrated about." Andrew's department chair handles student complaints, but he says that he hears "more of the complaints that originate with adjunct faculty regarding students," reinforcing the importance of the WPA for supporting writing instructors, even if in this case the WPA serves as something of a pressure-release valve. Answering more succinctly, when asked what kinds of interactions he has with students, John responds, "Not really any." The brevity of the response seems to echo in the chasm that separates most WPAs from undergraduate students.

Sarah, the WCD among my participants, offered a different perspective on working with undergraduates, although she first acknowledged that her role does not lead to regular interactions beyond managerial tasks: "I don't actually interface with (nontutor) student writers all that much" beyond addressing student complaints and issues using the online scheduling system. However, she has extensive experience working with undergraduate tutors, seeing "supporting tutors" through training and ongoing professional development as her primary work as a WCD. Among the participants, Sarah has the most positive interactions with undergraduate students, via tutor training. While our work as WPAs focuses first and foremost on the success of undergraduate students, we have little direct interaction with undergraduates in our administrative capacities.

Three of the participants have stronger relationships with graduate students, primarily because of their involvement with training and mentoring graduate teaching assistants and tutors. Sarah states that she sees graduate tutors' work "as essential professional development" before they move on to teach. In addition to training graduate tutors, Sarah also teaches a summer course that all first-time TAs across the disciplines must take. Sarah describes her work with graduate students as a rewarding aspect of her work as a writing center director. Similarly, Linda characterizes her work with graduate TAs as "generally more positive" than her interactions with undergraduates as WPA, "although it can be challenging." She describes the importance of a productive relationship with the director of graduate students "to make sure this is a good experience for both the TAs themselves and for the students in their classes." The importance of professional development for graduate students reflects all of the WPAs' work to provide professional development for the instructors and tutors in their programs. Their comments echo the importance of what Richard C. Gebhardt (2002) calls "macrolevel teaching" (35), of WPAs functioning as teachers of teachers. Even if in their day-to-day activities WPAs do not regularly engage with the undergraduates their programs serve, they provide support and writing pedagogy educational opportunities for the instructors and tutors who do interact with those students routinely. Perhaps here we can most clearly sense how the relationships WPAs cultivate with instructors function like roots running below the surface, supporting the ecosystem of the forest even when unseen. WPAs' macrolevel teaching functions to distribute disciplinary knowledge and expertise through the ecosystem as nutrients that enrich the soil in which writing students learn.

WORKING WITH THE WPA COMMUNITY

One of the recurring themes in the participants' responses was how important it is for WPAs to think about how their work aligns with their research. Their comments on methods for maintaining a productive research agenda suggest a need for developing research interests that grow out of or at least coincide with their work as WPAs. I put such emphasis here on the connections between WPA work and research because the participants' engagement in research appears to be reflective of their involvement and engagement with the WPA community and how vital this rhizomatic connection to the greater ecosystem of higher education can be. WPAs can draw sustenance from roots that extend beyond the rhizomatic relationships they form at their own institutions.

Four of the participants commented on the importance of establishing a synergistic relationship between WPA work and teaching. Linda, a pretenure WPA at a research-intensive institution, asserts that WPA work is a "double-edged sword" because administrative work can often have a deleterious effect on time for research and writing, a problem that is especially pronounced for pretenure WPAs, newly planted in their institutional forests. She negotiates this by "centering a lot of [her] research around WPA work, which helps blend these and make WPA work do double duty." Leslie, the other pretenure WPA among the participants, expresses a similar approach to a reciprocal relationship between research and administrative work: "luckily for me, ALL of my current research projects are directly related to my work as a WPA," but she also expresses some frustration in connection to research: "I prioritize basically everything before my own writing, because I see myself as a teacher and an administrator first and a writer second." Both John and Sarah comment that there is no research expectation for their positions, which they find in many ways liberating as they are able to determine their own research pace. Andrew, whose "research interests have traditionally been outside of WPA work and theory," argues that it would be helpful for anyone entering WPA work to "try to meld their research interests with their work as a WPA," echoing the other participants even as he acknowledges that his research interests lie elsewhere.

Participants also point to the need to cultivate and maintain professional relationships beyond their institutions to invigorate their work as WPAs. Linda notes that maintaining friendships with WPAs from other institutions "is very important to [her] in keeping perspective on things, especially in thinking about things that happen all over the place instead of being unique here," continuing to remark that many of those WPAs have become mentors who can help with advice on research and WPA issues.

John and Leslie stress the importance of CWPA as a source of professional support for their work that helps to sustain their intellectual interests and their research goals. John states, "CWPA has been really vital to me. These are my people. CWPA is very collaborative," and then describes how the organization helped him to engage in reading and producing scholarship to keep his position from becoming "just managerial." Leslie states that she is "forever grateful to be a part of CWPA, a professional community like I've never seen before." She also notes the importance of her connections with mentors and colleagues from her alma mater and the new relationships she forges by mentoring new WPAs.

Andrew, who is not as active in the broader WPA community, points toward a group of WPAs from his university system who meet regularly as an important avenue for interaction with other WPAs, noting that such meetings "have been immensely useful to me, and I would like to do this more often." His comments on research and on community, when contrasted with the other four participants, again highlight how vital it can be to cultivate relationships with WPAs from other institutions. These relationships fulfill numerous needs for WPAs, including mentorship, collegiality, friendship, and scholarly collaboration. The forests in which WPAs cultivate their academic lives extend beyond the borders of our own institutions.

SEEING THE FOREST AND THE TREES

As WPAs, we benefit from intentionally mapping our ecologies within our programs, our institutions, and our discipline. Being mindful of our relationships with others can help us not only to potentially do our work better but also to nurture the relationships that help us to grow. We are trees in a vast forest, and we need the sustenance of that interconnection and interrelation. The data I shared from the National Census of Writing suggests that WPAs almost inevitably face burnout (what could trees fear more than burning?), and while such intentional mapping of our rhizomatic relationships may not completely prevent that, it could help to mitigate some of the more negative emotional labor associated with writing program administration. Our lives as faculty members are cyclical, which we can use to our advantage by capitalizing on the relationships we build.

For example, as I write this chapter, I am currently a coeditor of *WPA: Writing Program Administration*, CWPA's journal, and a coeditor of two collections on writing program administration. The scholarly and editorial work involved in these positions has allowed me to form numerous connections with WPAs across the globe, and I consistently rely on those nodes of contact that form part of my own rhizomatic network, not just to help me do my own work as a WPA scholar but also to form a sense of comradery with others who face the same kinds of challenges I do and who take similar pleasure in the work. Like John and Leslie, I also credit CWPA as a major contributor to my ongoing growth as a member of the field. Like Andrew, I look forward to conversations with WPAs at other institutions in my university system. Even the "co-" prefix in the editorial roles I identify in this paragraph demonstrates how important connection and collaboration are to my own work. The WPA community is a vital part of my forest, and while I may be stepping away from my WPA position soon, I have no doubt that I will return to the position or assume another role that presents me with similar kinds of labor. This study suggests that WPAs share the sense that rhizomatic connections to other WPAs are important to their work.

Writing about her own WPA metaphor, a rocking chair, Susan Miller-Cochran (2018) describes the importance of listening: "one of my biggest responsibilities as an administrator is to listen to others while they share with me their thoughts, ideas, and concerns. When I listen, I understand more" (111). Her remark draws attention to the importance of tending to the relationships that energize our work as WPAs. We listen to others to understand. I would extend that metaphor to include listening to ourselves as we determine what makes WPA work sustainable for us.

When I first developed the concept of a rhizomatic metaphor for WPAs, I thought about the implied binary in the aphorism "can't see the forest for the trees," a binary that suggests people can only see at either the individual or collective level. However, for WPA work to be sustainable, we must be able to do both as we take stock of the relationships that make our work possible. The other consistent thread among the participants' responses was the concept that we must look after ourselves. Linda, who is especially adept at maintaining boundaries between her professional and personal life, observes, "I think often we can really lose sight of ourselves." Almost all of the participants commented on the need to make time for some combination of exercise and leisure activity to prevent being overwhelmed by WPA work. As someone who has held a WPA position for five years now, I strongly agree. Our labor will always be there, waiting for us, and we are all better able to serve our programs and the forests they exist within when we tend to ourselves. We may never attain the Zen-like status of Bob Ross's "happy little trees," but we can become trees that draw on the strength of the rhizomatic structure of our relationships with faculty, administrators, students, and our WPA colleagues to make our work more sustainable.

NOTES

1. Of the five participants in this study, two requested anonymity. Therefore, I have opted to use pseudonyms for all participants.
2. I embrace a broad definition of the term WPA that includes directors of writing across the curriculum and writing in the disciplines programs, directors of undergraduate majors in writing, and many others. The National Census of Writing, seeking to alleviate a narrow interpretation of the term WPA, approaches this challenge by establishing a spatially based approach by defining a WPA by "which site of writing [a] person administers rather than by the generic term writing program administrator."
3. In the demographics section of the two-year and four-year surveys, 108 out of 178 two-year respondents and 410 out of 612 four-year respondents direct first-year writing.

4. I should clarify that participants were asked to describe their interactions with students as WPAs rather than as teachers. All five participants teach undergraduate writing courses. I suspected their interactions with students as teachers are different than their interactions as WPAs, a suspicion confirmed by their responses.

REFERENCES

Acheson, Kris, Justin Taylor, and Kera Luna. 2016. "The Burnout Spiral: The Emotional Labor of Five Rural U.S. Foreign Language Teachers." *Modern Language Journal* 100 (2): 522–37.
Brewer, Meaghan, and Kristen di Gennaro. 2018. "Naming What We Feel: Hierarchical Microaggressions and the Relationship between Composition and English Studies." *Composition Studies* 46 (2): 15–34.
Charlton, Colin, Jonikka Charlton, Tarez Samra Graban, Kathleen J. Ryan, and Amy Ferdinandt Stolley. 2011. *GenAdmin: Theorizing WPA Identities in the Twenty-First Century.* Anderson, SC: Parlor Press.
Crocetti, Elizabeth, et al. 2014. "Personal and Social Facets of Job Identity: A Person-Centered Approach." *Journal of Business and Psychology* 29 (2): 281–300.
Elder, Cristyn L., and Bethany Davila, eds. 2019. *Defining, Locating, and Addressing Bullying in the WPA Workplace.* Logan: Utah State University Press.
Erickson, Rebecca J., and Christian Ritter. 2001. "Emotional Labor, Burnout, and Inauthenticity: Does Gender Matter?" *Social Psychology Quarterly* 64 (2) 146–63.
Fernet, Claude, Marylène Gagne, and Stéphanie Austin. 2010. "When Does Quality of Relationships with Coworkers Predict Burnout over Time? The Moderating Role of Work Motivation." *Journal of Organizational Behavior* 31 (8): 1163–80.
Gebhardt, Richard C. 2002. "Administration as Focus for Understanding the Teaching of Writing." In *The Allyn and Bacon Sourcebook for Writing Program Administrators*, edited by Irene Ward and William J. Carpenter, 34–37. New York: Longman.
Heckathorn, Amy. 2019. "The Professional *Is* Personal: Institutional Bullying and the WPA." In Elder and Davila, 151–71. Logan: Utah State University Press.
Ianetta, Melissa. 2015. "Absence and Action: Making Visible WPA Work." *WPA: Writing Program Administration* 38 (2): 141–58.
Miller-Cochran, Susan. 2018. "Innovation through Intentional Administration: Or, How to Lead a Writing Program without Losing Your Soul." *WPA: Writing Program Administration* 42 (1): 107–22.
Montgomery, Cameron, and André A. Rupp. 2005. "A Meta-Analysis for Exploring the Diverse Causes and Effects of Stress in Teachers." *Canadian Journal of Education* 28 (3): 458–86.
National Census of Writing. 2017. Accessed March 22, 2019. https://writingcensus.swarthmore.edu/.
Phillips, John R. 1984. "Faculty Burnout." *American Journal of Nursing* 84 (12): 1525–26.
Roach, Stephanie. 2019. "Tools of the Trade: Occupational Metaphors in the First Decade of WPA." *WPA: Writing Program Administration* 42 (3): 12–19.
Ryan, Kathleen J. 2012. "Thinking Ecologically: Rhetorical Ecological Feminist Agency and Writing Program Administration." *WPA: Writing Program Administration* 36 (1): 74–93.
Santoro, Doris A. 2011. "Good Teaching in Difficult Times: Demoralization in the Pursuit of Good Work." *American Journal of Education* 118 (1): 1–23.
Tregoning, Catherine and Paul Baker. 2015. "How to Undertake Research without Suffering Burnout." *BMJ: British Medical Journal* 351. doi.org/10.1136/bmj.h3932.
Vidali, Amy. 2015. "Disabling Writing Program Administration." *WPA: Writing Program Administration* 38 (2): 32–55.

3
LIGHT AND THE QUANTUM PHYSICS OF WPA WORK

Andrew Hollinger and Manny Piña

> "[I]ntra-activity is neither a matter of strict determinism nor unconstrained freedom. The future is radically open at every turn."
> —Karen Barad, "Posthuman Performativity: Toward and Understanding of How Matter Comes to Matter"

> "We choose to examine a phenomenon which is impossible, absolutely impossible, to explain in any classical way, and which has in it the heart of quantum mechanics. In reality, it contains only the mystery."
> —Richard Feynman

DUALITY

Isaac Newton believed light to be made of corpuscles, ether-like particles that traveled in straight lines. Although phenomena like refraction and diffraction were difficult to explain, it was obvious that light did not move through tubes or around corners the way sound does (Tretkoff 2008). Surely, light comprised particles.

The polymath Thomas Young, however, could not ignore the difficulties, and in 1801 devised an experiment to demonstrate a phenomenon that, over a century later, Richard Feynman (2013) would describe as "impossible, *absolutely* impossible, to explain in any classical way, and which has in it the heart of quantum mechanics" (p. 1–1). Young covered a window in paper with a single, small hole cut from it. As a beam of light shone through, he slid a thin card into the beam so that it split into two beams. Against the wall, instead of two discrete points of light, which a corpuscle theory predicts, the beams spread out and interfered with each other to create an

Donna Strickland argued for the managerial unconscious of the WPA, an argument that "the managerial has been an integral part of the development of the field" (2011, 4). Although "manager" was admittedly problematic, it was obvious that WPAs scheduled sections, filed paperwork, organized programs, and so on. Surely, the WPA was/is a manager.

At the same time, Charlton et al. argued that WPAs are "always in the process of becoming" (2011, 106) as opposed to *being*, and that "a becoming philosophy . . . emerge[s] from the choice to be engines of dissensus who continually learn to manage such an identity" (216) as continually shifting and diverse as "WPA." That is, *surely* the WPA is also scholar; surely the WPA is also advocate; surely the WPA is also teacher; surely the WPA is also—

In the 1960s, during his famous lectures, Richard Feynman (2013) declared that "Yes! physics has given up" (p. 1–10). He was

interference pattern of light and shadow (Tretkoff 2008). He would later, as would many physicists, recreate his experiment using two slits in a screen (see below). Light was certainly made of waves.

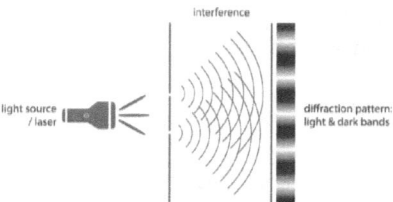

Figure 3.1. A diagram of the double-slit experiment showing interference pattern.

A hundred years after Young's experiments, scientists like Max Planck were studying the photoelectric effect in which individual electrons bounced off metal when light was directed at it. Albert Einstein first theorized that electromagnetic energy travels in packets of energy, which we now call *photons*, a discovery that earned him the 1921 Nobel Prize in Physics. Light, as it turned out, was certainly *also* particles. Einstein explains:

> But what is light really? Is it a wave or a shower of photons? There seems no likelihood for forming a consistent description of the phenomena of light by a choice of only one of the two languages. It seems as though we must use sometimes the one theory and sometimes the other, while at times we may use either. We are faced with a new kind of difficulty. We have two contradictory pictures of reality; separately neither of them fully explains the phenomena of light, but together they do (Einstein and Infeld 1939, 262–263).

To understand light, we must engage it as *both* wave *and* particle. Anything less is to misunderstand it.

discussing a quantum extension of Thomas Young's double slit experiment, this time with electrons instead of light. There is no way to predict the exact outcome and location of an electron, which is largely what Physics sets out to do: articulate the world as it is in order to know it and accurately anticipate the future. It seems that much WPA scholarship similarly seeks to articulate our rhetorical situation as it is in order to know it so that we might direct our futures. But how might we do that? How could we? Are WPAs enough alike that understanding one would allow us to generalize to the field? Or is there no way to predict the exact outcome of any WPA's efforts?

If writing programs are ecologies (and we think they are) and "emergence is what self-organizing, complex ecologies produce" (Reiff et al. 2015, 9), it follows that whatever the WPA is and does emerges from the relationships between the WPA and the curriculum, and the faculty, and the university structure, and the political climate, and student needs, and-and-and-and. Perhaps it is productive to borrow from and revise Einstein:

> It seems as though we must use sometimes one theory and sometimes another, while at times we may use any. We are faced with a new kind of difficulty. We have contradictory pictures of reality; separately no theory fully explains the rhetorical ecology and positionality of a/an/the WPA, but together they do.

To understand WPA work, we must engage *both* its contexts *and* the interconnected relationships that emerge from those contexts. Anything less is to misunderstand it.

PARTICLES, WAVES, AND WPAS

In their 2009 survey of the "WPA's progresses," Jonnika Charlton and Shirley Rose found that in the preceding twenty years there had been an "evolution," so to speak, of the conceptions of writing program administrator. Specifically, they find that what a WPA "is" had shifted away from commonplace job descriptions and monolithic responsibilities and more toward emergent and varied identities, that "there is not one narrative, but many" of WPA work (138). In our own lives, we are two WPAs who occupy strikingly similar professional positions at vastly different institutions: one of us a WPA at a large public R1-emergent university and the other at a small private liberal arts university. We feel daily the full weight of our professional experiences that are, at once, both parallel and divergent. That is, we recognize in our own lived experiences the diverse "portraits" of WPA work for which Charlton and Rose argue. For example, we both live out the "managerial functions" (Strickland 2011) typically associated with writing program administration, such as scheduling and mentoring a diverse faculty of full-time and part-time contingent labor. Further examining our portraits, we observe that one of us has, quite literally, no institutional authority to make decisions regarding section assignments (but instead makes recommendations to the department chair), whereas the other of us regularly assigns faculty (including tenured and tenure-track [T/TT], full-time non-tenure-track [FT-NTT], adjunct, and graduate instructors) to writing program sections. Additionally, one of us works with a relatively stable pool of full-time contingent faculty while the other has to navigate a more itinerant instructional staff; in addition to coordinating writing programs, both of us are ourselves non-tenure-track, full-time faculty that are, technically, considered "contingent"; we are both subject to navigating the paradox of administering the business side of a writing program in an age of austerity (Schell 2016, 178) wherein our professional voices are occasionally affected by our contingent status. We could continue parsing our portraits for similarities and differences. However our portraits overlap and diverge, though, the caption under each is, simply, "WPA." But again, what this actually looks like is itself contingent, indeterminate outside of our own locally constituting factors (compare this with Gunter's characterization of the WPA as "indeterminate, emergent, and provisional" improvisation, this volume). Our dual professional lives stand as a testament to Charlton and Rose's assertion that there is, in fact, no *determinate* portrait or narrative within which we can categorize or understand our work.

Therein lies the point: our simultaneously parallel yet wholly divergent experiences as WPAs demonstrate that even these diverse portraits of WPA narratives are, themselves, unstable, subject to local contingencies shifting from place to place and moment to moment. The National Census of Writing (Gladstein, 2013) confirms these diverse portraits: while 83 percent of reporting WPAs at four-year institutions are tenured or tenure-track (T/TT), 10 percent of writing programs are coordinated by NTT-FT faculty, 1 percent by NTT-PT (non-tenure-track part-time) faculty, 3 percent by hybrid faculty/staff positions, and 2 percent by full-time staff; at two-year institutions, 79 percent of WPAs are T/TT, while

7 percent of writing programs are coordinated by NTT-FT and 14 percent by hybrid faculty/staff positions. Some WPAs are "coordinators" and some are "directors" and some are "chairs" with other administrative duties. Whatever a WPA *is* seems to be necessarily constrained to the conditions and contexts in which a WPA is observed (there are many iterations of WPA and this one is mine). Add these shifting local settings to the various and specific requirements and possibilities of the job within those settings *and* our own professional and personal agendas, and what a WPA is and what it looks like becomes difficult to describe.

More to the point, what can explain why there are so many different kinds of WPA portraits? We return to light. Working behind and through the camera, governing aspects of color and pigment (if you prefer a painted portrait), affecting the scene and the subject, allowing us to *see*—is light.

We propose *light* as a metaphor to frame, focus, and understand the work of a WPA. Not only do the properties of quantum light speak to the dynamic, emergent, and performative dimensions of a WPA,[2] but light also supports many other metaphors operating within the field, including the metaphor of portraits, and speaks to its own potential sustainability and versatility.

COMPLEMENTARITY

The double-slit light experiment presents classical Newtonian physics with a deeply troubling paradox: the unassailable and observable reality that light demonstrates the physical properties of both particles and waves in turn. Perhaps Kenneth Burke (1984) was suggesting something far more material and physical when he argued that "a way of seeing is also a way of not seeing—a focus upon object A involves a neglect of object B" (70). The problem for classical physics is, like classical rhetoric with its often singular focus on *the* speaker or *the* audience, that classical physics dictates that a thing, such as light, cannot be both a particle *and* a wave. Light is incompatible with classical physics because in the classical sense "particles are localized objects that occupy a given location at each moment in time," while waves have an "entirely different nature: they are not even properly entities but rather disturbances in some medium or field" (Barad 2007, 100). Particles and waves, then, are mutually exclusive categories of being, and, as such, have different sets of determinate (and incompatible) characteristics. In and of themselves, these classical categories are unproblematic—as long as particles act like particles and not like waves, and vice versa. Light, however, troubles these categories because it is able to act as both a particle *and* a wave.

If we now frame a WPA as light, we find that they too may be incompatible with classical theorizations of program administration and writing pedagogy. The "classical" thinking (if there is such a thing) about WPAs is that writing program administration is knowable outside of a given moment in space and time. How often are program profiles or WPA scholarship presented in determinate ways that suggest they have something that could be replicated across any programmatic context? The truth is that as soon as we focus on a trait of WPA (management or curriculum development, perhaps), we make a choice not to see, even if only for a moment, the other characteristics that comprise the materiality, enactment, and emergence of *an/Other* WPA. Moreover, as a field we seem to also implicitly apply a determinate identity onto WPA work. The problem is not the ability to conceive of a WPA as something other than manager or curriculum developer. Instead, the problem is precisely the tendency to see the WPA in determinate ways, as an "essence," so to speak. Even classical physics could conceive of waves and particles, but it was not able to reconcile something being both/and. How, then are we to understand light and the WPA as both particle and wave? Or, perhaps a better question: why could they be *either*?

Quantum physics, it turns out, offers an elegant and rather simple solution to the philosophical complications posed by the double-slit experiment. The resolution, however, entails nothing less than a radical rethinking of our fundamental commitment to representationalism,[3] as well as of the assumed relationship between epistemology and ontology, which are often held to operate independently of each other. In other words, to understand how light—and writing program administration (WPA) work—can harmoniously exist in mutually contradictory states, we need to first call into question the classical assumption that objects have individual and independently existing determinant attributes or that we will ever be able to do more than piece together evidence *toward* a more complete understanding of light, or being a WPA, or what framing a WPA as light implies. Complementarity is a material expression of Burkean seeing. But it also supplies an indeterminate and contingent solution to the necessary "neglect of object B" by acknowledging the multiple natures of WPA to which we should return as we develop a fuller understanding of the ways in which a WPA emerges.

To this end, in this chapter we theorize *and model* writing program administration through the framework of Niels Bohr's quantum theory of complementarity. Bohr's rendering of the double-slit paradox affirms that, in fact, we can't have it both ways—at least not in the classical sense—that light is *not already* both a particle and a wave. Instead, complementarity is predicated on the idea of indeterminacy, which holds that objects do *not* have independently existing and a priori determinate characteristics. Instead, complementarity argues that "determinate entities emerge from their [local] *intra-actions*" (Barad 2007, 128; emphasis original).[4] So, what dictates whether light is a particle or a wave (for it is possible in some circumstances for it to exist as both) is *not* a predetermined quality of light itself, but *the specific ways in which light interacts, and is allowed to interact, with its immediate material environment.* Similarly, in this chapter we tack toward the material and argue that a quantum approach to understanding WPA work pays respect to the local, emergent, and indeed indeterminate identities that WPAs enact across all contexts. In other words, quantum physics suggests that we cannot know who or what a WPA is outside of the immediate conditions surrounding and constituting their existence as such.

If nothing else, the double-slit experiment evinces the limitations of classical ways of thinking about the nature of reality. There is simply no classical way to reconcile the existence of light as both a particle and a wave. We contend that, likewise, classical metaphors of WPA work have reached their natural limit. Only when we are attentive to the distributed and often contradictory means of administering a writing program can we pay respect to the complementary—and often mutually exclusive—ways in which WPA work manifests itself in its daily and embedded iterations. What are needed, then, are ways of understanding writing program administration that pay respect to the divergent ways in which WPA work is *emergent*. In the following sections, we unpack and critique a "classical" framing of metaphors to demonstrate how traditional definitions of metaphor are problematic; then, we present an updated "quantum" frame to understand metaphors that are sustainable while also articulating our metaphor of the WPA as light; finally, we close with implications and questions we hope understanding the WPA in a quantum state of light affords. Understanding light (and a WPA *as* light) requires engaging with complementarity and the shift between classical-traditional and quantum-emergent representations of physics as they help us (re)theorize ways to understand a WPA.

PARTICLE INTERLUDE

As part of our institution's most recent general education renewal, my campus colleague and I were tasked with spearheading a full redesign of the first-year writing program we "administer": new programmatic mission, new student learning outcomes, even new recommended writing assignments. I use scare quotes around *administer* because, to be honest, I'm playing a bit fast and loose with this word. Or, more precisely, it's difficult for me to characterize what it means to administer our new program in any singular or even any definitive sense. Program administration, on my campus, is necessarily *not* a monolith. To explain, while we were imbued with the institutional authority to oversee the development of this new writing curriculum, we were simultaneously stripped, for a variety of reasons (some self-imposed, some handed down to us), of any departmental apparatus or capacity to ensure its actual implementation across our diverse instructional staff. For example, we do have a departmental syllabus template which we can recommend instructors use but nothing in place to require them to do so.

There is, then, no official recourse for us to appeal to with which to ensure any kind of fidelity to even our programmatic mission; therefore, there is no official impetus for our instructional staff to actually teach our assignments or even to teach within the scope of the new curriculum. The resultant administrative environment is therefore understandably—and often frustratingly—capricious. We constantly find ourselves redefining how we are able to administer the new curriculum because even without structural recourse to ensure the new curriculum's implementation, we still believe it's important for *us* to function in ways that embody an ongoing commitment to pedagogical and theoretical growth as writing instructors. So, for example, even though we are still required to conduct evaluative departmental observations on our instructional staff, we've also restructured the ways in which those evaluations unfold and are presented to the faculty so that they are understood to be formative. We still have departmental meetings and professional development with our staff, but we've also implemented more informal "coffee meetings" with our instructional staff in the hopes of continuing conversations about the new curriculum. In one moment, administering the writing program feels akin to mentorship, but in the very next it waxes supervisory: sometimes a particle, sometimes a wave.

In an honest effort to be a "good" WPA, I used to ask myself, "What's the right way to be doing this whole program administration thing?" But then it became apparent that my thinking about being a WPA, much like the classical notion of light as always-already having a determinate character or quality, was premised on the faulty notion that there was a discrete and independently identifiable "thing" that a WPA is. But defining myself as a WPA is not a matter of slipping into notions of ungrounded relativity. Much to the contrary, my work administering our new curriculum has shown me that who I am as a WPA and the work I do toward that end emerges, moment to moment, in concert with and in relation to a myriad of co-constituting factors—as does the quantum understanding of light through Bohr's concept of complementarity. Each interaction is grounded in its material, institutional, and social (to name a few) surround.

MOVING BEYOND "CLASSICAL" METAPHORS

Metaphors necessarily create connections. Consider, for example, the classical metaphor of a WPA as a manager. This metaphor is tenable because it is able to locate instances of sameness between the roles typically associated with managerial work and roles taken up by a WPA. Unfortunately, classical metaphors often substitute one concept for another instead of simply inviting a richer consideration of the first idea. The net result of the "WPA as manager" metaphor is that, for most audiences, it substitutes a manager for a WPA, thereby obfuscating any potential alternative readings of a WPA. By developing connections, metaphors establish common ground—identification—between inherently disparate contexts or entities, a version of Kenneth Burke's (1984) concept of consubstantiality. Classical metaphors, then, by organizing through identification involve an unfortunate erasure of difference. Or, at best, classical metaphors often fail to fully acknowledge moments of difference and their potential rhetorical significance. Differences, in other words, are problematic for classical metaphors. Indeed, as Krista Ratcliffe (2005) notes, the Burkean conception of metaphor is limited precisely because "[i]t does not adequately address the coercive force of common ground that often haunts cross-cultural communication, nor does it adequately address how to identify and negotiate *troubled identifications*" (47–48; emphasis added). Following Ratcliffe, we too are skeptical about the ability of *classical* metaphors to adequately capture the fullness and complexity of "troubled identifications" such as writing program administration, precisely because metaphors *bind things together* (Lakoff and Johnson 1999) rather than acknowledge and embrace the spaces between. Classical metaphors suggest *the* WPA instead of *a* WPA.

As WPAs, our daily "individual" professional lives stand as a testament to the ways in which our work, indeed ourselves, are *not* made up by instances of Burkean identification and its insistence on moments of similarity but instead by the indeterminate ways in which we are consistently made new *and different* moment to moment. We wake up, for example, invested with institutional authority to conduct classroom observations one day, only to have that authority stripped the next day when we are reminded that these observations cannot factor into our (re)hiring decisions (see "Particle Interlude" above). This goes well beyond Tim Peeples's (1999) suggestion to construct multiple maps of the WPA's "simultaneous, fragmented, and fluid organizational positions" (155). Instead, following the quantum principle of complementarity, we suggest that a WPA, quite literally, emerges anew—and is different—in each situation. As such, any attempt to "identify" a WPA in a Burkean sense is necessarily inadequate, because it assumes the existence and imposition of a set of predetermined attributes that inhere in and across moments and places of being. Furthermore, such identifications involve an erasure of difference, ironic given that emergence is founded on inessential differences—small wonder that metaphors have difficulty sustaining across time and place!

How, then, are we to reframe the concept of metaphor as it applies to writing program administration so that these "troubled identifications do not simply vanish," but rather "perhaps become more audible . . . and then perhaps more visible . . . and then perhaps more possible to negotiate—with *perhaps*, of course, being the operative term" (Ratcliffe 2005, 66)? Again, the concept of light offers an elegant, if simple, solution in the form of diffraction. Diffraction is the physical phenomena that results when waves—be they light, sound, or water—bend and overlap after encountering an obstruction. In the case of light waves, diffraction results in a pattern of alternating light and dark lines such that even directly behind an object where one would expect to see full darkness, there is a telltale line of bright light. As a metaphor, light again works because diffraction, or an interference pattern, "does not map where differences appear, but rather maps where the *effects* of differences appear" (Haraway 1992, 300). Similarly, we are more interested in mapping *where* the effects of difference in writing program administration work manifest themselves, as opposed to trying to definitively qualify what that characteristic of difference might be, which would fall back into the same trap of representationalism that we are attempting to escape.

Moreover, as Karen Barad (2007) suggests in *Meeting the Universe Halfway*, the concept of diffraction is *more* than a metaphor for the effects of difference: "more profoundly, they [diffraction apparatuses] exhibit and make evident the entangled structure of the *changing and contingent ontology of the world* [emphasis added], including the ontology of knowing" (73). A diffraction pattern, in other words, is the result of the material environment within which waves operate as much as it is of the properties of waves itself; diffraction patterns of light are *materially entangled*. That is, when considered in concert with Bohr's concept of complementarity, a diffractive approach to understanding WPA work both dodges the problematic aspects of classical metaphors and embodies the physical reality of writing program administration as emergent and entangled. Therefore, in the following sections we offer a diffractive reading of our respective WPA experiences: we show moments of overlap *and* dissonance, and we show how the effects of our work are caught up inextricably with our immediate and constitutive conditions.

PARTICLE INTERLUDE

In 2015, my institution merged with another institution within our university system and we became, seemingly overnight, what feels like a very large school. In 2015, as part of the merger, the writing program split from literature and joined rhetoric, linguistics, and languages in a new department, Writing and Language Studies—effectively becoming an independent writing program. Also in 2015, I became the WPA.

Building a program from scratch might have been an easier task than creating a program from the elements of each contributing institution. Each university had a different pedagogical and curricular culture; each campus enacted service and scholarship with vastly different points of view; each campus related to each other and to students in nearly opposite ways. For example, one campus approached course development collaboratively, creating and piloting assignments together. Office doors in that hallway remained open, and colleagues had an open invitation to stop by to work out classroom strategies, discuss research, or even just to chat. The other campus approached curriculum development as an individual, proprietary, and personal task. Any effort toward collaboration was viewed with suspicion. Colleagues were friendly, but offices were personal spaces; colleagues could go an entire semester or year without running into each other. From this, I had to encourage and direct the creation of a first-year writing program: what was our mission, vision, curriculum, organization and structure, philosophy? What was our identity? What should it be? How many times did I drive to campus asking myself, "What am I doing? How am I supposed to do it?"

Some days, the work of program development required that I bear a torch and lead the way through difficult and unseen terrain. The person holding the light has to walk at the front. It does no good to shine the light from the back. The person holding the light encounters the unknown first, must respond and react first (similar to the way creating or consulting a map can help those in a writing program navigate; see O'Meara, this volume). The WPA enables the writing program faculty to do good work by lighting the way and responding to obstacles and danger first (danger might be changes in policy, assessment requirements, workload, evaluations, and so on).

Other days, being WPA of a program born from a merger meant shining a light back on ourselves. For me, building a "new" writing program was a call to develop a third culture. We weren't adopting the personality and character of either legacy writing program. We were creating our own, together. But along the way, there were moments where faculty felt lesser or marginalized (for being "from" one campus or the other, for getting certain course assignments, for policy changes enacted by the whole university system, for slights perceived and real). In those moments, it was important for me to illuminate ourselves, our relationships, the work we were doing and trying to do. In order for the program to survive and thrive, we had to look at ourselves to see who we wanted to be to and for each other, and like a physician peering into an ear or throat, it was my role as WPA to shine a light on those areas infected by hubris, isolation, insult.

That work continues; perhaps building a writing program has not an ending but milestones. Truthfully, my drive to work is still marked by a repeating refrain, "What am I doing? How am I supposed to do it?" What seems clearer now, though, is that whatever and however I am supposed to be a good WPA, it will require me to be light.

TOWARD SUSTAINABLE "QUANTUM" METAPHORS

Part of what makes a metaphor *sustainable* is its ability to do work across many contexts, to be invoked, recalled, alluded to, as well as its ability to find meaning in established idioms, facts, and trivia. In this way, WPAs and WPA work as light are made robust and given texture. What are the implications, for example, if our metaphor is extended one logical progression by suggesting that plants need light to grow hearty and fruitful? Or, what might it mean to suggest that someone lights up a room when they enter? Or to argue that a writing program is light-years ahead of where it once was? That new meanings and implications can be drawn from a metaphor means that it has legs: it will move, live, shift meaning, find strength anew. Sustainability isn't about finding one really good image or narrative to lean on (though we believe that is part of developing a good metaphor); sustainability is about crowdsourcing, reframing, reimagining, continual freshness. We're reminded that, each day as the Earth revolves around the sun and spins on its axis, the light fades and then returns. It's the same sun (the same idea), but the light seems new every morning.

A sustainable *quantum* metaphor is, like the WPAs it represents, an "engine of dissensus" that "create[s] spaces where dissensus can happen, giv[ing] stakeholders opportunities to question and disagree in ways that are heard" (Charlton et al. 2011, 217). We know that misconceptions about writing, and teaching writing, abound. The same is true of coordinating a writing program. How often have we heard *what students should be learning* in our classes from faculty across campus? But ignoring or shutting down questions and disagreement are not often productive or good for effecting change. A sustainable quantum metaphor for WPAs should be able to account for the many roles we have *and* the complex relationships we have with other faculty, with content, with assessment, with students. So, we recognize that light can *also* be blinding, intense, hot or cold / warm or cool, bent, or diffracted, and it can materialize in a variety of wavelengths which manifest along a range of visible and invisible light (infrared or UV). Light can provide much-needed vitamin D and also burn the skin (compare with the sometimes beneficial, sometimes devastating effects of fire and firefighting in Wilkes, this volume). A sustainable metaphor, to us, should be able to account for both the positive and negative aspects of WPA work and those who labor as WPAs. For example, a WPA who endorses racist assessment practices (whether intentional or not) is not a beacon of light. Rather, that WPA is, at least in that moment, destructive light bringing heat and cancer. A sustainable metaphor plays across all contexts and persists.

As engines of dissensus, sustainable quantum metaphors (light is both literally and figuratively a quantum metaphor) avoid the troubling identifications of classical metaphors. Of course, a sustainable metaphor can suggest identification—it's a metaphor! But, in the identification is also an acknowledgment of being and nonbeing, of other, possibly conflicting, narratives. It is a metaphor that winks at itself. It's a metaphor that suggests other possibilities even as it helps us understand our current situations. In its ambiguity, sustainable quantum metaphors are more true, more accurate, than classical metaphors. Light, as the quintessential quantum metaphor, illuminates WPAs and WPA work by acknowledging the various contexts and relationships that characterize WPAs across multiple contexts.

In light, we come to see that another's enactment of WPA work is not our own, and yet neither is it entirely inseparable from us: quantum conceptions of light posit the matter (its physical properties) of light as not only that of emergence but also *entanglement* with an/Other. We must tread carefully here, however, with the concept of entanglement because, as with most quantum language, it betrays and defies classical definitions. On its surface, it might seem that entanglement suggests two separate entities that are caught up in each other, twisted around one another. Yet quantum physics is rarely this simple. As Barad (2010) argues, entanglement is complex, both theoretically and practically: "*Quantum entanglements* are not the intertwining of two (or more) states/entities/events, but a calling into question of the very nature of two-ness, and ultimately one-ness as well. Duality, unity, multiplicity, being are undone . . . One is too few, two is too many" (251). By invoking the concept of entanglement, we are acknowledging that neither of us can be described or understood as a WPA independent of the other; but at the same time neither can we fully rely on the other to explain ourselves and the work we do in and across contexts. Thus, entanglement does not denote singularity, nor does it slide into pluralism, instead "it implies that the different realities *overlap and interfere with one another*. Their relations, partially coordinated, are complex and messy" (Law 2004, 61). While we admit that the concept of entanglement is perhaps messy, it also conveys a sense of dis/unity to the work that WPAs do across time and space, thereby making the metaphor of light more sustainable. What this suggests, practically, is that light is not particularly noticeable as a *single* particle. It is the rush of particles, the wave after wave of energy that appears to us as light—yet, that individual particle is not insignificant: without it, the light produced is literally less intense or bright. In this way, the emergence of a single WPA identity (as a "manager" perhaps) is not particularly bright; it is the confluence of identities that shines.

Thus far we have attempted to explain and narrate the various ways in which we can only understand the matter (its physical properties and metaphysical implications) of light and WPA work as they relate to their co-constituting surround, yet quantum field theory further suggests a radical re/framing of how we understand otherness and the self. This means that "the self" actually is (or becomes) in quantum physics "dispersed/diffracted through time and being" (Barad 2012, 211). Moreover, not only is *the self* diffracted in its surround, the self is also intimately caught up in and only understandable through *the other* because what were once separate elements—particles, fields, and the void—are, in quantum field theory, intra-related and connected. Barad argues, "physical particles are inseparable from the void, in particular they intra-act with the virtual particles of the void, and *they are thereby inseparable from it*" (2012, 211; emphasis added). Quantum field theory suggests that, across time and space, all matter—including the matter of both light and WPA work—is threaded together, the self intimately bound up in the other. Light as WPA / WPA as light is a materially rhetorical / rhetorically material proposition. We cannot separate the implications or ethics or physics from any of these strands, nor do we think we should. So, we ask: how is one of us to reasonably understand ourselves without also acknowledging and understanding the other *and* the ways in which the other makes us who we are while we simultaneously make them who they are? Along with Barad, we suggest that we simply cannot ignore the ways in which we are co-constitutive of and entangled with not only our surround but also each other (similar to the interconnectedness of a rhizome; see Babb, this volume). However, such an admission is not without an important call for response/ability.[5]

WAVES AND THE IMPLICATIONS OF INTERFERENCE PATTERNS

Here is the double-slit experiment: you will need a wall, a screen with two slits cut from it, and a light source. Shine the light at the wall and you will observe a circle of light, a bright center that grades back into darkness. Place the screen between the light and the wall and now you will observe a ripple pattern: lines of bright light, lines of dim light, and lines of shadow. Why? What's happening? When the light hits the screen, it stops. It does not pass through. But the lights that shines onto the slits—that's another matter! The light passes through each slit, squeezes through like a person turning sideways in a tight pass-through, and then spreads out, resuming its wave behavior. Only now, instead of one light source, there are two: two slits in the screen, two new origination points for light waves. Because the slits are close, the waves run into each other, very much like the waves at the beach are interrupted by the wake of a passing boat. The waves' interference with each other causes the ripple pattern on the wall behind the screen. Where the crest of one light wave meets the crest of another light wave, their light is amplified and a bright line is seen on the wall. When the crest of a wave meets the trough of another wave, their light is interfered with and a band of shadow is seen on the wall. The dim bands of light are explained by the meeting of waves not fully in crest or trough. The behavior of light is wondrous.

If WPAs and WPA work is light, the double-slit experiment is a reminder, an encouragement, and a warning. We should:

1. remember that although we may talk of *the* WPA, a single source of light, there are, in fact, many slits cut into the screen called "writing program administration." There are, in fact, many sources of light.
2. be encouraged that we make waves. What's more, we can amplify and be amplified by other WPAs, sources of light, and their work. We can shine brighter together than we can on our own. Far from being a cliché, this is material truth.
3. be cautious not to extinguish another's light. When we are out of phase (our trough matches another's crest and vice versa), we negate not only the work of others, but our own.

This is our response/ability: to conscientiously and carefully amplify *our* (not *my* or *your*) light. Perhaps this is what Barad means when she suggests that the other is always-already in us and we are always-already in the other. The WPA as light is not only a sustainable quantum metaphor. The WPA as light is an ethics of response and responsibility—response/ability.[6] To work as WPA is not only to schedule courses, develop curriculum, provide professional development, execute assessment, and conduct faculty observations, though it is definitely those things. To work as WPA is not only to advocate, mediate, model, and listen, though it is also definitely those things. To work as WPA is not only to be available, though perhaps that is most important. To work as WPA is to bear a torch, to illuminate our own deficiencies, to shine, to blaze, to bend, to diffract, to be both particle and wave, to show, to burn, to dispel darkness. To work as WPA is to embody the right role at the necessary moment. To be WPA is to be light.

NOTES

1. A note on structure: we have attempted to model rhetorical complementarity/Burkean seeing both textually and visually: we present information, evidence, and autoethnographic vignettes individually but also necessarily as part of some fuller, more meaningful and productive awareness of WPA work. To this end, we have concealed the identity of the writer of each "interlude." Additionally, our initial section, "Duality," presents complementary introductions side by side, requiring the reader to read each in turn. These are stylistic and rhetorical choices that require a material engagement with the content of our paper.
2. Our invocation of the performative aspects of WPA work follows from Karen Barad. Specifically, Barad points out that "[a] *performative* understanding of discursive practices challenges the representationalist belief in the power of word to represent preexisting things . . . [it] insists on understanding thinking, observing, and theorizing as practices of engagement with, and as part of, the world in which we have our being" (2007, 133). Likewise, framing a WPA as light challenges the concept of some determinate, preexisting quality and instead calls for us to understand the iterative ways in which a WPA *comes to be*. There is not, in other words, an "essence" of a WPA.

3. Representationalism is the nearly ubiquitous assumption in Western philosophy that scientific practices and observations "reveal *preexisting properties* [emphasis added] of an observation-independent reality" (Barad 2007, 97). In other words, the observer is *apart from* the natural work (as opposed to "a part of") the world they are observing. Important to note is that representationalism also pervades nearly all the social sciences and conceptions of language; both realists and social constructivists, that is, take it as a given that words are representative. The only difference is whether words represent an exterior and preexisting world or social structures of power (Barad 2008, 120). In both cases, representationalism is at play. In this chapter, we follow Barad and call into question the veracity of a *preexisting* and *observation-independent* reality. We instead argue for understanding how reality continually comes-to-be in "emergent and emplaced" (Rickert 2013) ways.
4. Here we borrow the term *intra-acting* from materialist scholarship (Gries 2013; Gries 2015; Latour 1999; Rickert 2013), using it instead of *interacting* in order to highlight our resistance to the representationalist trap of assuming that objects and persons come imbued with preexisting attributes. Moreover, *intra-action* highlights the ways in which rhetorical import is derived from an *interior* and *interdependent* assemblage or collective (Latour 1999) rather than an *inter*action of separate and independent entities.
5. We construct this word this way so as to capture both the ability to respond to the other, or "stranger within" (Barad 2012, 206), as well as our moral obligation to do so.
6. Our construction of response/ability follows from Diane Davis's articulation in "Creaturely Rhetorics." We use response/ability, as does Davis, to denote not only the ability to respond to an/Other but also the *obligation* to do so (2011, 89).

REFERENCES

Barad, Karen. 2007. *Meeting the Universe Halfway: Quantum Physics and the Entanglement of Matter and Meaning*. Durham, NC: Duke University Press.

Barad, Karen. 2008. "Posthumanist Performativity: Toward an Understanding of How Matter Comes to Matter." In *Material Feminisms*, edited by Stacy Alaimo and Susan Hekman, 120–54. Bloomington: Indiana University Press.

Barad, Karen. 2010. "Quantum Entanglements and Hauntological Relations of Inheritance: Dis/continuities, SpaceTime Enfoldings, and Justice-to-Come." *Derrida Today* 3 (2): 240–68.

Barad, Karen. 2012. "On Touching—The Inhuman that Therefore I Am." *differences* 23 (3): 206–23.

Burke, Kenneth. 1984. *Permanence and Change: An Anatomy of Purpose*. Berkeley: University of California Press.

Charlton, Colin, Jonikka Charlton, Tarez Samra Graban, Kathleen J. Ryan, and Amy Ferdinandt Stolley. 2011. *GenAdmin: Theorizing WPA Identities in the Twenty-First Century*. Anderson, SC: Parlor Press.

Charlton, Jonnika, and Shirley K. Rose. 2009. "Twenty More Years in the WPA's Progress." *Writing Program Administration* 33 (1–2): 114–45.

Davis, Diane. 2011. "Creaturely Rhetorics." *Philosophy and Rhetoric* 44 (1): 88–94.

Einstein, Albert, and Leopold Infeld. 1939. *The Evolution of Physics: The Growth of Ideas from Early Concepts to Relativity and Quanta*. Cambridge, UK: Cambridge University Press.

Feynman, Richard P., Robert B. Leighton, and Matthew Sands. 2015. *The Feynman Lectures on Physics*. Vol. 3. New York: Basic Books.

Gladstein, Jill. 2013. "National Census of Writing." https://writingcensus.swarthmore.edu/.

Gries, Laurie E. 2013. "Iconographic Tracking: A Digital Research Method for Visual Rhetoric and Circulation Studies." *Computers and Composition* 30:332–48.
Gries, Laurie E. 2015. *Still Life with Rhetoric: A New Materialist Approach for Visual Rhetorics*. Logan: Utah State University Press.
Haraway, Donna. 1992. "The Promises of Monsters: A Regenerative Politics for Inappropriate/d Others." In *Cultural Studies*, edited by Lawrence Grossberg, Cory Nelson, and Paula Treichler, 295–337. New York: Routledge.
Lakoff, George, and Johnson, Mark. 1999. *Philosophy in the Flesh: The Embodied Mind and Its Challenge to Western Thought*. New York: Basic Books.
Latour, Bruno. 1999. *Pandora's Hope: Essays on the Reality of Science Studies*. Cambridge, MA: Harvard University Press.
Law, John. 2004. *After Method: Mess in Social Science Research*. New York: Routledge.
Peeples, Tim. 1999. "'Seeing' the WPA with/through Postmodern Mapping." In *The Writing Program Administrator as Researcher: Inquiry in Action and Reflection*, edited by Shirley K. Rose and Irwin Weiser, 153–16. Portsmouth, NH: Boynton/Cook Publishers.
Ratcliffe, Krista. 2005. *Rhetorical Listening: Identification, Gender, Whiteness*. Carbondale: Southern Illinois University Press.
Reiff, Mary Jo, Anis Bawarshi, Michelle Ballif, and Christian Weisser. 2015. *Ecologies of Writing Programs: Program Profiles in Context*. Anderson, SC: Parlor Press.
Rickert, Thomas. 2013. *Ambient Rhetoric: The Attunements of Rhetorical Being*. Pittsburgh, PA: University of Pittsburgh Press.
Schell, Eileen E. 2016. "Austerity, Contingency, and Administrative Bloat: Writing Programs and Universities in an Age of Feast and Famine." In *Composition in the Age of Austerity*, edited by Nancy Welch and Tony Scott, 177–90. Boulder: University Press of Colorado.
Strickland, Donna. 2011. *The Managerial Unconscious in the History of Composition Studies*. Carbondale: Southern Illinois University Press.
Tretkoff, Ernie. 2008. "May 1801: Thomas Young and the Nature of Light." *APS News*, May 2008. https://www.aps.org/publications/apsnews/200805/physicshistory.cfm.

4
GROUNDING WPA WORK
A Phenomenology of Program Development as a Liminal WPA

Ryan J. Dippre

In considering the complex contexts through which a new writing program administrator must navigate, Sandee K. McGlaun (2007) offers the word "between," drawing in particular on everyday idioms across the US: "Between a rock and a hard place. Between the devil and the deep blue sea" (221). McGlaun's work on the concept of "between" in writing program administration highlights the intricate, nuanced work of writing program administrators who work in what Talinn Phillips, Paul Shovlin, and Megan Titus (2014) would call *liminal* positions: those that "engage in the high-stakes work" of WPAs with security of employment but "typically have an untenurable institutional rank: graduate student, contingent faculty, support staff, etc." (44). Amy Stolley (2015) carries the attention that McGlaun gives to the liminal WPA even further, suggesting that the "lore" (North 1987) surrounding such WPA work is in need of counternarratives—in particular, counternarratives told by liminal WPAs and "rooted in" (Stolley 25) Linda Adler-Kassner's (2008) concept of *principle*.

In this chapter, I propose *groundedness*—attending to, working with, and thinking through the local needs of teachers, students, and program members—as orienting language for liminal WPAs to think through their decisions when operating their writing programs. It is language that can help them think through the improvisatory (Gunter, this volume) challenges and the rhizomatic (Babb, this volume) complexity of developing and sustaining a writing program. I develop and dimensionalize this language through a phenomenological (Husserl 2013; Moustakas 1994; van Manen 1990, 2014) examination of my four-year role as a WPA. Though my current role has a path to tenure, I find the emphasis on liminality to be a useful way of bounding the circumstances of the specifics provided in this chapter. My work to ground my administrative choices may be useful to all manner of untenured

WPAs—graduate WPAs (gWPAs), student WPAs (sWPAs), junior WPAs (jWPAs), etc.—and the term *liminal* allows me to capture this.

My WPA work at the University of Maine began in fall 2015, but I began using the word *grounded* in my campus visit the previous spring. I found *grounded* to be a useful term to reference the local, contingent phenomenon of writing development that I was exploring in my dissertation research, that I was attending to in my teaching, and that I would aim to support at a programmatic level in an administrative position. For my campus visit to UMaine, I was asked to put together a presentation that would blend my research and administrative work, and *grounded* served as a useful concept for such blending: just as I had constructed a grounded theory of writing development, I would also engage with this site "from the ground up." My decision-making in the composition program would emerge from the local needs and concerns of students, teachers, and the program. When I was hired as the Associate Director of Composition in fall 2015, I began my administrative work in what I saw as a grounded manner: I observed classes, interviewed teachers, met with administrators, reviewed reports, and otherwise tried to get a sense of how the program operated on a day-to-day, semester-to-semester, and year-to-year basis. This work not only gave me a sense of the workings of the program but the directions in which the program would need to go when I stepped into the Director of Composition position in July 2017. In a sense, I was engaged in the cartographic work described by O'Meara (this volume).

As I transitioned into my second year as Director of Composition—my fourth overall in a liminal WPA space—I began to reflect on "grounded" phenomenologically. In particular, I drew on van Manen (1990, 2014) to drive my research decisions. Van Manen (1990) emphasizes that phenomenology is a *human* science—that is, for phenomenologists, "to do research is always to question the way we experience the world, to want to know the world in which we live as human beings" (5). Pursuing WPA research through a human science such as phenomenology seemed an appropriate approach for thinking through the managerial demands (Strickland 2011) of writing program administration, as it enables the challenging of prior assumptions through a close attention to the lived experience of program participants.

Using the procedures detailed by van Manen (1990), which I productively complicated through insights from Moustakas (1994), van Manen (2014), and Husserl and Lauer (1956), I identify specific experiences in my work as a liminal WPA when the sense of grounded work was perspicuous, and I look across those experiences (and their accompanying artifacts) for characteristics of grounded WPA work that remain invariant through curricular, assessment, and program-shaping decisions. The phenomenological examination of grounded WPA work identifies several themes that reduce (van Manen 1990, 78) the phenomenon productively for liminal WPAs to use in their administrative work in the future: uncertainty, trust, and mediation. While a phenomenological approach, and the characteristics that emerged for me from that approach, may be helpful for WPAs in positions that are not liminal, I have come to see my metaphor of groundedness as solving important problems that are particular for WPAs in liminal positions. Considering grounded WPA work through these themes suggest paths forward for liminal WPAs as they build their counternarratives about WPA work through principled administrative decisions.

PHENOMENOLOGICAL ANALYSIS: OVERVIEW OF A LOGIC-IN-USE

According to van Manen (1990), phenomenology is "a systematic, explicit, self-critical, and intersubjective study of its subject matter, our lived experience" (11). In being systematic, phenomenology uses specific "modes of questioning, reflecting, focusing, intuiting, etc." (11). In being explicit and self-critical, phenomenology aims to articulate "the structures of meaning embedded in lived experience" and, at the same time, "continually [examine] its own goals and methods in an attempt to come to terms with the strengths and shortcomings of its approach and achievements" (11). Finally, phenomenology is intersubjective in that it relies on an other—in this case, the reader—to validate new understandings that arise.

One of the aims of phenomenology is to understand the invariant structures, or essences, of consciousness. The broader vision of Husserl, in his establishment of phenomenology as it is taken up in this chapter, is to establish a body of work, a set of essences, through which the structures of consciousness could be understood. As Lauer (1965) notes, these essences would be, to some extent, independent, so particular essences could be disproven or replaced without the broader collection of essences being threatened. This building of a body of philosophical work never emerged in the way that Husserl intended, although the pursuit of invariant characteristics has remained very close to the heart of phenomenological inquiry, even as the discipline itself transformed through the later work of Sartre, Gadamer, and others in the middle of the twentieth century. Van Manen's uptake of phenomenological study attempts to locate the work of uncovering such characteristics in the daily work of education. For van Manen, phenomenology is a way to take the daily lived experience of teaching, living, and being on its own terms, with analysis beginning through the phenomena of interest that bubble up in the midst of that living.

Phenomenological analysis in the van Manen tradition, then, is a very different kind of analysis. Nevertheless, there is a logic to the tradition, a logic that becomes logical not in an abstract, taxonomic way but in the particular instances of its use, taking into account the many dimensions of human life that make up a given experience. In that using, the logic of a particular phenomenological study becomes accountable: in the writing up, the working through, of a phenomenological study, the researcher creates an account of the logic-in-use of a phenomenological analysis and, by extension, makes that account available for study, extension, complication, and critique. Below, I unpack the specific acts through which I lived through a phenomenological logic-in-use, to understand what it means to experience grounded WPA work as a liminal WPA. These acts lead to the particular instances I analyze in the next section.

As I mention above, the term "grounded" emerged from my dissertation work and served as a useful way to orient the audience at my job talk to both that research and my aims as a new WPA. Upon arriving to Orono, Maine, in August 2015, I found myself in the fortunate position of being able to take up the grounded perspective I had developed for that talk. The current Director of College Composition, Pat Burnes, was on phased retirement and would be stepping down at the end of the 2016–2017 academic year, giving me two years to watch her work and make sense of the ebb and flow of activity at UMaine.

In their preface to *The Discovery of Grounded Theory*, Barney Glaser and Anselm Strauss (1967) use the word "grounded" to signal "grounding theory in social research itself—for generating it from data" (viii). This approach—to study closely the data at hand and generate from it a more generalized account to inform future work—informed what I initially thought I was doing when I engaged in WPA work "from the ground up." I attended orientation for new English Department teaching assistants in fall 2015 and took extensive field notes on how the conversations unfolded. I did the same during the assessment "calibration sessions" that occurred during fall semester as well. These notes provided a starting point from which I began to understand what *counts* as the work of this composition program throughout the academic year.

These notes and the process of recording (and rereading) them served as the noun function of "ground," or the "basis, foundation" of the work that I came to understand as grounded writing program administration. As my roles and responsibilities increased across my two years as Associate Director, my conception of "grounded" expanded into verb form, becoming an action—I needed to not only *have grounds* for my WPA work at a local level, but *ground* my decisions actively, allowing them to emerge from my understanding of the situation at hand. In that work, "ground" took on its transitive verb definition—that is, to set on the earth—but that act of grounding was also caught up within an investigation, a critical look at, a breaking apart of the ground. In a sense, then, my active grounding of WPA work incorporated more of its Indo-European root *ghren*, meaning "to pulverize." In other words, my work to ground administrative decisions ended not with an understanding of how something worked locally but an investigation into why something worked locally as well. The act of grounding fractures, sorts, and organizes incoming information, time and time again, in order to get a sense of the lived experience of a particular site.

The move from considering what counts as composition program work to the why behind that which counts was not entirely a conscious choice. Instead, as I continued to engage in administrative tasks in ways that valued "grounded" work, I began to sense that what I was perceiving as grounded was transforming in ways I could not fully identify: the ground seemed to be shifting underfoot. By the start of my second year as Director of Composition, the perceived change in my notion of groundedness called out for investigation in my daily writing and appeared to be complicating the clarity of vision I had for my work with the program. Beginning with my new relationship to the dictionary definitions of "ground," I looked over my notebooks from my time as Director to identify strategic sites for an investigation into my revised enactment of grounded WPA work. Although I looked into several opportunities, I ended up focused on two specific "sites" of evident grounded WPA work: the development of teaching principles for our program, and the Portfolio Assessment Rubric (PAR) revision committee. These sites are strategic (Bazerman 2008) in nature, in that they make my grounded decisions particularly evident, more visible for further examination.

TWO INSTANCES OF "GROUNDED" WPA WORK

I present the two instances of grounded WPA work below in the order in which they occurred. Instance 1—the development of principles for teaching college composition at UMaine—unfolded across the course of the 2017–2018 academic year. Instance 2—the development of a PAR Revision Committee—unfolded over the course of May–August 2018. In each of these instances, I reflect on my own experiences, highlighting the particular moments that I will be able to turn to as I develop a set of invariant characteristics for acts of liminal WPA work that appear, phenomenally, as "grounded."

Instance 1: Teaching Principles for College Composition

One of the primary tasks I set for myself upon stepping into the role of Director of Composition was to explicate a set of teaching principles. Drawing on Peter Smagorinsky's (2009) (and, by extension, Applebee's [1986]) assertion that the idea of *best* practices is inherently problematic, as well as Adler-Kassner's (2008) suggestion that our work as teachers of writing needs to begin from principles—that is, the values we hold about writers and writing—I sought to uncover the principles shaping our program, from which we could begin to discuss the complex practices through which those principles could be taken up. I envisioned these principles as shaping our new instructor orientation, teaching observations, and—eventually, I hoped—the conversations that our teachers had about their teaching decisions.

My description of this instance does not, in the above paragraph, seem grounded at all. Rather, it appears as if I "read" the situation on the ground through research on writing program administration and, from there, developed a plan to go about outlining some principles for teachers to use as guides during their pedagogical decision-making. But such a reading was important for me, as a liminal WPA, in thinking through particular innovations in a well-established program. The language of the field—and the authority lent by the sources I drew from—gave power to my liminal presence that suggested such a move might be a beneficial one.

With the field as my starting point, in October 2017 I met with the two directors I work with in the College Composition program—the Associate Director for Assessment and Program Research, and the Assistant Director of College Composition—to discuss what our values were about teaching writing. My role in this discussion was to merely listen and take extensive notes on what values seemed to emerge from some deep thinking and discussion about the entirety of the program. In a subsequent meeting, I presented a list of principles that "consolidated" the work of our previous meeting, and we began to describe, expand, collapse, and otherwise revise these principles.

I brought the revised principles (what I tentatively called "Principles 1.0" in my notes) to several observations of teachers in the program and drew on the language in writing up my notes on observations and discussing what I saw with teachers afterward. These observations and meetings served as material to further revise the principles. This process culminated in a final copyedited document that all three directors agreed on at the end of April 2018. During the end-of-semester meeting in May 2018, these principles were presented to the teaching corps for discussion. The principles were adopted at the close of the meeting and were used throughout the subsequent year during new teacher orientation and teaching observations. I had aimed for our principles to be reflective of the work of the program at its best: what it aimed to do and, on its best days, accomplished.

My work to develop program principles, then, began with my own past experiences (accrued elsewhere) and the language of the discipline that I brought with me to UMaine. But by the time the principles were established, I had sufficiently pulverized records from various meetings and observations to sort the closely held values of those in the program from the chaff of unrelated information. The principles that our program ended up with, then, were set on the earth of the realities of classroom teachers and past administrative choices. They rendered visible commonly held beliefs, ideas, and knowledge in a new way that could be communicated to new program instructors with greater ease in coming years.

Instance 2: PAR Revision Committee

The work on the principles was largely confined to the directors of the program, with forays into observations and discussions with the teaching corps at large being carefully structured throughout the academic year. The PAR Revision Committee, however, introduced less structure into my work of "grounding" WPA decisions. The PAR (Portfolio Assessment Rubric) is the key document for the end-of-semester portfolio review in College Composition. At the end of each semester, all students in English 101 submit a collection of two academic essays and a critical reflection—work they have been developing throughout the semester. These portfolios are read by two teachers who are not the student's teacher and pass or fail according to the guidelines of the PAR. Since teachers are reading the work of one another's students, it is crucial that all teachers arrive at the portfolio review with a shared understanding of what the document is asking of students and their writing.

In response to changing curricula, changing outcomes, and changing times, the PAR is revised somewhat regularly—we are currently on PAR 5.0. The shift from PAR 4.0 to 5.0 happened from May through August 2018. A group of five instructors—two adjunct instructors, a first-year teaching assistant, and two second-year teaching assistants—were selected from the larger teaching corps to meet throughout the summer to write, test, and revise a new PAR. There was a unique exigence for this revision: the WPAs at six of the University of Maine System (UMS) campuses had, over the course of the 2017–2018 academic year, developed a set of joint outcomes to productively align first-year composition throughout the University of Maine System. This was the first joint outcomes statement of its kind for first-year writing in UMS history, and I thought it was important that the flagship campus take immediate steps to implement it.

Though revising the PAR was a common practice in our program, it happened infrequently enough that I had not witnessed it since my hiring: I arrived in Orono after the completion of PAR 4.0 and was not available for the meetings that led to its creation. I was thus incredibly unsure about the pace of the project, what sorts of changes it might lead to, and the time commitment required. I aimed to set up some early meetings that allowed us to discuss, first, the shortcomings, problems, and contradictions we saw in PAR 4.0. Then, I turned to the new UMS Outcomes Statement (UMS-OS), and we had further discussions about what the language of this document might offer further revisions. After feedback from the other directors in the program, outside consultations from University of Maine-Augusta's Elizabeth Powers, and several further rounds of discussions, we piloted the new PAR with a range of portfolios from past semesters to test its durability. This led to a further round of revisions, which we agreed on in early August. The new PAR was presented and discussed at the August staff meeting of College Composition teachers.

Like Instance 1, the PAR revisions remained grounded in several ways. They took into account the needs of instructors in the program; they were test-driven with past portfolios to assure consistency across the semester; they were examined by interested stakeholders outside of the committee but inside of the program in order to check for oversights. At each stage of our work, we were able to actively pulverize the data we were receiving. We ground them, in other words, into useful fragments that could be assembled into useful insights that productively shaped the revision of the PAR.

INVARIANT CHARACTERISTICS: UNCERTAINTY, TRUST, AND MEDIATION

In my reflections on these events and the process through which new documents—the teaching principles in Instance 1 and the PAR 5.0 in Instance 2—were created, I identified several recurring, seemingly invariant, characteristics. These characteristics are invariant aspects of my own lived experience of working through each of these instances from my position as a liminal WPA.

Uncertainty

Throughout the process of writing both the principles and the PAR 5.0, I was in a frequent state of uncertainty: uncertainty of the process, whether it was working, what it was working toward, and how other members of the activity were making sense of the work. How did the two directors working with me in College Composition, for instance, see the value in the work we were doing to establish particular principles? How did the members of the PAR Revision Committee see themselves working toward a set goal through our twice-monthly meetings?

This uncertainty carried through each project largely because the boundaries of the above-mentioned activities were not clear-cut. On the surface, the boundaries seemed easily marked only because of a clear idea of a final end product: a list of principles and an assessment rubric. However, each of these documents offered a wide range of possibilities that had to be winnowed down—and, for that matter, winnowed down according to a process that many involved were engaging with for the first time, due to the high levels of teacher turnover in our program.[1] The seeming certainty of a final product, in other words, masked the complexities of taking on the work to get to that product.

This uncertainty might be read as an opportunity to "fake it till you make it" in some way, but such a move would actually, based on my own reflection, work against the act of engaging in grounded WPA decision-making. Remaining grounded in my WPA work means not an obfuscating but rather an embracing of uncertainty, a willingness to work through that which does not make much (or any) sense in order to allow the needs and concerns of the unfolding moments shape one's choices as a WPA. In my work with the principles, for instance, I needed to attend carefully to how the principles worked in various places: with the directors, in the act of observing, and in discussion with the teachers in the program. Only in attending to the ways in which these principles failed—where problems arose, where disconnects were evident, where they were not doing the work for which they were needed—could I identify (and later take up) opportunities for revision of the principles.

The challenge with uncertainty is its visibility: it can easily be seen as indecisiveness, and only regular, frequent communication can keep that viewpoint from emerging as a consensus. Regular communication about next steps, public celebration about the progress that the program makes, and linking our ongoing work to broader themes that the program is moving toward has allowed me to frame uncertainty as a strategic choice, a willingness to engage with the opinions of other perspectives in the program.

Trust

On the flip side of such an embrace of uncertainty is the invariant characteristic of trust: a willingness to step back from a particular aspect of a project and have faith that the participants will engage in the project in ways responsive to local needs. My work to bring together the PAR Revision Committee, for instance, was limited—deliberately—to doing very little aside from scheduling meeting times, setting agendas, and—at times—keeping the conversation from veering too far away from the rubric. But the bulk of the work—deciding on problems with the current PAR, cross-walking the UMS-OS to the PAR 4.0, negotiating language choices—emerged from the discussions that the members of the group had during our meetings. It was their language, the values that they were working through, that shaped the new PAR.

Such trust might seem to be an invitation to chaos, particularly when committee meetings are involved. In my work with the PAR Revision Committee, I often thought back to a story that my wife's family tells about her grandfather. When her father and his siblings were younger, her grandfather began renovating the bottom of the staircase, putting in tile flooring. When his children saw what he was doing, they insisted on helping. Rather than shoo them away, he gave each child one section of the floor and a pile of tiles to work with. He then coordinated their work so that, at the end of the work, the available tile covered the necessary flooring. This coordinating work proved crucial to my engagement with grounded WPA work—I needed to keep myself in the position to provide infrastructure for work, without being overly determinative in the way that work is assigned. Lindsey's grandfather did not have a crystallized vision of what the final flooring would look like—or, rather, he did not after his children jumped in to help—but the general setup and his strategic interventions allowed the eventual product to meet the needs of the situation with a careful attention to the situation on the ground, so to speak.

The work of the PAR revisions went ahead without any particular chaos, and certainly without the kind that children working with tile are capable of producing. Indeed, the embrace of trust—of asking, at the end of meetings, what the group felt had to happen next in order to accomplish our goals—seemed to reduce the likelihood of such chaos on its own. The committee was not asked to carry out someone else's vision; rather, they were asked to determine, based on their experiences with teaching and the values that emerged from their work in the program, what their vision would be, and work together to make it happen.

Mediation

My work of dealing with uncertainty and extending trust to other members of the program was supported by what I call *mediation*—that is, developing decisions through a series of interstitial steps. The development of the principles—up to and including their rollout at the end of the year—came one step at a time, with uncertainty dealt with from one moment to the next, and trust extended from one moment to the next. Even the broader structures of work that I put up to support the trust I extended were malleable, able to be reorganized if needed as a project developed.

Acts of mediation can be traced in each of the projects I indicate above: at each stage, opportunities to revel in uncertainty and extend trust were made with the broader work of the project in mind (without being overly determinative). Such acts of mediating a long-term project allowed each of these instances of WPA work to remain tightly grounded, responsive to local needs and, at the same time, operating in conjunction with the broader knowledge of the field that I brought with me to this particular site. Mediation is essentially the deferral of particular kinds of decision-making to free up one's attention to focus on the particularities of a given moment. Such a focus does more than simply create smaller, more manageable tasks: it allows the actual project to morph in response to emerging concerns with interested stakeholders.

In conjunction with "trust," mediation may seem to suggest a certain nebulousness in the long-term goals of the WPA, which is something that I do not intend. Mediation, as a characteristic of grounded WPA activity, works with the characteristic of trust to keep the long-term goals of both the WPA and the program in sync with the unfolding, moment-to-moment needs of the program. If writing programs—and those who administer them—are to successfully pursue new avenues of insight, to break new ground in the teaching and learning of writing, then WPAs will need to be responsive both to broader goals and local needs. Mediation serves as the concept that brings these two together.

Each of these characteristics represent the invariant essences of my lived experience of engaging in grounded WPA work. They were not goals of my work, but rather the recurring features that shaped my intentional engagement with the many tasks set before me as a WPA. They proved to be self-reinforcing characteristics: embracing uncertainty leads to small steps of establishing consensus, which further develops the trust I have in the colleagues I share this program with. It would be inaccurate to suggest that my WPA work was *always* grounded, or that I have not had challenges with implementing such an approach. But the work that I have come to fondly recall as grounded in nature has invariantly involved uncertainty, trust, and mediation.

A METAPHOR TO LIVE BY? GROUNDING LIMINAL WPA WORK

As is likely already clear to the reader from the rest of the chapter, I stepped into a WPA role in a high-quality, well-run first-year writing program. The program, in fact, went on to receive the 2018 CCCC Writing Program Certificate of Excellence. Though the award was given in my first year as Director of College Composition, I have joked that I "earned" that award the same way that Reagan "won" the Cold War: after others put in about a half-century of work,[2] I showed up at the end and ate a lot of jelly beans. I bring this up now to highlight the complex space I found myself in as a novice WPA. I was new to the field, new to the university, and new to a highly successful program with a rich history—that I was now running. Treating my work as a WPA as "grounded"—even if unevenly, even if in a way that was frequently undergoing a transformation—was a way to navigate this complex space in a liminal position.

Thinking through my work as a liminal WPA through this metaphor, then, has been effective for me given the specifics of my context. But is it a useful metaphor more widely? Might it have analytic heft for other WPAs in sometimes radically different but still liminal situations, particularly through a phenomenological lens? I would argue that such a perspective—that is, to live one's WPA work through a metaphor of groundedness—might prove a productive avenue for liminal WPAs attempting to establish themselves in both their programs and their fields. Liminal WPAs engaged in grounded WPA work have the opportunity to ask questions about their programs, to identify effective instructors, helpful stakeholders, and valuable opportunities so that they might begin the tough, exacting work of informed program development with the aid of those in the program. Such work has the opportunity to encourage ownership of the program throughout the teaching ranks, as well.

Liminal WPAs interested in taking on the work of grounded writing program administration can begin by reflecting on their administrative work with the three invariant characteristics of grounded administration in mind: how is the work that they do embracing uncertainty, extending trust, and providing a range of mediation to support both of those? Such responsiveness to local sites of administration can recruit additional support for liminal WPAs, bring in other stakeholders, and serve as a starting point for establishing broader counter-stories about engaging in liminal WPA work.

At the close of this chapter, I would like to return to the broader phenomenological project that Husserl imagined and consider its import for liminal WPAs. There were a number of aspects of grounded WPA work that I could not perceive for a range of reasons. For instance, my bodily presence as a larger, white male no doubt had an impact on how I am able to engage in grounded WPA work. Only through other phenomenological analyses by other liminal WPAs in a range of different circumstances can we build a robust, well-rounded sense of what it means to engage in grounded WPA work. Perhaps continued attention to such groundedness, continued applications of this method across sites, can enable a set of localized studies to generate flexible, productive characteristics that liminal WPAs can draw upon in a wider range of situations, in response to a greater variety of circumstances.

NOTES

1. Such turnover is by design: roughly two-thirds of our teaching corps consists of graduate teaching assistants completing a two-year MA program.
2. In particular, Pat Burnes, who served as the WPA at UMaine from 1972–2017, with only brief time away to temporarily take on other administrative duties. Dylan B. Dryer and Mary Plymale Larlee also spent over a decade developing the program before the award was issued.

REFERENCES

Adler-Kassner, Linda. 2008. *The Activist WPA: Changing Stories about Writing and Writers.* Logan, UT: Utah State University Press.

Applebee, Arthur N. 1986. "Musings . . . Principled Practice." *Research in the Teaching of English* 20 (1): 5–7.

Bazerman, Charles. 2008. "Theories of the Middle Range in Historical Studies of Writing Practice." *Written Communication* 25 (3): 298–318.
Glaser, Barney, and Anselm Strauss. 1967. *The Discovery of Grounded Theory: Strategies for Qualitative Research.* New York: Routledge.
Husserl, Edmund. 2013. *Ideas: General Introduction to a Pure Phenomenology.* New York: Routledge.
Husserl, Edmund, and Quentin Lauer. 1956. "Phenomenology as a Strict Science." *Cross-Currents* 6 (4): 325–44.
Lauer, Quentin. 1965. *Phenomenology: Its Genesis and Prospect.* New York: Harper.
McGlaun, Sandee K. 2007. "Administering Writing Programs in the 'Betweens': A jWPA Narrative." In *Untenured Faculty as Writing Program Administrators,* edited by Deborah Frank Dew and Alice Horning, 219–48. West Lafayette, IN: Parlor Press.
Moustakas, Clark. 1994. *Phenomenological Research Methods.* Thousand Oaks, CA: SAGE.
North, Stephen. 1987. *The Making of Knowledge in Composition: Portrait of an Emerging Field.* New York: Heinemann.
Phillips, Talinn, Paul Shovlin, and Megan Titus. 2014. "Thinking Liminally: Exploring the (com)Promising Positions of the Liminal WPA." *WPA: Writing Program Administration* 38 (1): 42–64.
Smagorinsky, Peter. 2009. "EJ Extra: Is It Time to Abandon the Idea of 'Best Practices' in the Teaching of English?" *The English Journal* 98 (6): 15–22.
Stolley, Amy Ferdinandt. 2015. "Narratives, Administrative Identity, and the Early Career WPA." *WPA: Writing Program Administration* 39 (1): 18–31.
Strickland, Donna. 2011. *The Managerial Unconscious in the History of Composition Studies.* Urbana, IL: NCTE.
van Manen, Max. 1990. *Researching Lived Experience: Human Science for an Action-Sensitive Pedagogy.* Albany: State University of New York Press.
van Manen, Max. 2014. *Phenomenology of Practice: Meaning-Giving Methods in Phenomenological Research and Writing.* New York: Routledge.

SECTION II

Institutional Landscapes

5
THE WPA AS LABOR ACTIVIST

John Belk

It has been almost three decades since the Council of Writing Program Administrators' Portland Resolution provided guidelines recognizing the diverse work of program administration that nonetheless falls outside of traditional academic labor models. In those decades, a number of metaphors have arisen to reflect the unique positions (and conditions) of WPAs: the WPA as intellectual (Council of Writing Program Administrators 1998), as professional (Olson and Ashton-Jones 1988), as researcher (Rose and Weiser 2002a), as theorist (Rose and Weiser 2002b), as middle manager (Malenczyk 2004), as father/husband/ex (Hesse 1999), as worker (Council of Writing Program Administrators 2014), and as activist broadly conceived (Addler-Kassner 2008). This essay adds to that list "WPA as labor activist," arguing that the history and rhetoric of organized labor offers a productive and more sustainable framework for considering the difficult-to-metaphorize work of WPAs across institutional contexts.

Labor activism historically has played an influential, though often overlooked, role in American rhetorical praxis, from contemporary trade unions to the more radical industrial unions of the early twentieth century. However, despite unionization efforts in higher education today, the discourse of organized labor has made few inroads into scholarship on academic administration, where the dominant metaphors tend to be filled with business-speak or managerial jargon (Deem and Brehony 2005).[1] For the hybrid roles of WPAs—often caught between the market strategies of upper administration, significant faculty responsibilities, and the needs of our students—the literal labor activist might serve as a metaphor that encompasses the WPA's paradoxical orientations toward bureaucracy, management, curriculum, and personnel.

To elucidate this claim, this piece begins by detailing a tradition of American labor rhetoric rooted in guiding principles of radical collectivity, anti-exploitation, and diversity, demonstrating how these roots might serve as new key principles for grounding the varied work of WPAs in the increasingly corporatized world of higher education. I then offer a heuristic for applying these guiding principles in the contemporary context of writing program administration, offering the metaphor of the labor activist as a way of reconceiving the work of the WPA. Finally, I illustrate an application of this heuristic in a brief case study of my first three years as a jWPA at a midsized regional university, focusing particularly on the twinned responsibilities of advocating for faculty and strengthening morale while simultaneously (and sometimes oppositionally) building relationships with upper administration, faculty colleagues in other disciplines, and departmental colleagues from other specializations of English studies. In doing so, I show how a metaphorical framework that focuses on radical collectivity, anti-exploitation, and diversity might recast old and familiar WPA narratives in fresh and inspiring ways. Ultimately, this essay not only offers a new set of metaphors for WPA labor, but also a means for applying those metaphors, demonstrating the pressing need for labor's voice in the contemporary neoliberal university.

RADICAL COLLECTIVITY, ANTI-EXPLOITATION, AND DIVERSITY: A TRADITION OF AMERICAN LABOR RHETORIC FOR WPAS

Perhaps the greatest tension in the early twentieth-century American labor movement was between the moderate trade unionism of the American Federation of Labor (AFL) and the revolutionary industrial unionism of radical organizations like the Industrial Workers of the World (IWW). Trade unionists focused on achieving pragmatic gains, such as the eight-hour workday for skilled laborers, within a framework of democratic capitalism. Their opponents criticized them for being exclusive, exclusionary, and even agents of capitalism itself (Foner 1965, 32–33). Industrial unionists, on the other hand, argued for a radical collectivity across trade lines (e.g., electricians joining with carpenters joining with unskilled factory workers) to bring about the revolutionary overthrow of the wage system and capitalism as a whole.[2] Their opponents criticized them as bomb hurlers, rainbow chasers, and unsavory rabble-rousers (Richard 2012). Both groups had designs on the soul of the American labor movement, and the tensions between them would play a major role in shaping the discourse of organized labor in ways that continue to hold great import for the work of WPAs. In particular, the activism of industrial unionism and the IWW would contribute three key principles to the larger tradition of American labor rhetoric: radical collectivity, anti-exploitation, and diversity. Furthermore, the literal examples of these principles in labor history provide a metaphorical framework for helping WPAs translate our own political commitments to effective action that resists exploitation and inequity at our institutions, in our disciplines, and in society as a whole.

The first principle, radical collectivity, might seem the most far-removed from the work of WPAs, as union strength and the efficacy of collective bargaining has waned in recent decades. However, the need for radical collectivity in the early twentieth century emerged out of material circumstances that look quite similar to the labor landscape of higher education today. For example, founded on the premise of universal labor solidarity across trade and craft lines, the IWW criticized the inherent worker divisions that employers leveraged to separate, stratify, and thereby exploit labor: craft versus industrial, skilled versus unskilled, experienced versus new, Anglo versus immigrant, and so on (Industrial Workers of the World 1905). Such divisions were further reinforced by the trade union system itself, which controlled job openings and charged high dues for laborers seeking to switch trades or migrate to new areas. These divisions disrupted the possibility of radical collectivity among workers, rendering efforts for improved working conditions "limited in scope and disconnected in action" and thereby ineffectual (Industrial Workers of the World 1905).

To anyone working off the tenure track in higher education today, these concerns most likely resonate all too well. From prohibitively high professional organization dues to stratified promotion and tenure systems to the unspoken "shelf life" of a terminal degree to a tightly vetted and controlled job market, it often seems as though the deck is stacked in favor of a segregated labor structure bent on maintaining a divided status quo: teaching versus research faculty, STEM versus humanities, contingent versus tenured, Student Affairs versus Academic Affairs, and so forth. Such stratifications in higher education have preserved a labor model collapsing under its own weight, as evidenced by the ongoing hiring crisis that seems to spread to new and previously "safe" disciplines with each academic year (McKenna 2016; National Science Foundation 2015). For WPAs then, the notion of radical collectivity asks us to consider our complicity in the segregated labor structures of academia, which hinder collective action and, by extension, improved working conditions for all.

With this notion of radical collectivity in mind, the second central tenet of American labor rhetoric for WPAs is a commitment to anti-exploitation. If collective action is the means by which labor achieves positive change, such collectivity must be rooted in anti-exploitative principles lest we sacrifice working conditions for some to improve working conditions for others. This was the central dilemma of the trade unions like the AFL, whose efforts in collective bargaining drew criticism for excluding unskilled laborers in order to secure better conditions for skilled trades. But while these more moderate trade unions focused their efforts on reducing economic exploitation of their members exclusively, more radical unions like the IWW took their efforts a step further. For the IWW, exploitation in any form—whether rooted, for example, in race, immigration status, linguistic background, geography, or education—was a danger to the solidarity (and therefore efficacy) of collective action. Because of this, the IWW saw the cause of anti-exploitation to be as much a cultural, political, and social battle as a pragmatic one limited to the workplace (Richard 2012). In other words, to eliminate workplace exploitation more narrowly, the example of the IWW demonstrates that we must commit to battling exploitation in society (or at the very least, higher education) as a whole.

Examples of the IWW's anti-exploitative commitments are numerous and well discussed in labor histories (see Foner 1965; Milton 1982; Richard 2012); however, the defining feature across all examples was an unwillingness to accept victories or compromises at the expense of other workers, especially the unskilled and foreign-born. In fact, the unwaveringness of this commitment would ultimately contribute to the IWW's decline, as established skilled laborers who participated in early IWW strikes viewed the swelling ranks as a symbol of union deterioration (Foner 1965, 552)—the promise of One Big Union was no match for the ingrained racism of American society. Nonetheless, the IWW's commitment to anti-exploitation has its greatest implication for WPAs in expanding the scope of labor organization beyond the narrow interests of particular crafts and trades—or in the terms of the contemporary university, beyond disciplinary boundaries and tenure status.

Tied to anti-exploitation, the final core principle for WPAs in the tradition of American labor rhetoric is diversity. Calls for increased and genuine diversity have been on the rise in the scholarship of writing program administration in recent years: one only need to look at Christy Wenger's 2014 article on "Feminism, Mindfulness, and the Small University jWPA," Amy Vidali's 2015 article on "Disabling Writing Program Administration," the entire Spring 2016 issue of *Writing Program Administration* on "Challenging Whiteness" (L'Eplattentier et al. 2016), the increasing scholarship on graduate student perspectives in writing program administration, or the immense body of work on inclusion, assessment, and retention that spans the top journals of rhetoric and writing studies. To extend that research, I suggest that this framework of labor rhetoric might offer valuable ways of discussing diversity in writing program administration (as well as instructive pitfalls to avoid).

More specifically, the IWW's commitments to diversity, while not without oversights, are particularly instructive for WPAs seeking to translate ideology into concrete action. For example, the IWW accepted membership cards from all foreign unions, minimizing logistical membership barriers for immigrants (Foner 1965, 18). Furthermore, IWW periodicals circulated in twenty-four different US cities and were published in nineteen different languages, radically increasing access to IWW messaging (Zimmer 2015). Finally, the IWW made well-documented use of poets and songwriters, providing increased accessibility for populations with low levels of reading and writing literacy.[3] Such policies and operational decisions may seem mundane to us today, but they are important examples of how the IWW translated their ideological commitments into tangible practice, a translation activity that well-meaning WPAs might engage in more deeply and more often.

Such translation of ideology to practice, however, raises the question of specifics: how might the principles of radical collectivity, anti-exploitation, and diversity exemplified here inform the work we do as WPAs? In the remainder of this piece, I build on the framework of this section to provide WPAs with a heuristic for action based on the principles above, highlighting the conversation between WPA work and how such work might be informed by the metaphor of labor activism. Because when labor activism is viewed as a guiding metaphor for WPAs, the grounding principles developed in this section offer new paths forward for making our individual workplaces—and our discipline as a whole—better.

LABOR ACTIVIST AS METAPHOR: A HEURISTIC FOR ACTION

Labor activism is a standpoint that can easily apply nonmetaphorically to the work of WPAs.[4] Often we are tasked with negotiating and implementing the literal material concerns of organized labor: collective bargaining (whether formal or informal), faculty contracts, leave approvals, group insurance policies, and more. Despite engaging in *aspects* of labor activism, however, most WPAs are not literally organizing workers, not even our own faculty. Many campuses are already unionized, and even for those that aren't, WPAs inhabit a paradoxical role of both advocate and manager when it comes to faculty interests. In light of this inherently paradoxical role, approaching the idea of "labor activist" as a metaphor (rather than a literal role) allows us to generate an even richer vocabulary that accounts for the slippery aspects of writing program administration, applying the diversity-focused, anti-exploitative, and collective framework detailed above to situations where WPAs must balance the interests of individual faculty with the interests of an entire writing program.

It is no surprise that WPAs are regularly faced with difficult and often contradictory decisions—the devil's deal is ever present. Consider the following scenario: for several years, a WPA has been arguing for a reduction of course caps to bring writing program teaching loads more in-line with national disciplinary standards. Many reports and much deliberation later, upper administration agrees to a formal request for lowered course caps, resulting in a predicted shortage of twelve sections for the upcoming academic year.[5] The condition of the lowered caps, however, is that the section shortage it creates must be made up using adjunct labor rather than new full-time teaching lines. This leaves the WPA with a difficult decision: secure lower course caps for full-time faculty by staffing more courses with adjuncts or settle for more onerous full-time teaching loads in order to resist reliance on adjuncts. These are obviously not the literal concerns of an automotive plant or textile mill, but nonetheless, the metaphor of labor activism—and the guiding principles of radical collectivity, anti-exploitation, and diversity it provides—offers a heuristic by which we might navigate such difficult decisions.

Simply writing out the above scenario, my instinct, training, and pragmatism screamed to take the deal. The managerial side of writing program administration makes the rational decision of securing long-term improvements to working conditions seem like a victory—even if it means sacrificing to the altar of increased adjunctification. However, the framework of radical collectivity and anti-exploitation suggests otherwise. How long will gains remain gains if they come at the expense of other workers? Will moving from 5 percent adjuncts to 10 percent mean that, with each new enrollment surge, adding adjuncts becomes the new default solution? And how do we argue effectively for the value of our labor when we are so quick to fill roles with underpaid and exploited versions of ourselves? Furthermore, the decisions we make at our institutions have import and influence beyond our walls. The increased reliance on statistical comparison between peer institutions means our labor practices directly affect those of our neighbors (both metaphorical and geographical), so that our increased reliance on cheap labor becomes justification for theirs and vice versa.

This is not to say that the problem is unsolvable, or that in attempting to solve it we are destined for Rachel Riedner and Kevin Mahoney's "cycle of despair" (2008), which Seth Kahn takes up eloquently in a WPA context to show how progress can be paralyzed by specious calls to reason and moderation (2015, 114). Looking to ecological models of writing program administration (Cooper 1986; Kahn 2015; Kipling and Murphy 1992; Ryan 2012), localized conditions might offer partial solutions to the most intransigent of thought experiments. For example, a midsized comprehensive university might still lower course caps by absorbing overage through increased scheduling efficiency. A small liberal arts college (SLAC) might consider curricular change or improved placement procedures to offset the increased time to graduation created by fewer sections of required writing. A research-intensive university might offer more summer sections to unionized graduate students to supplement stipend packages. All of these institutions have unique variables that offer possible (if partial) relief to adjunctification. Often, though, it is true that no good solutions exist—no amount of placement finagling or grad-student teaching will solve the issue. In these cases with no *good* solutions, it should be our goal at the very least to avoid increasingly bad solutions, particularly solutions that increase exploitation and decrease solidarity among faculty, thereby devaluing the labor of our colleagues and ourselves.

Ultimately, what we must ask ourselves when faced with the complex and often "unwinnable" decisions of writing program administration is this:

1. Is our decision radically collective—does it hold the various manifestations of labor in our program equal, and does it support that labor to the inclusion, rather than exclusion, of the laborers in our program?[6]

2. Is our decision anti-exploitative—does it reduce or resist inequities, inequality, and exploitative tendencies in our immediate programmatic context?

3. Is our decision rooted in diverse ways of knowing and doing—do we draw on the expertise and lived experiences of the faculty in our program, rather than assuming our own training or background offers the best solution?

Even with such a heuristic, though, we will inevitably have to make difficult decisions. The R1 offering more summer classes to graduate students could be seen as perpetuating inadequate compensation in their standard-term contracts. Improved placement procedures at the SLAC may create an opportunity for un- or undercompensated labor in the form of scoring placement exams. But if the history of labor rhetoric presented in this paper is any example, we cannot see the partialities and impossibilities of our decisions as an excuse to fall into Riedner and Mahoney's paralyzing cycle of despair, where no good is possible because no change can occur in the face of our inaction. If we operate in good faith, guided by the principles of the above heuristic, we can certainly limit the harm of the decisions we must make while spreading "optimism and humaneness" rather than "despair, frustration, and toxic sludge" (Kahn 2015, 118). And that, more than anything, should be the goal of anyone who takes on the role—literal or metaphorical—of labor activist.

THE JWPA AS LABOR ACTIVIST: A CASE STUDY

So far, I have outlined a tradition of labor rhetoric rooted in radical collectivity, anti-exploitation, and diversity, and I have demonstrated how the metaphor of labor activism grounded in these concepts offers a decision-making heuristic for WPAs. But what does the application of such a heuristic look like in practice? To answer that, I will detail a brief case study of how in my first three years as jWPA at a mid-sized, teaching-intensive university the principles outlined above have pervaded my own decision-making while blurring the lines between the metaphor and praxis of labor activism.[7]

The Writing Program at Southern Utah University (SUU) is housed under the administrative umbrella of the English Department. The department is made up of twenty-six full-time faculty, half of whom are non-tenure-track, with first-year writing as their primary teaching load. As WPA, I have a direct supervisory role over these thirteen faculty, but I also have the more important role of ensuring their voices are heard through the governance structures of the department and university. As a result, my first three years as WPA were spent largely doing the work of a union representative: building morale, providing advocacy, and generally representing the needs and interests of writing faculty to English department and university administration.

The first place our writing program illustrates the principles laid out in this article is in its actual labor structure. Writing faculty at SUU are full-time non-tenure-track (FTNTT) faculty with benefits and a promotion structure that parallels the tenure track: lecturer → assistant professor (NTT) → associate professor (NTT). While FTNTT faculty are not eligible for tenure, they do (thanks to recent policy revisions) move to a five-year performance-review cycle upon advancement to associate professor (NTT), which provides a form of de facto security and stability that parallels tenure.[8] Such a structure, modeled on principles of anti-exploitation, has allowed us to hire experienced, long-term career teachers with diverse backgrounds into our writing program. These hiring decisions, however, have led to another way my WPA work has come to mirror the work of labor activism.

Experienced FTNTT faculty require little managerial oversight but do require more advocacy, particularly because they are granted more liberal autonomy in how and what they teach. Rather than training graduate students or ensuring consistency among adjuncts who might be teaching at multiple schools with multiple curricula, I am required to do very little day to day in the way of supervising full-time faculty. Instead, I spend more time advocating for the needs and interests of those faculty: arguing for special teaching assignments, increased travel allocations for scholarship and professional development, protections against student complaints, and so forth. Furthermore, despite being full-time and benefitted, our faculty are no less contingent, as Richard Colby and Rebekah Shultz Colby (2017) point out about the FTNTT faculty of the similarly structured University of Denver Writing Program (61). And this contingency too requires added advocacy demands.

Like those in the University of Denver's Writing Program, our FTNTT lines are approved directly through the provost's office, and are largely dependent on the financial exigencies of the state legislature. While we have never cut an FTNTT line in my time as WPA, those lines are nonetheless still one-year contracts, even after promotion to associate professor (NTT) moves the line to a five-year review cycle.[9] Within this context, then, even scheduling becomes a form of labor activism—while many programs consistently push for new lines, viewing growth as a positive, we have been deliberately conservative in both our scheduling practices and budget requests. We maintain a 95 percent fill-rate across all of our sections with a 10–15 percent drop/fail/withdraw rate, running deliberately "lean" so that the necessity of FTNTT lines is apparent: there is no scheduling buffer to absorb a cut faculty line, no empty seats for those unserved students to fill. There is also no way to make up the loss in efficiency and concomitant increase in time-to-graduation for students forced to delay their required writing because of fewer seats offered. This approach has resulted in a slower rate of faculty growth but much greater assurance that lines will be permanent in practice if not in contract. The choice to put added energy into scheduling, then, is one drawn out of radical collectivity: the overall health and efficiency of our program has direct correlation to the stability and material circumstances of the faculty lines we employ.

Finally, we have made a concerted effort toward diversity in our writing program over the last three years, supported by SUU hiring a woman of color as the first Vice President for Diversity and Inclusion in 2016. Because SUU is a rural campus in a small, predominantly white community, it can be difficult to recruit and retain faculty with a diversity of lived experiences, especially for non-tenure track positions. However, the decision to put added energy into faculty recruitment and retention is, like the energy put into scheduling, a conscious political decision in the spirit of the heuristic detailed above. By recruiting diverse faculty, we not only benefit our students but the overall health of the writing program and the deliberative decisions we make via faculty governance. And as seen in the IWW's ideological commitments, such decisions extend beyond the workplace, improving our larger community in tangible and intangible ways.

If it sounds like I am tooting our writing program's collective horn, I am—a bit. We have managed to achieve a work environment and labor structure in our program that suits the faculty involved and represents their interests in ethical and positive ways. But is it enough? As detailed in this section, the majority of our writing faculty are still contingent, even if they enjoy far greater protections than many. And that is unlikely to change anytime soon. Likewise, when asked, the writing faculty at SUU still offer a number of ways that they could feel more included in governance decisions, more protected in review processes, more fairly compensated, and more satisfied all-around with the valuing of their labor.

So the entire argument of this essay leads to an inevitable question: is the framework presented here even possible under the current conditions of higher education? Put differently, can radical collectivity, anti-exploitation, and true diversity even be achieved short of revolutionary means? To be clear, I'm not calling for the armed overthrow of boards of trustees across the country. However, the call to reconsider the foundations of our shared enterprise—to truly rethink the systems and hierarchies of higher education from the ground up—is perhaps the biggest challenge offered by considering the WPA as literal and metaphorical labor activist. Because to ignore the radical, revolutionary elements of the labor movement is in many ways to disregard the engine of its successes.

CONCLUSIONS

My greatest sense of guilt stems from this lack of revolutionary change: we (all of us involved in our writing program at SUU) have worked hard to ensure fair labor practices over the last three years. Our course caps have decreased, resulting in a 10 percent reduction in teaching-load headcount. Our writing classes are taught almost entirely (95 percent) by full-time, benefitted faculty. Salary discrepancy between full-time teaching faculty and tenure-track faculty has reduced by 15 percent. And within the constraint-driven decision-making contexts of writing program administration, I have in many ways embodied Mark McBeth and Tim McCormack's (2017) reassurance that "the WPA's goals cannot simply resist bureaucratic imperatives, but must alternatively re-envision judicious solutions to them, even if not legibly revolutionary" (43). But in the activist framework presented by this piece, I can't help but feel that I haven't been revolutionary enough.

And maybe this is where the *metaphor* of labor activism is useful. Like any good metaphor, the principles of radical collectivity, anti-exploitation, and diversity can be applied literally, serving as a generative heuristic toward direct action. But metaphors offer more than utilitarian guides to decision-making—they underscore the larger values we, and our discipline as a whole, should strive toward. So even for WPAs who don't position themselves as literal activists (or for those of us who feel we could do more), the metaphor of labor activism can still reveal, shape, and reinforce our underlying values and commitments as administrators. Through the metaphor of labor activism, we hold our own roles within the complex ecologies of higher education in high relief. And in considering how that metaphor applies to our literal work, we might realize how each decision we face is not simply business as usual, but a political opportunity for improving working conditions and lives—of our colleagues, our students, and ourselves.

Likewise, there are many angles to labor activism left undiscussed here that might benefit WPAs. There is a robust and growing body of literature on organizer burnout that mirrors and in many ways extends discussions of burnout in our own discipline, especially for hybrid faculty-administrators like WPAs and department chairs. There is also a stunning body of literature on community outreach for labor activists that dovetails nicely with our own movement in writing studies toward service learning, engaged learning, and community-based learning. Furthermore, the literature of labor offers wonderfully creative, pragmatic, and accessible strategies for organizational improvement that could benefit writing studies immensely. But none of these conversations will magically create a worker's utopia in higher education, or fair compensation across stratified faculty, or humane working conditions for faculty and staff overnight. And maybe that's okay.

There is a famous IWW saying that "labor is entitled to all it produces" (Industrial Workers of the World 1924), and perhaps the flip side is that there is always more labor to be produced. Maybe it's okay to not fix all the inequities of higher education at once, or to not be the vanguard of a higher education revolution. Maybe all we can do is be our best selves, guided by principles of collectivity and anti-exploitation and diversity, laboring together to make a better world—or at least better writing programs. Because in the end, there is still so much work to be done.

NOTES

1. Interestingly, the opposite is true for faculty discourse: David Deshler's 1985 study of eighty-three extensive interview transcripts with higher-ed employees found that faculty often use labor language to discuss their own work while using business terms to metaphorically denote negative feelings toward administration (25–27). For example, the desire for "solidarity, unity, collaboration, reconciliation, and interdependence can be inferred" from many of the faculty-used metaphors in the study (24), while faculty metaphors for administration were more commerce-oriented, including phrases like "MBA accounting mentality," "bankruptcy," and "gobbled up in market values" (27).
2. For a more detailed statement of the IWW's goals and philosophies see Industrial Workers of the World's *Industrial Union Manifesto*, penned by IWW leadership at the 1905 Conference of Industrial Unionists at Chicago.
3. For more on the social role of poetry and song in the early twentieth-century labor movement, see Marsh (2007), 15–18; Harrington (2002). For more on the IWW philosophy of poetry and song, see Wilson (1908).
4. It is worth reiterating that, in addition to labor activism serving a useful metaphorical function for writing program administration, many WPAs also engage regularly in overt labor activism, serving as union representatives, generating and disseminating more equitable hiring and evaluation documents, and liaising with professional organizations on behalf of workers (Council of Writing Program Administrators, n.d.).
5. For more on the intricacies of how a decision on an issue like course caps might result in such a drastic effect on scheduling, see Reiff et al.
6. Mirroring the IWW's radical openness, the term "laborer" here is used in a spirit of inclusivity to include students and other workers who might not directly inhabit the literal role of "employee."
7. While I have maintained a distinction throughout this piece between the metaphor of labor activism and its praxis, it is worth noting that in the complex ecosystems of higher education, such distinctions often blur. Furthermore, while I have focused my argument on the metaphor of labor activism, it is the translation of metaphor into action that ultimately creates lasting change, as Paulo Freire notes in *Pedagogy of the Oppressed*: "Liberation is a praxis: the action and reflection of men and women upon their world in order to transform it" (79).
8. FTNTT faculty also receive base-salary raises equivalent to tenure-line faculty upon promotion. For more details on the structure of the SUU Writing Program, see Belk (2018).
9. There is an added form of labor activism that arises here: the emotional labor of advocacy—assuring that FTNTT faculty voices are heard in policy discussions

(particularly pertaining to yearly evaluation criteria), reassuring those faculty in times of change or uncertainty, and maintaining morale among those faculty via a listening ear and transparent decision-making.

REFERENCES

Adler-Kassner, Linda. 2008. *The Activist WPA: Changing Stories about Writing and Writers.* Logan: Utah State University Press.

Belk, John. 2018. "Maintaining a Humanistic Center: Rhetorical Humanism as a Holistic Framework for Writing Programs." *Composition Forum*, no. 40 (Fall). http://compositionforum.com/issue/40/southern-utah.php.

Colby, Richard, and Rebekah Shultz Colby. 2017. "Real Faculty but Not: The Full-Time Non-Tenure-Track Position as Contingent Labor." In *Contingency, Exploitation and Solidarity: Labor and Action in English Composition*, edited by Seth Kahn, William Lalicker, and Amy Lynch-Biniek, 57–70. Fort Collins: The WAC Clearinghouse, University Press of Colorado.

Cooper, Marilyn M. 1986. "The Ecology of Writing." *College English* 48 (4): 364–75.

Council of Writing Program Administrators. n.d. "Labor Resource Center." Updated July 2, 2020. https://csal.colostate.edu/resources/cwpa/.

Council of Writing Program Administrators. 1998. "Evaluating the Intellectual Work of Writing Program Administration." http://wpacouncil.org/positions/intellectualwork.html.

Council of Writing Program Administrators. 2014. "CWPA 2014: Call for Proposals." http://wpacouncil.org/CWPA-conference-2014-CFP.

Deem, Rosemary, and Kevin J. Brehony. 2005. "Management as Ideology: The Case of 'New Managerialism' in Higher Education." *Oxford Review of Education* 31, no. 2: 217–35.

Deshler, David. 1985. "Metaphors and Values in Higher Education." *Academe* 71, no. 1: 22–28.

Foner, Philip S. 1965. *History of the Labor Movement in the United States, Vol. 4: The Industrial Workers of the World, 1905–1917.* New York: International Publishers.

Freire, Paulo. 1970. *Pedagogy of the Oppressed.* Translated by Myra Bergman Ramos. 30th anniv. ed. London: Continuum.

Harrington, Joseph. 2002. *Poetry and the Public: The Social Form of Modern U.S. Poetics.* Middletown, CT: Wesleyan University Press.

Hesse, Douglas. 1999. "The WPA as Father, Husband, Ex." In *Kitchen Cooks, Plate Twirlers, and Troubadours: Writing Program Administrators Tell Their Stories*, edited by Diana George, 44–55. Portsmouth, NH: Boynton.

Industrial Workers of the World. 1905. *Industrial Union Manifesto.* https://archive.iww.org/history/library/iww/industrial_union_manifesto/.

Industrial Workers of the World. 1924. *Education and System: the Basis of Organization.* Chicago, IL: Printing and Publishing Workers Industrial Union no. 450. http://archive.lib.msu.edu/DMC/AmRad/educationsystembasis.pdf.

Kahn, Seth. 2015. "Towards an Ecology of Sustainable Labor Practices (and Other Places)." *Writing Program Administration* 39, no. 1 (Fall): 109–21.

Kipling, Kim J., and Richard J. Murphy. 1992. *Symbiosis: Writing and an Academic Culture.* Portsmouth, NH: Boynton/Cook.

L'Eplattentier, Barbara, Sherry Rankins Robinson, and Lisa Mastrangelo, editors. 2016. "Symposium: Challenging Whiteness and/in Writing Program Administration and Writing Programs." *Writing Program Administration* 39, no. 2 (Spring).

Malenczyk, Rita. 2004. "Doin' the Managerial Exclusion: What WPAs Might Need to Know about Collective Bargaining." *WPA: Writing Program Administration* 27, no. 3 (Spring): 23–33.

Marsh, John. 2007. *You Work Tomorrow: An Anthology of American Labor Poetry, 1929–41*. Ann Arbor: University of Michigan Press.

McBeth, Mark, and Tim McCormack. 2017. "An Apologia and a Way Forward: In Defense of the Lecturer Line in Writing Programs." In *Contingency, Exploitation and Solidarity: Labor and Action in English Composition*, edited by Seth Kahn, William Lalicker, and Amy Lynch-Biniek, 41–55. Fort Collins: The WAC Clearinghouse, University Press of Colorado.

McKenna, Laura. 2016. "The Ever-Tightening Job Market for Ph.D.s." *The Atlantic*, April 21, 2016. https://www.theatlantic.com/education/archive/2016/04/bad-job-market-phds/479205/.

Milton, David. 1982. *The Politics of U.S. Labor*. New York: Monthly Review Press.

National Science Foundation. 2015. "Doctorate Recipients from U.S. Universities." National Center for Science and Engineering Statistics and the Directorate for Social, Behavioral, and Economic Sciences. December 2015. https://www.nsf.gov/statistics/doctorates/.

Olson, Gary A., and Evelyn Ashton-Jones. 1988. "Writing Center Directors: The Search for Professional Status." *Writing Program Administration* 12, nos. 1–2 (Fall/Winter): 19–28.

Reiff, Mary Jo, Anis Bawarshi, Michelle Ballif, and Christian Weisser. 2015. *Ecologies of Writing Programs: Program Profiles in Context*. Anderson, SC: Parlor Press.

Richard, Joe. 2012. "The Legacy of the IWW." *International Socialist Review* 86 (November). https://isreview.org/issue/86/legacy-iww/index.html.

Riedner, Rachel, and Kevin Mahoney. 2008. *Democracies to Come: Rhetorical Action, Neoliberalism, and Communities of Resistance*. Lanham, MD: Lexington/Rowman and Littlefield.

Rose, Shirley K., and Irwin Weiser. 2002a. "The WPA as Researcher and Archivist." In *The Writing Program Administrator's Resource*, edited by Stuart C. Brown and Theresa Enos, 275–302. Mahwah, NJ: Lawrence Erlbaum.

Rose, Shirley K., and Irwin Weiser, editors. 2002b. *The Writing Program Administrator as Theorist*. Portsmouth, NH: Boynton/Cook/Heinemann.

Ryan, Kathleen J. 2012. "Thinking Ecologically: Rhetorical Ecological Feminist Agency and Writing Program Administration." *Writing Program Administration* 36, no. 1 (Fall/Winter): 74–94.

Vidali, Amy. 2015. "Feminism, Mindfulness, and the Small University jWPA." *Writing Program Administration* 38, no. 2 (Spring): 32–55.

Wenger, Christy I. 2014. "Feminism, Mindfulness, and the Small University jWPA." *Writing Program Administration* 37, no. 1 (Fall): 117–40.

Wilson, James. 1908. "The Value of Music in I.W.W. Meetings." *Industrial Union Bulletin*, May 1908.

Zimmer, Kenyon. 2015. "IWW Newspapers, 1906–1946." *IWW History Project*. http://depts.washington.edu/iww/map_newspapers.shtml.

6
LEARNING, REPRESENTING, AND ENDORSING THE LANDSCAPE
WPA as Cartographer

Katherine Daily O'Meara

> *"I've always been fascinated by maps and cartography. A map tells you where you've been, where you are, and where you're going—in a sense it's three tenses in one."*
> —Peter Greenaway, *Film Comment*
> (May/June 1990)

The nature of the cartographer is to create maps and report what is there. They are responsible for map *projection*: representing the terrain accurately. Cartographers are also accountable for what's known as *generalization*: determining the relevance of objects on the map and reducing complexity for viewers and users. And lastly, they help implement *design*: orchestrating the salient components of the map for its intended audience. Cartographers have historically been tasked with mapmaking to help others "define, explain, and navigate their way through the world" ("History of Cartography" 2018).

The metaphor of the cartographer is an apt one for a WPA. WPAs are frequently called upon to represent and advocate for the ever-changing landscape of their writing program and its positionality in the larger university. Historical knowledge of how an institutional map used to be is beneficial for any WPA, hence why the enculturation period is such a vital step for a new administrator. Furthermore, these cartographer-WPAs use what they learn to make recommendations and plan for the futures of their programs, teachers, and students. Institutional and programmatic changes and initiatives condition the topography of the WPA's map, and so these wily cartographers persist in their commitment to re-envisioning the landscape as changes occur over time. The institutional structures and interpersonal relationships that enable a program to sustain itself can be made visible on maps created by WPAs (or, as we will see in the pages that follow, maps created by others for WPA use). Thus, cartography as a skill and as a metaphor for writing program administrators proves to be a viable method for WPAs to create and maintain programs (and curricula, and assessments, and relationships across the university and beyond) that are dynamic and ultimately sustainable.

I came to this metaphor organically through a variety of disparate situations. Cartography, or mapmaking as I originally thought of it in popular terms, seemed to come into the mix naturally, based on the methodologies I used first as a doctoral student specializing in writing program administration and now as the Director of Composition in my small Midwestern university. Initially, cartography was tied to the research methodology institutional ethnography (IE), a natural venue for making maps that "seeks to uncover *how things happen*—how institutional discourse compels and shapes" individuals' lived realities in a complex organization such as a writing program, department, or university (LaFrance and Nicolas 2012, 130). As a new jWPA in my third year of a tenure-track position, I found mapmaking such an informative and generative practice, particularly in learning a landscape in order to assess it, that I employed mapping as a hands-on student activity in my "Intro to Writing Program Administration" graduate course. Each of my cartography experiences proved to be a beneficial and eye-opening experience.

This chapter shares the two cartography experiences from my WPA life. Both of these mapmaking experiences make visible the WPA's (and others') positionalities within and without the writing program, situating actors in their lived realities and helping administrators learn, represent, and endorse their programmatic landscapes for the common good. As the latter sections of this chapter will detail, I was doing map-related things before I even knew to give a name to my practice. It was only when I read the CFP for this edited collection that these experiences fell into place as one particular application: cartography. The identity of "WPA as Cartographer" (i.e., the value of the actual practice of mapmaking, as well as the metaphor in general) has proven to be essential in my own visualization of my writing program and my place in it, as well as the ways in which different mapping scenarios inform decisions that WPAs in general make about their work environments and the futures of their programs.

WHY CARTOGRAPHY?

In their article on institutional critique, Porter and colleagues (2000) advocate for authentic institutional change through rhetorical action. Though universities tend to move at a glacial pace, they are indeed malleable: "[Universities] are not monoliths; they are rhetorically constructed human designs (whose power is reinforced by buildings, laws, traditions, and knowledge-making practices) and so are changeable" (Porter et al. 2000, 611). But where does one start, when an institutional change is desired, requested, or demanded? The first step, often, is to find out what's already there. Institutional history is paramount, whether that means learning the actual historical timeline of events or establishing who works well with whom (or not). A WPA's ability to "read a writing program" can be made more transparent and tangible through mapmaking (Peters 1998, 123). Furthermore, if the WPA is the cartographer, she can then share her map with relevant interested parties, allies and advocates, and even adversaries, to receive feedback, direction, and critique. Programmatic and institutional cartography can be a collaborative effort.

Mapmaking makes visible the complex landscape of a writing program and other institutional writing spaces, and the cartographer-WPA is responsible for presenting and situating this complexity. Porter and coauthors (2000) employ the notion of spatial critique in their article, as do Porter and Sullivan (2007), who note that mapping visualizes the diverse views, perceptions, and experiences of writing program teachers and other stakeholders. Individuals do not always look at the same situation in exactly the same way; they may situate their experiences "in different places and according to varied hierarchies" (Porter and Sullivan 2007, 20). The better WPAs can represent people's "local and discursive" (e.g., complex, lived, day-to-day, "in the trenches") experiences, the more accurately we can portray what's happening in and around our programs. Mapmaking does this for WPAs naturally.

Risks

Peeples (1999) notes both the promise and possible perils of map creation in his chapter "'Seeing' the WPA With/Through Postmodern Mapping." It is true that "identities arise out of the spaces in which people live, work, and play" (153), and map-generation helps portray these spaces and can often give voice to the invisible, marginalized, or lower-prestige actors on the map. However, mapping strategies have continually been critiqued for the relative ease with which the cartographer may choose to conceal, misrepresent, and even "colonize" the spaces and people contained within a map (Peeples 1999, 154; see also Porter 1998; Porter and Sullivan 2007; Sullivan and Porter 1993). In this way, the WPA as cartographer holds a subjective and potentially controversial role in the mapmaking endeavor, and this knowledge should prompt them to move forward carefully and thoughtfully. This important concept of colonization, particularly in the obligation of humans (WPAs included) not only to accurately represent but also to care for all moving parts, both human and nonhuman, is discussed at length in Wilkes's chapter in the present volume.

Mapmaking is a messy practice at best. When being created, maps are dependent upon the cartographer to accurately portray and represent the information therein. Then, once a map is created, it is more often than not a static artifact—edits are not necessarily made often or with real-time changes. Maps may also be interpreted in myriad ways, read through different lenses and angles and for different exigencies and purposes. Mapmakers get to decide what to portray and what to obscure. It is therefore the cartographer's responsibility to ensure the most accurate and up-to-date rendering possible, making clear what and who are being represented, by whom, and for whom. Maps portray a snapshot by a particular mapmaker, from a particular perspective, and of a particular time. It is this situated and potentially privileged positionality that makes the metaphor of WPA as cartographer so significant. WPAs assume this responsibility whether they explicitly acknowledge it or not, and so it is important to be aware of the inherent risks of mapmaking and address them. And furthermore, while WPAs at all stages of their careers can use mapmaking to facilitate their work, new WPAs (like me) may find cartography a useful endeavor in enculturating to a new landscape.

Many (new) WPAs experience what Peters (1998) calls an *enculturation*: a three-stage process to condition themselves to their positions, including critically reading their program, finding allies (and adversaries), and working toward building a "coherent community identity" (123). I realized as I was in the thick of my own enculturation experiences (first as a graduate student WPA, then as the new WPA at a four-year university) just how beneficial a mapmaking inquiry could be to learn how things happen in people's everyday work lives—who our allies and stakeholders are, what texts and tools help us achieve our goals, where writing happens, and how to locate the other spaces that facilitate our writing and teaching of writing. Cartography was a tool that I could use to better understand and assess a writing program, to help my writing program connect with other spaces of writing across the university, and to "pay it forward" and teach grad students how to use mapmaking to better their own institutional and classroom contexts. Overall, the "WPA as Cartographer" metaphor can be shared with all writing program administrators to help conceptualize our roles within the institution and, for new WPAs especially, to facilitate enculturation and to inform decisions that they make about their work environment and the future of their programs.

The next sections detail my two actual mapmaking experiences: first from my dissertation-writing days as a PhD student and graduate WPA, and next from a mapmaking assignment I included in a graduate-level "Intro to WPA" course I currently teach.

MAPMAKING SCENARIO 1: DISSERTATION STUDY

My full dissertation study was an institutional ethnography investigating the "everyday/everynight" (Campbell and Gregor 2004, 27) experiences of nine second-language (L2) teachers in the Writing Programs at Arizona State University.[1] Because they are viewed as a WPA's "ethical obligation" (Huot and Schendel 2007, 207), program evaluation and assessment procedures that consider individual experiences should be carefully devised and implemented. Many complex overlapping factors interact and contribute to a writing teacher's everyday work life; therefore, multiple data-collection tools were necessary to fully capture the ways that teachers describe their jobs. To mitigate this complexity, I devised a mapping activity or heuristic for participants to complete during data collection to organize the interpersonal relationships, materials and texts, and spaces and places inherent in their jobs as L2 writing teachers (see appendix 6.A for this mapping heuristic). Smith asks institutional ethnographers to initially situate their research by "looking up from where [they] are" within the institution (2006, 5). Researchers can then determine how individual participants' perceptions and experiences inform a larger social organization. I created the mapping heuristic after I "looked up" from my own understanding of the program as I had viewed it and regarded the differences in perception of work experiences felt by other writing teachers of different roles and ranks in my writing program—namely, the graduate student teaching assistants (TAs) and the part- and full-time non-tenure-track (NTT) faculty members who were also teaching in the program. The NTT faculty's experiences *felt* different to me, complicated and layered and different from my own as a TA, but I struggled to create interview questions that adequately got to the root of their differences. To tease out their subtle variations of perception and experience, I took a cue from Peeples's (1999) chapter on WPAs and postmodern mapping, as well as a mapping activity Ortmeier-Hooper (2007) used in her doctoral dissertation.

The task of mapmaking was relatively simple. Each participant was asked to map out their work lives. They were given Post-It notes of three different colors: the darkest color (dark) for people involved in their day-to-day work lives, the medium color (medium) for the places and spaces in which they worked, and the lightest color (light) for the materials and texts inherent in their positions. Participants were presented with a large piece of drawing paper—what Peeples refers to as *static background* (2007). I chose Post-Its because they could be easily moved around, and I suggested that participants use pen or pencil to write down details or clarifications or draw connections among Post-Its as needed. Participants were given no "starting point" or central controlling location for their maps. They were asked to use twenty minutes to create their best maps of their L2-writing-teacher lives, and later in the interview to use their maps to help explain their work experiences.

For the purposes of my dissertation research and this chapter, I focused on three of the nine participants: Becky, Sam, and Lex (pseudonyms). Becky was a full-time NTT faculty member; Sam, a PhD student in rhetoric and composition; Lex, a part-time NTT adjunct. These differing roles and ranks of writing played an integral part in the participants' map creation and overall conceptualization of their work lives, including and especially their central controlling organization and their inclusion of people (and nonpeople who were counted as people, as you will see).

Where Did They Begin?

The first meaningful finding was in simply looking at the initial organization of Becky's, Sam's, and Lex's Post-It maps.

Becky and Lex, NTT instructors in the writing program, began their maps with a dark "people" Post-It for "students" and organized the rest of their maps around that central note. Becky connected the "students" Post-It to the places and spaces in which she interacted with them: "Google hangouts—digital meeting," "Social media—Facebook, Twitter, and Instagram," "My office," and "My classroom." Lex included three separate dark Post-Its for her students' major first-language groups. Lex then connected these dark Post-Its to light "materials/texts" Post-Its for the assignments she used in FYC and for other sources such as the Internet and access to the campus library, as well as to a medium Post-It for her classroom meeting space.

Learning, Representing, and Endorsing the Landscape   103

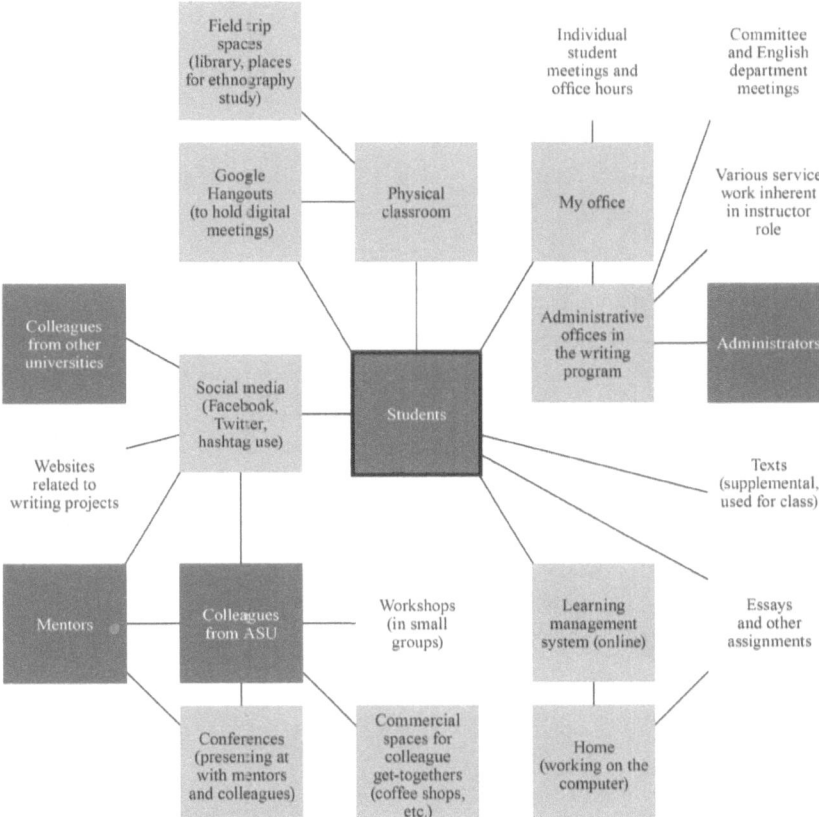

Figure 6.1. Becky's Work Map. Key: dark = people; medium = places/spaces; light = materials/texts.

Contrasted with instructors Becky and Lex, TA Sam chose a different central organization: in the center of his map is a Post-It for "curriculum," on which he also wrote "purposes, goals, objectives, definitions of writing and literacy" and drew arrows toward the eventual "assignment sequence" for his FYC course. The central "curriculum" Post-It was then immediately connected to two other light "texts/materials" Post-Its for "Textbooks and materials" and "Resources for common activities" including peer review as well as grammar and citation lessons. When reflecting upon his map-construction, Sam noted that "[c]urriculum is always at the center for [him]; purposes, goals, and objectives; definitions of what writing is, what literacy is, and *how* those components are encapsulated in the assignment sequence or arc for the semester."

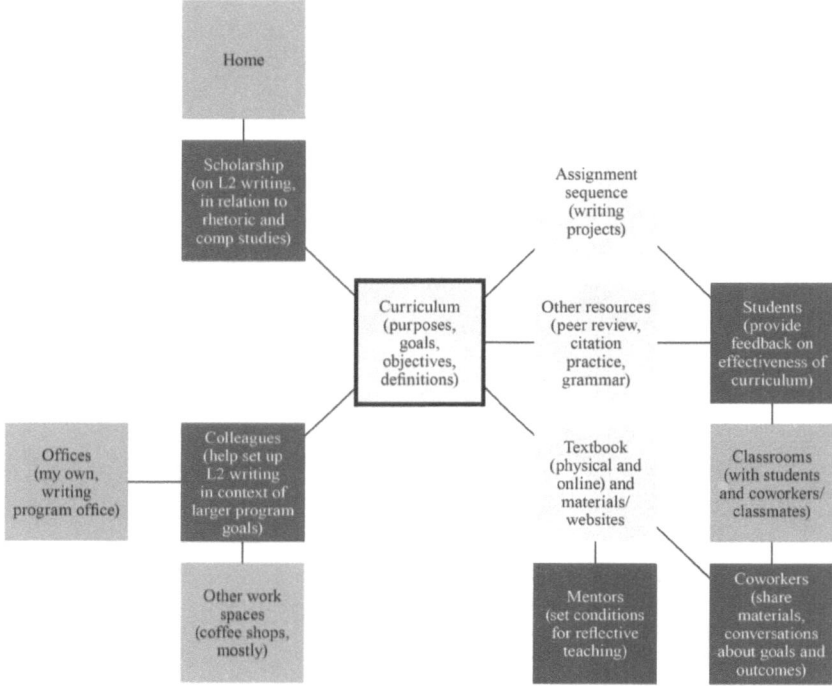

Figure 6.2. Sam's Work Map. Key: dark = people; medium = places/spaces; light = materials/texts.

He continued, "Talking about these purposes and objectives and goals [of the curriculum] and relating them to assignment sequences is really important."

The differences in central organization between the two NTT writing teachers and the graduate TA may be reflective of what the individual participants value first and foremost in thinking about their work within the writing program. Another practical reason for this discrepancy is the differences of responsibilities between instructors and TAs. Because instructors Becky and Lex are faculty and not PhD students, they spend the majority of their days at work doing teaching-related tasks, including planning and creating materials for classes, teaching, holding office hours, and meeting with and providing support for students. In contrast,

Learning, Representing, and Endorsing the Landscape 105

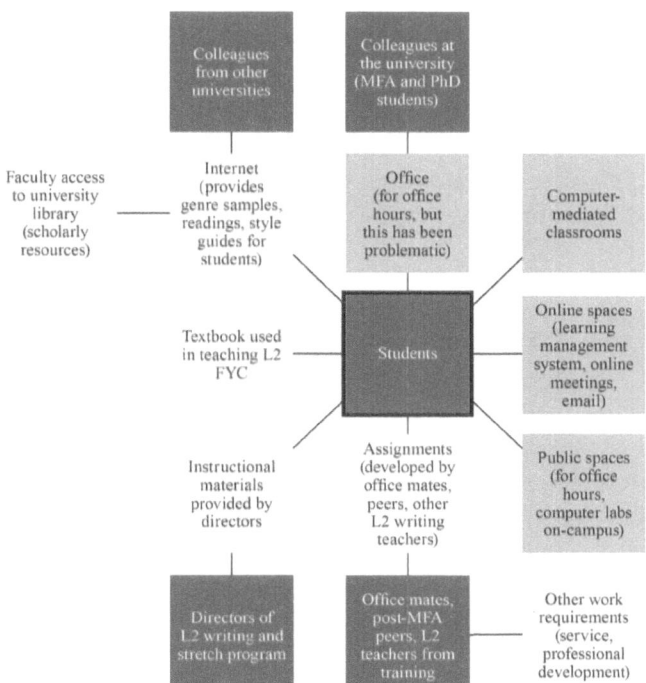

Figure 6.3. Lex's Work Map. Key: dark = people; medium = places/spaces; light = materials/texts.

Sam's map is very different organizationally from the maps of Becky and Lex. His organization was more or less like a set of concentric circles, with light "texts/materials" at the center, followed by dark "people" and ending with medium "places/spaces" on the periphery. As a graduate student, Sam not only has fewer class sections and students to worry about—he also has the responsibilities inherent in his work toward his PhD, including completing coursework and writing his dissertation.

Perhaps the most surprising organizational finding was that Sam included his knowledge of L2 writing "scholarship" as one of his dark "people" Post-It notes—a reflection of his engagement with his scholarly work. He saw the published authors and scholars that he engaged with in his studies to be actual people that helped inform his teaching. There were also marked differences in how TAs and NTT faculty engaged with scholarship in the field, particularly in the role that scholarship played in their teaching and day-to-day lives as L2 writing teachers. Furthermore, where Becky's and Lex's experiences and reflections were centered around students, Sam placed students in the bottom right-hand corner of his map, the farthest away from the center where he started from. The way in which the three participants "organizationally positioned" their students, spaces, and materials (Peeples 1999, 156) in the overall picture of their work lives lends some insight into what they prioritize in their jobs—though all three participants are L2 writing teachers, their central focuses differed depending on what particular teaching role and rank they held.

Colleagues, Mentors, and Others in the Writing Program

Another item of interest among participant work maps was whom, beyond the students they taught, they chose to include on the rest of their dark "people" Post-It notes, as well as the commentary they provided for the interpersonal relationships associated with their jobs and how these relationships related to their teaching of L2 writing. While all three participants included the same *kinds* of relationships with people (e.g., coworkers, students, and administrators), their explanations of and perceptions about those relationships differed greatly depending on individual experiences (past and present) and contexts.

Becky named the following groups of people on her dark Post-Its: "mentors," "colleagues from ASU," "colleagues from other universities" (whom she had met through attending conferences during her MFA program), and "administrators" (e.g., the WPA and director of L2 writing within the writing program). She also discussed her past experience as a TA in the writing program, attributing her success as a full-time instructor in this specific context to the training and support she received as a TA: "It has been amazing preparation for academic work in general. . . . [I]f I have a problem, I have backup, and I know *who* to go to, and if I have any questions, I just feel super supported." The support Becky felt she received as a graduate TA helped her to feel confident in navigating relationships and protocol within the writing program (e.g., who to contact if a student plagiarizes), and it also forged positive relationships with coworkers in the writing program early on in her teaching life that persisted up to the time of the study. Becky noted that her coworker relationships were "*hugely* important to [her]." She continues:

I'm in an office right now with some pretty experienced instructors. [We share] advice about what kinds of comments are helpful in a workshop, methods for creating more understanding in the classroom, and just unique situations—you know, "What would you do when *this* happens?" If I have questions I can go to them. I lean on them heavily.

Lex also acknowledged the presence of colleagues and mentors in her work map, though she organized them a bit differently and was less positive in her reflections. She separated her Post-Its into those she felt she obtained L2 resources and knowledge from: the WAC and L2 writing directors were on one Post-It, and next to it is one that reads "office mates, post-MFA peers, and second-language teachers that [she] met in [L2-specific teacher training experiences]." She also included a note for what she referred to as "facilitators" between herself and her students—the WPA and the writing program manager and administrative assistant. Lastly, Lex included a final dark "people" Post-It for the "MA and PhD students at ASU and other universities," stating in her interview that they "have helped me more than anything else to access the rhetorical traditions of [her multilingual] students." However, when asked to elaborate on the collegial connections she experienced in the writing program, Lex's responses were largely negative, due to her role and rank in the writing program as an adjunct faculty member. Overall, Lex felt undervalued by the writing program and the larger institution because of her adjunct role. She noted that as an adjunct, "I felt *really* isolated. You know, I felt like it had to be a *big deal* to go seek out someone" like a coworker or administrator for support. "I felt like I wasn't justified in seeking out any mentor figures, and I didn't have access to any peers." Because she felt unable to connect to colleagues as an adjunct, Lex focused her Post-It map discussion on the students. Her frustration with the part-time adjunct position carried over into the asymmetrical relationship between herself and the university, and the mismatch in the responsibility she felt she had for her L2 writing students:

> I really feel like with [multilingual] writers, you do need to take more time with them. And when you're already getting paid so *little*, and are so *clearly dispensable* to the university—it's a hard position to be in. To be like, I *know* I need to put more into these students, because they *need* more help . . . and at the same time, anything that I put into them will help them, and on some level it will help *me* as a person too, because I'll feel like I've fulfilled my obligations toward them and toward myself, but then you feel like you're getting screwed over [by the school]. I can see how [adjuncts] would *not* want to teach L2 writing.

The rampant and systematic exploitation of adjuncts in higher education was brought into sharp focus on Lex's map.[2]

Finally, Sam's dark "people" Post-It notes were clearly separated from one another: "Colleagues" were a part of his work life to "Help set L2 writing in context with larger program goals"; "Mentors" were there to "set conditions for reflective teaching"; and "Coworkers" (e.g., his fellow L2 and mainstream teachers, the new TAs with whom he worked) were a means to "share/provide helpful materials" for the classroom and to "question complexities" that occurred with regard to teaching L2 students and the overarching "goals, purposes, and outcomes" of the program. Surprisingly, Sam did not feel the need to discuss his relationships with coworkers or administrators; instead, he focused on his experiences working with the new TA teaching practicum. He noted that helping new TAs in "developing a reflective practice," including "developing strategies for reading a classroom, taking in data, analyzing and interpreting that data, and adjusting your practice accordingly," were things he discussed with the new TAs and then directly "appl[y] . . . to [his] second-language writing class."

Overall, the three participants' work relationships varied depending on their past learning and teaching experiences, the amount of time and previous roles they held within the writing program, and their current situations related to their job (e.g., who was in their offices, and whom they worked with and talked to on a regular basis). Another large factor in their perception of interpersonal work relationships was how supported by their colleagues, administrators, and the overall program or institution they felt.

Scenario 1's Implications for WPAs

The first mapmaking scenario revealed differing priorities of writing teachers in three different configurations of roles and ranks: full-time NTT instructor, PhD student TA, and part-time NTT adjunct. Becky and Lex placed "students" at the center of their maps and created a visual representation of their work lives around that central group. However, the fact that Sam, a graduate student, chose to put "curriculum" in the center of his map suggests that the organizing principles of his work as a graduate-student writing teacher begin in a very different place from Becky and Lex. These findings suggest that the training and professional development offerings of a writing program should consider the organizing principles of writing teachers by role and rank and be sensitive to their prioritizations. What these PhD-seeking TAs, who may have more investment (and more recent experience) in working with theoretical underpinnings, expect to learn in a program-wide workshop for writing teachers, for example, may fall flat with adjunct and full-time faculty members, who may be anticipating things to be suited for a more immediate and student-centric purpose. WPAs and others responsible for professional development strategies should then keep in mind the differences in what individuals and groups of teachers prioritize and find most practical.

Furthermore, the roles and ranks of teachers also affected their interpersonal work connections. Becky's confidence in being able to lean heavily on her colleagues, administrators, and friends within the program as a full-time instructor starkly contrasted Lex's described interpersonal experiences as an adjunct faculty member within the program. As a part-time writing teacher, Lex did not feel her individual experiences warranted her any voice in the writing program or with her colleagues. Because she was "only a part-timer," Lex was reluctant to make connections with office-mates and other writing teachers. Her rhetoric about leaning heavily on technology and other "equalizing" sources and spaces in her work life is another hint at how she positioned herself. And different still was Sam, the grad student, whose interpersonal relationships within his organization of his work map seemed to function more as connections to the curriculum and less as collegial relationships than the instructors'. Overall, Sam's map organization was much more methodical and rigidly organized than Becky's or Lex's maps, and therefore the relationships with colleagues came off as more functional than collegial. The fact that Sam's interpersonal connections on his map and his commentary regarding these relationships differed from Becky's and Lex's perceptions suggests that taking individual teachers' knowledge and experiences into account can be an eye-opening approach for WPAs in determining what writing teachers of different roles or ranks prioritize, what they need, and what factors may contribute to their job satisfaction.

Ultimately, the cartographer-WPA must decide what to do with the knowledge gained from these maps. The three positionalities of Becky, Sam, and Lex can inform administrative decisions including initial training and sustained support for writing teachers in different roles and ranks, the configuration of shared offices to maximize collaboration, and ways to improve communication across the landscape of the writing program as a whole. To be fair, the WPA would not necessarily *have* to create maps such as these for the WPA as cartographer metaphor to be useful; she could prioritize getting to know individual teachers at various roles and ranks and glean this information without a map. However, it was through the physical act of mapmaking that certain intricacies of individual experience became visible, and because of this, I do suggest actually creating a map if there are time, space, and resources available.

I had such success with cartography in terms of helping to articulate and visualize one's programmatic and institutional surroundings that, once hired as a WPA in my first tenure-track position, I decided to implement the practice in a teaching context to explore how mapmaking benefits students as well.

MAPMAKING SCENARIO 2: ENCULTURATION MAPS (INTRO TO WPA COURSE)

Currently, I teach a graduate-level "Introduction to Writing Program Administration" class for online master's students in English, and almost all these graduate students are concurrently working full-time jobs in varied K–12 or university teaching contexts. As mentioned, I found cartography to be so beneficial for myself as a graduate-student WPA that I wondered to what extent this practice would benefit my own grad students in their own teaching and work contexts. One of the goals or themes that emerged from the Intro to WPA course was for students to conceptualize and visualize themselves *as writing program administrators*, whether or not they held that official title. In almost every case, these full-time teachers pursuing an MA in English were already expected to perform many of the duties delineated in "The Portland Resolution," including assessment, advising, and various instances of articulation (Hult et al. 1992). This, to me, was another opportunity for would-be WPAs to identify enculturation experiences (Peters 1998) as they acclimated to understanding the bigger picture of their institutional contexts.

To give my students a place to begin, I took a cue from a heuristic offered at the 2016 CWPA Workshop led by Sheila Carter-Tod, Heidi Estrem, Peggy O'Neill, and Chuck Paine. Their heuristic was originally titled "Campus Writing Map Worksheet," but I renamed it "Where Writing Happens" for the Intro to WPA course.[3] This table-style heuristic was an effective way to list out the key places that writing was happening at one's institution, the people or groups they could identify as possible allies, and the ways in which those places and contacts supported (or could support) writing at their institution. There was also space for articulating possible alignment with a writing program's current goals. To me, this was another method to organize much of the same information that a mapmaking activity could do, and so I offered both the CWPA Workshop heuristic and my dissertation Post-It mapping heuristic (appendix 6.A) to my graduate students as options to complete the assignment. In addition to their maps, they were asked to compose a narrative write-up of their process and their findings or takeaways from the activity—another chance for them to "look up" from where they currently stood to think about the larger landscape (Smith 2006). As with my dissertation mapmaking scenario, the grad students were not given a place to start; instead, they made these rhetorical and organizational choices themselves. Included in this chapter are samples from two students, Tanith and Grady (pseudonyms), whose differing complex institutional situations were made more comprehensible, and whose personal situatedness was better understood through cartography.

Tanith's Maps

Graduate student Tanith was pursuing a second master's degree in English, after first earning a master's in TESOL. She was a full-time teacher in the university intensive English program (IEP) and thus created her map of where writing happened in this realm "to better understand where we are and the factors that influence and are influenced by" the IEP. Ever an overachiever, Tanith created three maps: "Academic Progress," "Financial and Administrative Matters," and "Policy and Curriculum." This choice was intentional: "I thought it would be more useful to divide the information into categories to make it easier [for me] to understand."

As Tanith started mapmaking, even more differences surfaced. She discovered:

> [T]he stakeholders [e.g., IEP students] and the decisions [made in the IEP] are somewhat divided. The people making decisions are concerned with student retention, whereas the stakeholders are often more concerned with student success and writing development. So, the people who are making decisions about allocations of resources are most concerned with the number of students enrolled, and their primary focus isn't going to be the same as it would be for stakeholders that want to see students developing their writing and critical thinking.

Tanith used a newspaper page layout in Microsoft Word to create color-coded shapes that distinguished among the "Decision Makers" for the IEP, the "Influencers," the "Support," and the "Stakeholders," depending on the focus of each map. She also color-coded arrows for connections and for specific relationships where feedback was given from one entity to another, and also for budgeting decisions.

Tanith's maps reveal many aspects of the IEP that the naked eye could not see—and that a full-time teacher would not normally think

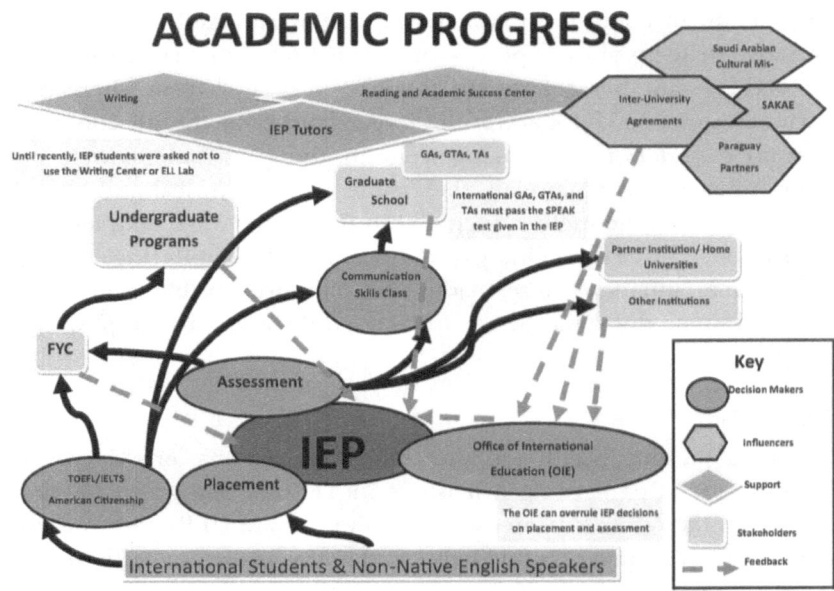

Figure 6.4. Tanith's Maps (1 of 3): "Academic Progress."

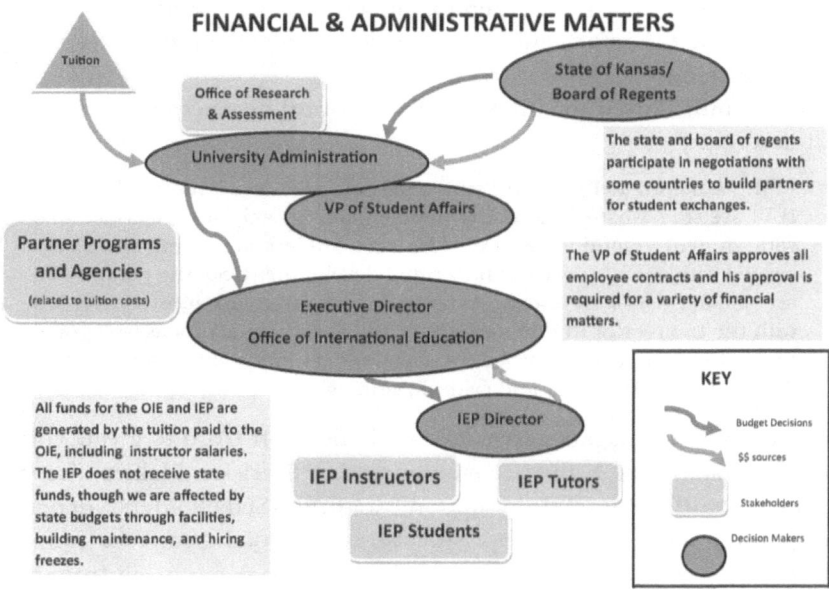

Figure 6.5. Tanith's Maps (2 of 3): "Financial & Administrative Matters."

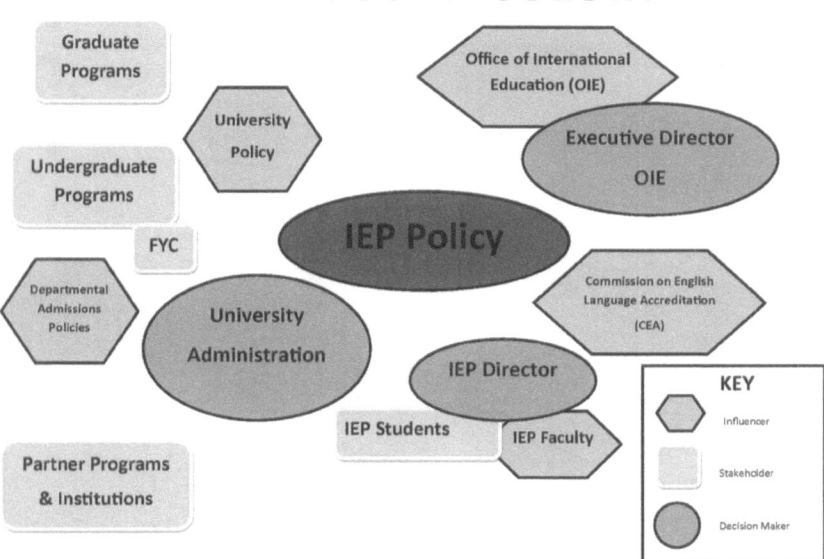

Figure 6.6. Tanith's Maps (3 of 3): "Policy & Curriculum."

about. She learned that the IEP is a pipeline for students to move into both undergraduate and graduate programs; to move on from the IEP to programs in her university, partner institutions, or other universities; and for students to assume the roles of composition student and graduate assistant. In the "Academic Progress" map, Tanith identified three areas of support for IEP students: writing support, IEP tutoring, and the university academic success center. The "Financial and Administrative Matters" map helped her to articulate the cash flow of the Intensive English Program, as it related to the state board of regents, student tuition, and salaries of the IEP director, instructors, and tutors. And through the "Policy and Curriculum" map, she remarked that she was "happy with the direction the IEP is headed" with regard to work conditions and facilities as well as "job security for existing faculty."

Overall, Tanith's mapmaking helped her locate specific "IEP policies and practices [that] are still influenced by times past and stakeholders who do not embrace change," pointing to potential areas of improvement for more successful future initiatives. Overall, the mapping activity allowed her to critique her current landscape and recognize that "tremendous progress is being made and that the IEP is on-track to continue to progress."

114 KATHERINE DAILY O'MEARA

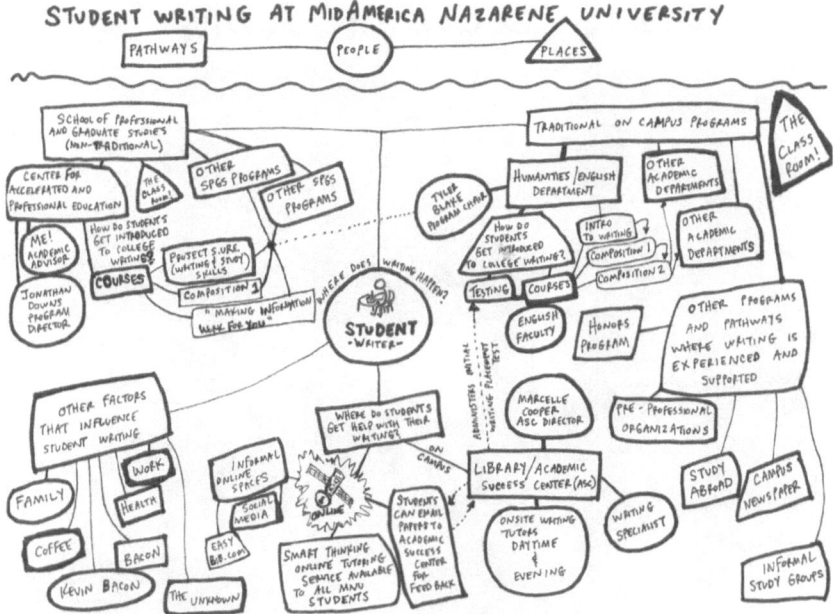

Figure 6.7. Grady's Map: "Student Writing at MidAmerica Nazarene University."

Grady's Map

Graduate student Grady was also working full-time while in school; his position was as an academic advisor in a private four-year institution, focusing on the success of nontraditional students in his university's School of Professional and Graduate Studies. Grady writes, "My biggest concern is that many of the spaces and advocates that benefit our traditional students are not equally positioned to serve our nontraditional students."

In his hand-drawn map (figure 6.7) that he based off his table heuristic (table 6.1), Grady put his university's students at the center, drawing connections to three major areas of writing: nontraditional campus programs, traditional campus programs, and other spaces where students get help with their writing. He said he was "particularly interested in how [his campus's] nontraditional students fit into the map." He used different shapes to designate pathways for student success (rectangles), people (circles), and places (triangles). Grady's sense of humor radiated through the map, though in his reflective write-up, he was all business.

As Grady considered his cartography experience, he illustrated his institution's benefits and challenges in his assignment write-up:

Table 6.1. Grady's table heuristic

Writing "Place" / Key Contact(s)	Description	How this Place Supports Writing

Mabee Learning Commons (Library)
    Lauren Hays—Instructional and Research Librarian
    Lon Dagley—Computer Services Librarian
	In the past year, the library was completely redesigned and remodeled to function as a learning commons. The new space has an open design that is more technology-friendly and has study spaces that are more versatile and better accommodate group work. I would be remiss if I did not mention that the campus coffee shop, the Dewey Book and Bean, is also located here. Personally, this is where I go on my lunch breaks to get some serious reading and writing done.	The overall effect of this repurposed space is an inviting atmosphere that allows students to focus on their research and writing, or to collaborate with their peers. I like to think of this space as a lab where students experiment with the writing process.

Academic Success Center
    Marcelle Cooper—ASC Director
    Writing Specialist
    Peer Writing Tutors
	Housed in the Mabee Learning Commons, the Academic Success Center is essentially a writing center, math center, and testing center rolled into one.	Writing tutors are available to provide students with feedback and to walk them through the writing process if needed. Providing this service in the same space as the Learning Commons aligns with the writing program's goal to make writing more accessible to students.

First-Year Writing Courses
Traditional Campus:
    o *Intro to Writing*
    o *Composition I*
    o *Composition II*
School of Professional and Graduate Studies:
    o *Project S.U.R.E.*
    o *Composition I*
    o *Making Information Work for You*
Writing Program Faculty:
    Tyler Blake
    Shanti Thomas
    Cathy Ream
	The classroom is the one writing space that is not optional (unless you're an online student). While students get to choose where they work on their homework and whether they use the writing tutoring at all, the classroom is the one place where we know students will experience writing. This is one reason we can justify the need for classes that focus specifically on writing, and it seems logical that students benefit from these the most at the start of their college experience.	Two of the three first-year writing courses offered by our nontraditional program are different than what you'll find on our traditional campus. There are probably several reasons for this. Since our nontraditional courses are smaller in size, we have a hard time filling non-credit developmental courses like "Intro to Writing." This is also because adult students seem particularly resistant to paying for a class they know they won't receive credit for. Instead, we have developed two courses (*Project SURE, Making Information Work for You*) that combine developmental writing skills with other material that justifies a credit-bearing course.

The mission of the university is to be "a transformative university that nurtures Christ-like community, pursues academic excellence, and cultivates a passion to serve." As a small, private university, our size allows us to cultivate a sense of community that is more difficult to attain at a larger institution. Conversely, our small size also makes it a struggle to provide the variety of resources and support that might be available to students at a state school that receives more funding. This certainly impacts the shape of our writing program, which influences our ability to fulfill our commitment to "pursue academic excellence."

This cartography activity allowed Grady to lay out a full picture of his institution and, in particular, the places where the experiences of nontraditional students could be considered, analyzed, and improved. The experience helped inform his full-time job as an academic advisor, and it worked as a springboard to his master's thesis project (in progress), which focuses on the success of nontraditional students at his university.

Longer-Term Benefits of the Assignment

I contacted both Tanith and Grady for further reflection on their maps, asking them to speak directly to the ways in which the cartography experience had benefited their current understanding and day-to-day tasks in their positions.

Tanith was able to employ her cartography experience to understanding the way the Intensive English Program worked and how she fit into the larger picture. She writes, "Mapping the information helped me to visualize a lot of information that I knew as separate data points, but the maps helped me to visualize it as a whole picture and see how areas interacted." She continued, "One of the biggest takeaways for me was how interconnected we [the IEP] are with other entities. Our program tends to seem fairly isolated from the rest of the campus, and the map helped remind me that we are part of a bigger organization with a shared goal." Tanith was able to see the forest for the trees and ended up feeling reinvigorated in her day-to-day roles of teaching and student support when set against the backdrop of the entire university.

As an academic advisor of mostly nontraditional university students, Grady also became better acclimated to his landscape as a whole. He learned that his institution employed writing specialists that could help struggling students. He noted, "A large part of my job involves listening to student concerns, identifying the core issues underlying those concerns, and then connecting students with resources that will help them address those issues. The mapmaking activity really helped broaden my understanding of the writing resources available on campus that I can recommend to my students." Finally, Grady was able to share the knowledge he gained from the mapping experience with fellow student advisors in his department and across his university campus.

Scenario 2's Implications for WPAs

For both Tanith and Grady, the mapping activity they completed in their "Intro to WPA" graduate class helped them to "understand the complexities of [their] own positions within [their] local contexts" (Peeples 1999, 165)—even though neither one held an official title of writing program administrator. The mapmaking experience gave them more programmatic knowledge than the average IEP teacher or academic advisor is normally equipped with, and this ability to see and understand the nuanced, often latent complexities of their work organization gave them each the chance to participate in a reflective process that Peeples (1999) notes as imperative for a postmodern administrator, even when the official title is not there. In addition, the fact that Tanith and Grady were seeking master's degrees in English (in contrast to Sam from the first example, who was on his PhD quest) was telling: PhD students are more focused on theories and scholarship (e.g., Sam), while Tanith's and Grady's maps were centered around their more hands-on roles in teaching and advising, respectively. This distinction (teacher versus student roles, responsibilities, and focuses) can be another site for WPA consideration—especially at larger institutions where multiple roles and ranks of teachers and students coexist and teach within a single writing program.

In a sense, this harkens back to Phelps's "Turtles All the Way Down" (2002), which notes that the official definition of the WPA is unclear, and that many people do the work of WPAs without formal recognition. Phelps's chapter also asserts that leaders—doers, advocates, changemakers—can be found at any level in an institution. Mapping out the lived realities of people, places, and spaces can be used as a way to recognize all of the WPA-like work that is done all over the university, and by folks from all different roles, ranks, pay grades, and levels of prestige. Cartography makes so much all the more visible.

CONCLUSIONS

The two mapping scenarios offer a few key insights for WPAs and those who do similar kinds of administrative labor. By viewing the visual representations of what constitutes "work" for multiple individuals within a specific unit that functions inside a larger institution, such as a writing program, WPAs may be able to tease out any notable similarities and differences in values, ideologies, and spatial relations and how they contribute to a larger perception of what is working in the program and larger institution (and what is not). The WPA as cartographer is empowered to shed light on, as Peeples (1999) says, "what is privileged and what is obscured" in a "complexly organized" institutional space like a writing program (155). Cartography can act as a window into the complexities of people's positionalities, with the ultimate goal of "construct[ing] better spaces/practices" for all—students, staff, teachers, and administrators (Peeples 1999, 155).

Benefits and Considerations

Cartography can help people observe and understand *positionality* within an institution or writing program, a request that many WPAs are tasked with and trusted to explain to other stakeholders across the university. Mapmaking makes visible what WPAs (and everyone else) *do* by making visible connections to other spaces, stakeholders, allies and adversaries, majors and departments, as well as the lived experiences of faculty, staff, and students. The WPA as cartographer can make visible the impact of writing programs beyond their specific academic unit. WPAs can show administrators, provosts, and others who hold the purse strings how vital writing well is to student success in all disciplines and future careers. Maps make the connections among points that might otherwise seem to be quite disparate, a substantial benefit of mapmaking activities for writing program administrators (and those with whom they work, teach, and collaborate). Mapmaking creates opportunities for WPAs and others to see how interconnected stakeholders are in a university ecosystem and to reflect on stakeholders' positionalities within that ecosystem. These are the most important affordances of cartographic activities for all parties involved, and they can boost interconnectivity among stakeholders, open conversations about positionality, and move the writing program to a more visible and more sustainable place within the university.

This leads to some questions that might further develop the metaphor of WPA as cartographer. Through mapmaking, WPAs can become aware of the different positionalities and experiences of faculty and other stakeholders in their programs. How might WPAs utilize and draw upon others' maps in their planning? How might the maps that WPAs and others make inform major tasks in WPA life, such as curriculum development, professional development, assessment, and more? How might the WPA-as-cartographer metaphor use others' maps to create bigger, more inclusive, comprehensive maps that can be shared, drawn, and redrawn by all? Might "crowdsourced" maps be possible? Could different stakeholders collaborate to overlay different visualizations on the same shared map? And how might the future of WPA cartography contribute to a more sustainable conceptualization of the writing program administrator overall?

When we see maps, often we think of them as objective representations of space. The reality, though, is far from it—maps are just as subjectively situated as their contexts of space and time. Maps can tell their own stories, but it is the mapmaker's responsibility to choose which angles to represent and how. The cartographer is inherently implicated in the narration and representation, and the authority to choose what makes the map and what doesn't creates a weighty responsibility for a WPA.

In envisioning institutional ethnographic work for WPAs, LaFrance (2016) states that "an individual's social alliances, experiences, and sensibilities play an important role in how that individual negotiates everyday institutional settings (such as classrooms, programs or departments)" (110). Peeples (1999) asserts that (like the methodologies inherent in institutional ethnography), the act of mapmaking is "an effective way of representing the fragmentation and fluidity of human subjects" (154). Cartography, then, may be a useful tool for WPAs to reveal the "dynamism of individuals" (LaFrance 2016, 110) in their own writing programs and across the university landscape, to recognize the good already happening, to identify areas of improvement, and to advocate for positive change. And beyond the physical act of mapmaking, WPAs who envision themselves as cartographers inherently assume responsibility to learn, represent, and endorse the landscapes of their writing programs and the wild university beyond. Ultimately, cartographer-WPAs can indeed "define, explain, and navigate their way through the world" ("History of Cartography" 2018). Mapmaking can better equip us to see the forest for the trees and to recognize the often latent but steadfast social connections inherent in sustainable WPA work.

APPENDIX 6.A

Mapping heuristic from dissertation (Post-Its)

Mapping exercise (adapted from Christina Ortmeier-Hooper's dissertation, 2007)

Materials:
- Colored Post-It notes
  - [color 1] ☐ people (coworkers, administrators, mentors, students)
  - [color 2] ☐ places (classroom, office, admin offices, other rooms/buildings)

- [color 3] ☐ materials (texts, textbooks, assignments, forms/paperwork, classes/training, meetings, other work requirements)
- Large poster paper
- Writing utensil (marker, sharpie, pen/pencil)

Directions:
1. Participant writes names of people, places, and materials used in his/her work on the appropriate Post-It notes.
2. Participant writes name on the poster paper.
3. Participant arranges Post-It notes to map out his/her work experience.
4. Participant draws lines/connections/notes to add clarification to arrangement, if needed.

Participant and interviewer discuss the Work Map.

APPENDIX 6.B

"Where Writing Happens" directions from "Intro to WPA" course

"Where Writing Happens" institutional mapping exercise (directions)

Topics and Activities
- Positioning your WP and institutions as part of the broader landscape of your institution
- Completing your institutional map
- Consider the mission and/or values of your program and/or institution
- Analysis/Discussion: What are frames surrounding current stories about writing and writers on your campus and beyond? What do these have to do with the larger landscape?

Outcomes
- To situate your writing program in the context of your campus/institution
- To consider the potential relevance of larger conversations about writing and writers happening on your campus
- To better understand institutional and program practices that affect—and can be affected by—the work of a WPA
- To locate these conversations in issues of particular relevance in the larger conversations
- To think about mission statements and long-range planning of your writing program and your institution

Key Questions to Consider
- Why have your prioritized things as you have?
- How will your priorities help you enact your values and those of your institution?
- How is your WP situated in your institution curricularly? Administratively? Geographically?
- What are the broader conversations about writing and writers happening on your campus? In the larger landscape?
- How can WPAs and writing instructors position ourselves within these conversations?
- Are there possible alliances/allies on your campus that are visible on your map?
- How can we identify ways to advocate for the principles and practices critical to our programs without becoming overwhelmed (or morose)?
- How is your institution positioned in the larger higher-ed landscape? How might this influence your writing program?

APPENDIX 6.C

"Where Writing Happens" table heuristic from "Intro to WPA" course

"Where Writing Happens" at your Institution [heuristic]

Writing "Place" / Key Contact(s)	How That Place Supports (or could support) Writing	Possible Alignment with Writing Program Goals

NOTES

1. The choice to study L2 writing teachers (vs. mainstream writing teachers) was related to my personal parallel interests in both L2 writing theory and WPA theory. I do not think this designation had any affect on the participants' map creations or in how they used the heuristic. It just so happens that all of the teachers had L2 writing background in common.
2. For more discussion of self-conceptions of subordination, see Teagarden's chapter, "Representing the Basement," this volume.
3. See appendixes 6.B and 6.C for the directions and heuristic from the "Where Writing Happens" activity, respectively.

REFERENCES

Campbell, Marie, and Frances Gregor. 2004. *Mapping Social Relations: A Primer in Doing Institutional Ethnography*. US ed. Walnut Creek, CA: AltaMira Press.

"History of Cartography." 2018. *Wikipedia.* Last modified November 25, 2018. https://en.wikipedia.org/wiki/History_of_cartography.

Hult, Christine, David Joliffe, Kathleen Kelly, Dana Mead, and Charles Schuster. 1992. "The Portland Resolution: Guidelines for Writing Program Administrator Positions." http://162.241.207.49/positions/portlandres.html.

Huot, Brian A., and Ellen E. Schendel. 2007. "A Working Methodology of Assessment for Writing Program Administrators." In *The Longman Sourcebook for Writing Program Administrators*, edited by Irene Ward and William J. Carpenter, 207–27. New York: Longman.

LaFrance, Michelle. 2016. "An Institutional Ethnography of Information Literacy Instruction: Key Terms, Local/Material Contexts, and Instructional Practice." *WPA: Writing Program Administration*, vol. 39, no. 2 (Spring): 105–23.

LaFrance, Michelle, and Melissa Nicolas. 2012. "Institutional Ethnography as Materialist Framework for Writing Program Research and the Faculty-Staff Work Standpoints Project." *College Composition and Communication*, vol. 64, no. 1 (September): 130–50.

Ortmeier-Hooper, Christina. 2007. "Beyond 'ELL': Second Language Writers, Academic Literacy, and Issues of Identity in the U.S. High School." PhD diss., University of New Hampshire.

Peeples, Tim. 1999. "'Seeing' the WPA with/through Postmodern Mapping." In *The Writing Program Administrator as Researcher*, edited by Shirley K. Rose and Irwin Weiser, 153–67. Portsmouth, NH: Heinemann.

Peters, Bradley. 1998. "Enculturation, Not Alchemy: Professionalizing Novice Writing Program Administrators." *WPA: Writing Program Administration*, vol. 21, nos. 2–3 (Fall): 121–36.

Phelps, Louise Weatherbee. 2002. "Turtles All the Way Down: Educating Academic Leaders." In *The Writing Program Administrator's Resource*, edited by Stuart C. Brown and Theresa Enos, 3–39. Mahwah, NJ: Lawrence Erlbaum.

Porter, James E. 1998. *Rhetorical Ethics and Internetworked Writing.* Norwood, NJ: Ablex.

Porter, James E., and Patricia Sullivan. 2007. "'Remapping Curricular Geography': A Retrospection." *Journal of Business and Technical Communication* 21 (1): 15–20.

Porter, James E., Patricia Sullivan, Stuart Blythe, Jeffrey T. Grabill, and Libby Miles. 2000. "Institutional Critique: A Rhetorical Methodology for Change." *College Composition and Communication*, vol. 51, no. 4 (June): 610–42.

Smith, Dorothy E. 2006. *Institutional Ethnography as Practice.* Lanham, MD: Rowman and Littlefield.

Sullivan, Patricia A., and James E. Porter. 1993. "Remapping Curricular Geography: Professional Writing in/and English." *Journal of Business and Technical Communication* 7:389–422.

7
APPROACHING WPA LABOR WITH *AHIMSA*
Mapping Emotional Geographies through Sustainable Leadership

Christy I. Wenger

I've had a lot of yoga teachers over the past thirteen years, two states, and five towns. They have all imparted wisdom as unique and varied as themselves, and yet all have been held together by a shared conviction to the yogic philosophy of *ahimsa*, or nonviolent, mindful consideration for oneself and for others. Despite their differing motivations, practices, and commitments, all of my teachers held sacred this core tenet of yoga that can be traced back to the original five *yamas*, the ethical code for yogis (Satchidananda 2011, 2.30: 125). The ancient Indian author of the Yoga Sutras, Sri Patanjali (Satchidananda 2011), refers to ahimsa as nonviolence, though yogis functionally understand ahimsa as this and more: as also compassionate consideration that employs the act of mindfulness, or moment-to-moment nonjudgmental attention turned in awareness to both the self and to others. Mindfulness encourages ahimsa as we wake up to the present moment, and ahimsa becomes a tool by which we can practice mindfulness. My teachers all stressed ahimsa because they knew that without it there can be no mindfulness—and therefore no yoga.[1]

Yoga is meant to be lived off the mat. Ahimsa is both a metaphor and a concrete practice: it suggests a way of approaching life so that violence is minimized; the goal of complete nonviolence remains resolutely metaphoric in its loftiness. Rather than suggesting a negative absolute, concepts like ahimsa can be applied as a model of positive behavior just as useful for when we are flowing through a sequence of poses as when we are wrangling children or running a writing program. Ahimsa is metaphoric because it helps us make a useful comparison between life and yoga. Yogi and writer Judith Lasater (2000) reminds us that "living our yoga" means recognizing that each moment of our lives is a potential moment for practice and that mindfulness, the core value espoused by yoga, is, like other contemplative practices, a way of life. I forward Lasater's approach here. I offer the metaphoric concept of ahimsa, or nonviolent, conscious consideration, a core value of mindfulness, as one that will help WPAs live their professional lives in more sustainable ways, in ways that minimize violence with both lived and metaphoric consequences. Practicing ahimsa, I argue, can help WPAs construct safer, more sustainable spaces from which to lead by helping them enact nonviolence toward themselves and others within their programs. As a practice of mindfulness, ahimsa metaphorically wakes us up to our own presence and also makes us aware of the intersubjective nature of well-being, as ours is connected to those around us. Ahimsa as a thoughtful, relational practice of awareness that yet respects the primacy of the self is a particularly useful tool for WPAs to identify the emotional geographies of their programs in order to create sustainable spaces that invite ongoing self-reflection. Like the yogi who learns to first check in with herself before attempting a pose to enact the self-care of ahimsa, WPAs can use mindfulness of the emotional terrain of our workplaces to help us better gauge our feelings and negotiate our responsibilities to our own and others' well-being.

While I draw from my personal experiences as a yogi in these pages, WPAs don't have to be practicing yogis to enact these principles of mindfulness. The metaphoric practice of "living our yoga" is applicable to all. WPAs can still can benefit from learning to be less self-judgmental and more aware of their emotional states by applying ahimsa to the practice of administration. All that is needed is the intention of mindful awareness. This awareness translates into learning how to better act for the success of our programs and how to maintain boundaries around our work so that we do not allow our heavy administrative workloads to negatively impinge on our emotional well-being. WPAs can practice ahimsa in their programs in the spirit of living our mindfulness practices and as a way to enable us to reshape the whole of our lives and not only the hour a few days a week we may or may not devote to contemplative practices like yoga, meditation, or nature walks.[2]

Grounding my analysis of how ahimsa might be strategically applied to our workplaces is my leadership of a small, unsupported writing program situated in a literature department that relies heavily on the use of contingent labor, all within a liberal arts university where I am the first and only WPA. In what follows, I examine how the mindful emotional practice of ahimsa makes visible emotional geographies, the spaces constructed by the ways emotions move between bodies and create attachments of feeling and felt communities, as identified by

Andy Hargreaves's (2001) educational leadership theory. Since WPA administration is entrenched in emotion work, despite the latter being largely absent from our training and academic professionalism, we should do more to attend to the dimensions of that work. Drawing on examples from my university as contextualized by the cultural dynamics of academic workplaces at large, I suggest that navigating these geographies with ahimsa helps WPAs exchange unexamined and automatic emotional labor for mindful awareness of their emotional boundaries, self-compassion practices, and efforts toward emotional understanding. Ahimsa helps WPAs identify and label the specifics of their local emotional geographies, making visible the emotional labor they already perform, and provides new, mindful ways for them to manage that labor toward the end of promoting their own and their programs' well-being.

EMOTIONAL LABOR AND *AHIMSA*

Ahimsa as a practice of mindfulness promises WPAs a tangible strategy to reclaim our embodied location and to work toward increased emotional well-being. Ahimsa does this by first having us acknowledge the emotion work we do in ways that promote self-reflection and boundary setting. Education theorist Andy Hargreaves reminds us that "the recurrent emotional experiences that people have in their respective occupations affect their identities and their relationships . . . Each occupation and its culture has different emotional expectations, contours, and effects" (2011, 1057). And while we might argue about its usefulness, writing program administration is heavily invested in a caregiving ethos and related expectations.

For the position I currently hold, I was told when I interviewed that administration had finally agreed upon the need for an officially designated WPA on campus, because they wanted someone to "care for writing and the writing instructors." That language choice has stuck with me over the years because it was so telling. They were seeking to hire someone, first, not as a leader or visionary per se—though those things in time might prove to be nice too—but as a *caretaker*. It is no wonder that many WPAs like myself take up administrative work by taking on the role of caretaker and caregiver. This is an identity largely accepted by the field. Wendy Bishop notes of WPAs, "We care: about writing, writing students, writing teachers, reading and writing connections, writing within and across and outside the university" (1999, 2). Bishop captures in this sentiment the need for us to pay attention to the emotional labor we perform through our jobs, because we are often cast into roles of caretaking. Just as often, we willingly take up this role because no one else seems able or willing except us. No one has asked me, for example, to serve as an unofficial advisor for our increasingly numerous dual-enrollment students who are flocking in disproportionate numbers to first-year writing courses. Yet, I have found myself in that role, because I am the only one who found it disturbing enough that the university didn't provide any formal faculty mentors for these students that I began working with them, out of concern for their success and a duty to care for my contingent instructors who were trying to take on this role themselves—despite labor and working conditions that made even informal advisement of these students untenable.

Notably, the care that WPAs take on is in the form of managing emotions and building relationships that inspire confidence among teachers and students, continuity among curricula, and comradery within programs. This may be especially true at smaller schools, where the WPA may "think of himself/herself less as a 'program administrator' and more as a 'people advocate' . . . [because] the people *are* the program" (Hebb 2005, 99, original emphasis). Doug Hesse agrees on the centrality of serving people as the central aim of our positions, noting, "I think that a certain kind of valuable ethos derives from being a steward to a writing program" (2015, 134). Hesse's language makes explicit the ways the emotional labor performed by WPAs, though certainly white-collar, is akin to other service positions like flight attendants, nurses, or customer service representatives, all of whom serve as "stewards" in their respective positions. Because Laura Micciche lists emotional labor as one of the "troubling work conditions" for WPAs and classifies it as "largely invisible" (2002, 434), it's important to understand the implications of emotional labor to WPA work.

Arlie Hochschild's groundbreaking study of flight attendants led her to define emotional labor simply as "the management of feeling to create a publicly observable facial and bodily display" (1983, 7). Emotional labor includes any performance of emotion where "the emotional style of offering the service is part of the service itself" (5), such as attending to other's feelings, downplaying one's own emotions to conform, maintaining a supportive communicative environment, counseling and mentoring others, developing and maintaining personal relationships, supporting others' feelings of well-being, among other acts. Emotional labor is a capitalist effect of the service industry because it "is sold for a wage and therefore has exchange value" (7). Hochschild's analysis helps us approach emotional labor as a matter of performance in that emotional management occurs as we attempt to accommodate emotional norms and align "what we feel" with how we are "supposed" to feel. For WPAs, it might mean working to express and inhabit the prescribed feeling rules, "a set of shared, albeit often latent, rules" of our jobs based on our professional identities (Hochschild, 1983, 268). In WPA work, the unwritten emotional expectations of our work include the dictum to care for our students and teachers and to work happily and collaboratively with other departments on our campuses to promote writing values across the university.

WPAs engage in emotional labor any time they attempt to change their emotions to align with what is deemed as appropriate for a given situation. Eileen Schell explores this self-management of emotion in her study of part-time faculty and finds that workplace emotions become yet another means of exploitation for these teachers (1998, 76). While WPAs may be positioned within universities in more privileged labor dynamics than contingent instructors—I, for example, am tenured—awareness of that privilege can propel us to perform even more emotional labor in the spirit of self-sacrifice. That's why I've taken on advisement of my university's dual-enrollment students: I am sacrificing my time and emotional well-being for the sake of my overworked contingent instructors, who were being overrun by their dual-enrolled students' emotional, social, and financial questions about university resources, course planning, and logistics. To make my instructors' working conditions more bearable, I told them to defer students' problems and queries to me. I engage in this increased workload and emotional labor despite feelings that my university should provide such services to students through the dual enrollment program, which has its own staff and greater resources than the writing program.

Service workers like WPAs, who regularly perform emotional labor, are at risk of confusing their professional and personal identities and of losing awareness of how they feel in the moment, Hochschild explains, since "seeming to 'love the job' becomes part of the job; and actually trying to love it, and to enjoy the customers, helps the worker in this effort" (6). This labor requires "a coordination of mind and feeling" and "draws on a source of self that we honor as deep and integral to our individuality" (7). For this reason, emotional labor deeply impacts the worker's state of mind, identity, and sense of self both on and off the job. This puts the emotional laborer in a constant state of giving, of outwardly expressing the appropriate emotions that are expected of her. Emotional labor, in other words, capitalizes on mind*less*ness and makes it harder for the WPA to identify and label her feelings, the more naturalized her emotional performance is.

The emotional labor I take on, by decision or by decree, of course impacts the boundaries of my work by creating the very edges of my practice, which can be as violently damaging to my well-being as an overly zealous yoga practice that leaves me injured. If emotions are not only "within" or "without" but both, creating the very effect of the surfaces or boundaries of bodies and worlds (Ahmed 2004, 117), mindfulness urges me to approach this boundary-making with full awareness. And ahimsa calls me to navigate this process gently and to remember that I cannot care for another's emotions without sufficiently attending to my own, since they are interconnected.

Ultimately then, increasing awareness of the ways we are emotionally mapped into our spaces through mindfulness is the first step in renegotiating those spaces sustainably. Taking into account the boundaries of our emotion work is necessary if we are to make this work visible and tangible and target it in our professional training. Such a targeted approach can give current and future WPAs means of attending to emotional labor in the spirit of ahimsa, changing the ways they manage it to increase their own and their programs' well-being. Mapping emotional labor, in other words, is a means of not only making our labor visible through the conscious consideration of ahimsa but also of moving toward awareness of how we feel and how we might better respond with mindful intention to these feelings. Since the concepts of ahimsa and mindfulness may be new to many WPAs, I explore them in more detail and connect them to contemporary trends in academic workplaces that naturalize our tendency for reckless overwork and mindlessness as we approach the emotional expectations of our jobs. I then turn to my own leadership as a counterexample of mindfulness to provide specific strategies of manifesting ahimsa in our workspaces.

AHIMSA AND SUSTAINING OURSELVES

For WPAs, emotional labor reveals a politics of intersubjective relationality in our work environments and an opening for ahimsa. Ahimsa transfers well to professional spaces because it is a pragmatic practice of cultivating well-being. When asking students to move our bodies in new ways, my yoga teachers want us to bring awareness to those bodies and to respect what they can and cannot do in any given moment. Ahimsa teaches me that my downward-facing dog may not look like yours because my hamstrings may be tight, limiting my ability to straighten my legs and sink back into my hips. It's easy to get caught up in negative judgment that leaves me with a defeatist attitude about my abilities. But rather than harshly judging my pose as inferior because I cannot release as deeply, ahimsa teaches me that I should embrace this difference as nonjudgmentally as I can and remain gentle with myself in the pose to respect my body's boundaries. Similarly, I should approach with curiosity and open awareness my hesitation to perform an intense pose like headstand. If my hesitation stems from an old neck injury and speaks to a truth about my body's limits in practice, I should enact ahimsa by accepting this hesitation and choosing another, safer pose. Ahimsa can similarly become a metaphor-in-action for my WPA work too. I can sometimes feel defensive when comparing the dynamics of my WPA work to others'. For example, I've felt shame when WPA colleagues find out that I do not complete scheduling alone, that I work with my department chair to set the writing schedule but let her take the lead since our department is small and our writing program even more so. Rather than seeing this shared duty as somehow a reflection of my reduced position on campus, which I have admittedly done in the past, I can chose to instead see it with ahimsa as simply a difference in how I strike my WPA pose locally, which looks different than some other WPAs' poses on their respective campuses.

Ahimsa doesn't just guide the intrapersonal; it also works interpersonally and relationally. Ahimsa teaches me to act with compassion when a classmate in the yoga studio cuts in front on me to quickly grab a yoga mat and block when I've been waiting patiently in line. Instead of stewing upon my momentary feelings of anger or judgment, I might instead notice my classmate's unfocused eyes, which hint at how she is too busy ruminating over some life trouble to see the line she cut in front of, and remember how she rushed into class late and is trying to hastily set up her station before we begin. I lose nothing by choosing kindness and forgiveness in this moment; indeed, I will likely regain inner peace once more. As a WPA, I might similarly do well to remember that a strong rebuke by a campus colleague on the declining state of student writing is likely more a sign of my colleague's insecurities about teaching writing in her own classes than it is a critique of my writing program.

I accordingly approach my professional application of contemplative concepts like ahimsa through a larger feminist framework of sustainability. To this end, I apply Lorraine Code's "ecological thinking" (2006), which is not only a means of thinking about sustainability and the environment but also a way to approach communities of practice as ecologies "both physical and social where people endeavor to live well together" (2006, 24). Ecological thinking can be enacted in communities of practice like writing programs by applying ahimsa to the ecology, where "living well together" in cohabitation is a pragmatic goal to keep programs sustainable and successful by keeping the people that run them "healthy," as measured by well-being, or the ability of individuals to flourish together and individually. Of this type of thinking, Code says, it is "not simply thinking about ecology or about the environment"; instead, "thinking ecologically carries with it a large measure of responsibility . . . about imagining, crafting, articulating, endeavoring to enact principles of ideal cohabitation" (2006, 24). Ecological thinking is therefore responsible, feminist thinking that values the importance of relationships and networks between people so that they might live well together and in ways that promote justice.

Ahimsa is a natural ally to ecological thinking, because it is a means of respecting our presence at the same time we respect our interdependence on others: to live well, we must live well together. When yogis practice vegetarianism, for instance, they often do so because of the ethical implications of ahimsa. These implications point to the need to cohabitate in ways that increase an ecology's well-being, which some do not see advanced by the practice of eating meat. B. K. S. Iyengar describes yoga in such ecological terms as "an integrated science which can lead [wo/]man's divided being back into wholeness and health" (2002, 85). At the heart of yogic philosophy and practice is therefore an interconnected nondualism best illustrated by the greeting built into the end and beginning of yoga practice, "*namaste*," which means "[t]he divine spirit in me honors the divine spirit in you" and is an acknowledgment of the fundamental connection between individuals (Geno 2017). Practicing ahimsa as an administrator is a means of applying this type of nondualistic thinking to our administrative spaces, which necessarily changes our relationship to our duties and the people we serve. Ahimsa questions the sustainability of normalized WPA selflessness that prioritizes serving others to the detriment of the WPA's own well-being, as this mindless behavior ignores the ways WPA well-being is ecologically tied to instructor and program well-being. It also changes the ways we understand the ramifications of how we are emotionally mapped into administrative spaces and how this creates closeness to and distance from others within our programs and departments.

As a skill of mindfulness, ahimsa makes us aware of the intersubjective nature of well-being, as ours is connected to those around us. Ahimsa helps us to create spaces of self-reflection that help us better understand the negotiation of feeling in our workspaces to promote well-being for ourselves and for others. WPAs can use ahimsa to promote self- and other-care by creating awareness of the emotional terrain of our workspaces and by providing us a tool that increases mindfulness and decreases the violence unattended emotional labor can bring to these spaces.

Ahimsa is a leaf on the larger branch of mindfulness. Mindfulness is "moment-to-moment, non-judgmental awareness, cultivated by paying attention in a specific way . . . in the present moment, and as non-reactively, as non-judgmentally, and as openheartedly as possible" (Kabat-Zinn 2005, 108). Mindfulness is not simply relaxation, nor is it the attempt to erase our thoughts. These are common misconceptions. Instead, we might think of mindfulness more fully as a centering awareness that changes the quality of our interactions with our thoughts and with others, a "gesture that inclines the heart and mind (seen as one seamless whole) toward a full-spectrum awareness of the present moment just as it is, accepting whatever is happening simply because it is already happening" (Kabat-Zinn 2005, 61). This gesture is so powerful that repeated practice can alter the shape and functioning of our brains so that we are better able to focus and less reactive to thoughts, emotions, and events, especially when these are disturbing or do not align with our desires or expectations, as evidenced by fMRI brain scans (Baime 2011, 47).

Connecting it directly to the practice of ahimsa, Jon Kabat-Zinn has defined mindfulness as an "act of love" and a "gesture of benevolence and kindness toward ourselves and toward others" (2005, 69). We can see mindfulness as an enactment of self-love and a perfect illustration of ahimsa because it pulls us from habituated thinking, where we often react to turbulences in our day by filtering them directly through narratives about how we feel ("I am sad") or a larger narrative about how our day is going ("Today is a bad day") instead of appreciating moments genuinely as they unfold and responding to them without hurtful ruminations and preconceived filters. I may, for instance, feel overwhelmed by my large "to do" list when I run into my department chair who asks me if I've observed our newest teacher yet, since consistent mentoring and observations of teachers are part of my job as WPA. While her question may have been innocent and a simple query, without mindfulness of my feelings going into this encounter, I may hear condemnation in this question ("Why *haven't* you observed the new teacher yet?"), which projects violence on our encounter, and I may react with increased stress ("Will today get better already?? One MORE item to add to my list!!"), a reaction that isn't compassionate to my well-being. To practice ahimsa, I need to approach this encounter with open mindfulness and a generous acceptance of the present moment to better manage my emotional well-being. To address this situation with ahimsa, I might begin by first becoming aware of any negative mental scripts that overtake this encounter and consciously rewrite them to disturb my habituated ways of thinking and to create new, mindful thinking: "My chair values my mentoring of new faculty. I will set up an observation next week when I have more time."

We all already have the capacity for the focused awareness of mindfulness. However, our contemporary society compels us toward violent emotional habits that move us further from it as we increase the speed of our living and the demands on our days. While we should, according to Thich Nhat Hanh, be focused on slowing down and putting our full energy toward each daily task, so that while "washing the dishes, washing the dishes must be the most important thing in your life" (1976, 21), we are more like the tea drinker who anticipates the cup of tea with which she will reward herself for washing the dishes. Ahimsa disappears in this case and the dishwasher effectively removes herself from the moment of washing the dishes and diminishes her joy from the act as she works to complete it as quickly as possible (1976, 24). If few of us approach washing dishes in this way, likely even fewer of us approach our WPA work with such mindfulness. Myself included.

I know the value of ahimsa because of the ways I have fallen short of enacting it in my own practice, personal and professional. While I respect others' desire to enact nonviolence, I've often tossed ahimsa to the side in my WPA and yoga practice because of my attachment to pride and ego. My tenuous relationship with ahimsa is not surprising, for what first drew me to yoga was the calm, intentional practice it promised. I need(ed) mindfulness because I am a classic "type A" WPA who constantly pushes herself beyond healthy boundaries. In my years of practicing yoga, I ignored ahimsa more often than not, determined as I was to be the best yogi I could be. I threw myself into poses I wasn't entirely ready for and drowned out my body's whisper of "Not yet. Be patient. Be kind" with a motivated and unhearing "I can and will do this." Incidentally, it's this refusal of ahimsa that recently lead me to develop tendonitis in both elbows, a chronic overuse injury that has taken over a year to manage with physical therapy and that will forevermore shape my yoga practice. No longer can I push myself through poses without regard to the consequences as I did before. As a result of my injury, I have learned to be kinder to myself by being more aware of the emotional struggle when my ego desires that I push, but my body demands that I don't. I have become more compassionate of my boundaries and more aware of my edge—the point at which a challenge remains positive and not unhealthy or unwise.

If ahimsa can guide yogis like me toward self-compassion and communal well-being, it can similarly help WPAs construct safer, more sustainable spaces from which to lead and can help them enact nonviolence toward themselves *and* others within their programs. "Violence" may seem a strong word to use in the context of running writing programs, but it is fitting and in-line with my focus on WPA well-being. Like yogis new to their practice, many WPAs find themselves violently disregarding their physical and emotional boundaries as they carry out their duties, working long hours that mean too much sitting and no time for exercise, or carrying disproportionate levels of work stress based on overwhelming responsibilities, to only mention a few examples. Perhaps most problematic in this overwork equation are the ways that WPAs are often unaware of their emotional boundaries: they want to stop an endless cycle of giving, but they remain unable to articulate ways to renegotiate the edges of their practice.

Evidence of the habituated mindlessness that leads to such violence present within academic workplaces appears in the 2019 *Inside Higher Education* article "The Zero-Sum Game of Faculty Productivity" by Michael S. Harris. Harris argues that we need to talk more openly and frankly about the trade-offs in our productivity if we are to balance an ever-increasing workload that requires multitasking while proving our efficiency and productivity against traditional markers of success like tenure and publication. Harris's article illustrates the cultural backdrop of our work as WPAs and is therefore important to consider briefly before moving to the specifics of my own workplace. Harris's unquestioned acceptance of endless multitasking and the sped-up nature of academic work may seem pragmatic to some readers, but a mindful perspective reveals that this acceptance can cloud the violence that these habits may do to our emotional well-being, forestalling the ability to see mindfulness as another option. Certainly when Harris starkly observes that "[s]aying yes to staying late for a committee meeting means saying no to your son's baseball game" but ultimately reminds us that "you will struggle if you do not prioritize the work that your institution and tenure committee value," we can see the dangerous ways he naturalizes overwork tendencies that can threaten academics—especially WPAs who already feel vulnerable to increased pressures and demands. For the WPA, Harris's "zero-sum game" is fraught: it's rarely as easy as "decid[ing] to focus on creating value for our students or in our research endeavors rather than letting busywork take over our day, week and semester" (2019).

Harris's comments are not unique; they are a product of contemporary neoliberal economic and political ideologies that, according to

Nancy Welch and Tony Scott (2016), have taken over higher education. Harris's mindless emotion management encourages a reckless work-life balance that impinges on academics' emotional well-being. He evades the question of how we might be approaching academic time and work-life balance violently and thus leading to the degradation of emotional well-being, one example of the negative ramifications of Welch and Scott's identified "austerity politics" (2016). Lil Brannon states in her "Afterword" in Welch and Scott's book that we might work against austerity politics to "[reclaim] our embodied locations" and establish a new way of working in higher education (2016, 225). Mindfulness suggests a means of doing this work, and ahimsa offers a sustainable administrative strategy to help us to name and navigate the emotion work of WPA labor in order to promote emotional well-being.

In the next section, I explore how WPAs might better control their emotional environments by first becoming fully aware of their emotional geographies through mindfulness, attending with ahimsa to the spaces of these environments and the resulting emotional relationships. We might, in other words, illustrate alternatives to the mindlessness promoted by our overwork culture and echoed by academics like Harris and begin to question the normalization of the "zero-sum" emotional game. Emotion work has been regarded as a form of hegemonic control (Ahmed 2015; Jagger 1992), and attending to the emotional impact of oppressive structures is one way to create more just alternatives that enact ahimsa in our work environments. Yogis practice mindfulness meditation on the breath to cultivate awareness of the moment as it is so they can respond to it through the conscious consideration of intentional response and not automatic or habitual reaction. WPAs who enact a mindful mapping of their emotional geographies can similarly learn to assess their emotional environments so that they too can better control their own well-being by understanding its relationship to their workplace's emotional geographies.

AHIMSA AS A MAPPING STRATEGY

We can apply ahimsa to map our emotional experiences by reflecting on our emotional spaces using educational theorist Andy Hargreaves's notion of emotional geographies. Emotional geographies are themselves real and metaphoric, extending Kat O'Meara's analysis of the WPA as cartographer in this collection. Emotional geographies help us map how emotional closeness and distance are created through material boundaries as well as felt conditions, both of which shape individuals' interactions. Hargreaves defines emotional geographies as "the spatial and experiential patterns of closeness and/or distance in human interactions and relationships that help create, configure and color the feelings and emotions we experience about ourselves, our world and each other" (Hargreaves 2001, 1061). Emotional geographies take into account that emotions are social and constructed through interactions between bodies and material environments. This concept helps us to examine the intersubjective impact of emotions and the ways relationships help to construct an emotional environment. This understanding of emotion is consistent with Ahmed's widely-accepted social theory of emotion (2004; 2015). Of the psychological, material, and social effects of emotion, Ahmed explains, "emotions do things, and they align individuals with communities—or bodily space with social space—through the very intensity of their attachments. Rather than seeing emotions as psychological dispositions, we need to consider how they work, in concrete and particular ways, to mediate the relationship between the psychic and the social, and between the individual and the collective" (2004, 118).

Emotional geographies are therefore spaces constructed by how emotions move between bodies and how emotions align certain bodies with other bodies and individuals within communities through attachments of feeling. This understanding resonates with yogic concepts of self which assume that we are both integral wholes, that we have centers which need the protections of ahimsa, but also that we are connected intimately and fundamentally to others as part of the whole of the world through our material and social natures. We must therefore extend ahimsa outward beyond the self. In his analysis, Hargreaves divides emotional geographies into six categories:

1. sociocultural: differences in race, culture, gender, etc., that create or dismantle distance between people
2. moral: common goals, shared purposes, and accomplishments or disagreements over goals and purposes
3. professional: definitions and norms of professionalism, setting colleagues apart, or creating opportunities for collaboration
4. physical: issues of time and space that promote or hinder cooperation
5. political: differences in power and status
6. personal: closeness of personal relationships

For the sake of space, I will outline two of these geographies in the next section: sociocultural and professional. I will take liberties to expand Hargreaves's original concepts to fit my local context. For instance, in my exploration of sociocultural geographies, I will examine the value systems in the department of literature where my writing program lives, since these tend to differ from the value systems prevalent in writing studies. My analysis will illustrate the connections between these geographies, which can be understood separately but, like an ecology, work together to form a networked and connected whole. While we can certainly think of positive examples of how emotional geographies might work to bind people in communities together, I will focus on the challenges of these emotional boundaries and the ways they invite conflict and violence. In my final section, I use these outlines to explore how ahimsa provides us a way of reconceiving these distances. I suggest that navigating these geographies with awareness helps WPAs exchange unexamined and automatic emotional labor for ahimsa, which becomes a means of enacting microresistance against the emotional violence of our workplaces, creating space for us to carve out administrative presence and seek well-being.

BOUNDARIES OF EMOTIONAL UNDERSTANDING: SOCIOCULTURAL DISTANCE AND POLITICAL DISTANCE

Professional Distance

Emotional geographies are structured by professional distance, which Hargreaves defines as a social process by which norms of professionalism are established, setting colleagues apart or creating opportunities for collaboration. He adds that norms for professional distance may constrain meaningful interaction and connection and notes that in his study of teachers, they experienced the greatest degree of negative emotion and labor "when their expertise, instructional knowledge, and judgments for which they felt uniquely qualified were questioned" (2001, 1069). Hargreaves importantly identifies the caretaking ethos that requires close emotional understanding through rigorous emotional labor as a professional norm that shapes the emotional well-being of teachers. WPAs are trained as teachers first and often approach their administrative work through the pedagogical lens of macrolevel teaching, making Hargreaves's analysis easily applied to the emotional spaces of administrative work.

One way I am expected to "care" for my program and the teachers in it is by willingly devoting whatever time and energy is necessary to perform all incumbent duties to keep the writing program running and successful, regardless of how problematic this load might be for just one person to complete. Take the matter of assessment. Over the years, my colleagues have heard my pleas for an established assessment budget that would allow me to pay stipends to the contingent instructors who teach 85 percent of our writing courses any given semester. When it became clear, after initial requests to upper administration to conduct larger-scale assessments of our first-year writing portfolios, that I was not going to be granted consistent or dependable funding, I was told I would have to assess these portfolios myself. When I pressed against this, it was pointed out to me that such administrative tasks are what justifies my teaching load reduction as WPA. Everyone agreed that as a compositionist "I like assessment anyway," so that this shouldn't be much of a burden. Incidentally, this stereotype has also made it such that I have been given leadership of all departmental assessment as the appointed assessment coordinator. In addition to the ethical problems of the WPA being the sole assessor of her own program, the resulting situation disregards my well-being as I attempt to complete a portfolio assessment single-handedly each spring. When I see others handing out multiple-choice assessment surveys in other classes, I feel resentful, defeated by my allegiance to best practices and marginalized by my professional identity.

Sociocultural Distance

Hargreaves defines sociocultural distance, one interest of his application, in terms of the teacher-student and teacher-parent dimensions of teaching. Hargreaves notes that "all too often, teachers look at students and parents with growing incomprehension. They are physically, socially, and culturally removed from the communities in which they teach . . . [which] often leads teachers to stereotype and be stereotyped by the communities they serve" (2001, 1062). While Hargreaves is cognizant of the differences of race, class, and gender, he is also interested in a myriad of other differences that can spawn feelings of distance, such as educational background, upbringing, and age. Sociocultural distance breeds uncertainty and stunts meaningful communication, which is why it often leads to stereotyping the "other" community. Of course, these are all factors that shape emotional labor and emotional well-being performed in our workplaces.

The ramifications of sociocultural distance equally impact university environments, inviting us to examine these factors in academic relationships between university faculty and instructors, as well as the emotional well-being of WPAs, who often stand at the nexus of these relationships. One way that sociocultural difference is manifested in WPA work is the disciplinary marginalization of the WPA, who may be situated within a larger English program that emphasizes literature or another discipline outside of writing. This is a common occurrence in teaching-oriented liberal arts schools like mine who just don't have enough faculty to justify freestanding writing departments and who have retained traditional disciplinary divisions. The "growing incomprehension" that Hargreaves targets as creating distance between two varied "cultural" groups applies not only to parents and teachers, then, but also to teachers of varied disciplines and especially to those who are administratively motivated by leadership positions to represent and serve their field, like WPAs. This can invite conflict.

Like many other state universities, mine has been hit hard recently, with lower enrollments and progressively less state funding each year. In my English department, where I am the only tenured faculty member with a writing studies degree and am outnumbered by colleagues in literature, that has meant that "streamlining" the offerings of upper-level courses for our majors has disproportionately impacted me, the WPA and only full-time, tenured writing studies faculty member. While offering fewer upper-division classes each semester has certainly impacted my literature colleagues as well, often resulting in them teaching more survey courses and waiting three or four semesters to teach a desired topical course, I am the only one in the department who faced the actual disappearance of her sole consistently offered, non-service-bound, upper-level course—not coincidentally, since I am also the only one, as WPA, who is perceived as "preferring" first-year writing. Three years ago, I found out in a department meeting that I would no longer be teaching an advanced composition course for our majors, a course that was on the books before I took my job—and was incidentally a reason I chose to take it, since I saw a commitment to a vertical writing curriculum in the major. When a new course rotation list was passed around and approved at an earlier department meeting at which I was not in attendance because I was at a conference, it was voted on and accepted by a majority. This was a violent disappearance, since no one alerted me to the change. Indeed, I only found out *weeks later* when I was reviewing the course rotation list on my own and noticed the absence. I felt sideswiped; I went home angry and upset.

AHIMSA AS MICRORESISTANCE

These examples mapped by emotional geographies illustrate moments of violence in my position that negatively impact my emotional well-being and call for me to engage in emotional labor to manage my feelings so I can productively run my writing program and maintain community within my department. They can be understood to represent examples of what Meaghan Brewer and Kristen di Gennaro describe as discrimination of composition within literature, where "composition is [seen as] a class or an administrative position, not a discipline with its own set of research and content knowledge" (2018, 16). Collectively, English department colleagues are allied in sociocultural social justice pursuits and explicitly focused on racism, sexism, and other marginalizations, but they are "less aware of how class-based, hierarchical prejudices play into the relationship between composition and literature" (17). Brewer and di Gennaro label the outcomes of these prejudices "microagressions," or insults and slurs that occur in everyday interactions and conversations (17). Cristyn Elder and Bethany Davila (2019) remind us that it's dangerous to naturalize these microaggressions as just part of the working conditions of our job when, these authors claim, they are examples of bullying in our workplaces. It might seem odd to classify compositionists, especially those tenured and in administrative positions of "power," as a target of bullying microaggressions, a term that has been used to also analyze gender and racial discrimination, but as Brewer and di Gennaro note, while universities situate composition more centrally, departments of English often simultaneously view it as less important than literature, fostering an environment that contributes to microaggressions against compositionists in departments of literature (2018, 20). That microaggressions are common experiences which help to structure the emotional geographies of our workplaces testifies to just how needed ahimsa is in our administrative work. Analogous to what Mwenja says in her chapter within this collection about restorative composition pedagogies and how they offer circles of support to practitioners, ahimsa becomes a means of creating a more inclusive and restorative community of practice.

I'm not suggesting ahimsa is a magic pill that makes the challenges and difficulties of WPA emotion work disappear. My examples in the last section prove the situation is more challenging than that. My goals are more humble. Ahimsa doesn't eradicate the emotional labor of administration, but it does change our orientation to it and provides us a pragmatic tool to use: mindfulness. WPAs who practice ahimsa as part of a larger practice of sustainable leadership engage their work differently and therefore open up news ways of responsibly navigating the emotional labor of that work, which promotes the well-being of their programs and the people within them, including the WPA. We can develop mindfulness through meditation on the breath, fully attending to the in-breath as it moves into the body, in through the nose and into the lungs and belly, expanding and filling us internally with air, and then reversing the process of attending to notice the collapse of the belly and the movement of air outward from the lungs and out through the nose. This awareness anchors our attention to the present moment of the breath. The goal is to keep focus on the breath, not by suppressing other thoughts that will naturally arise, even for the most experienced practitioners, but by instead gently redirecting the attention back to the breath every time it wanders. We practice ahimsa in these moments of gentle redirection. Because we have a limited capacity to attend, by narrowing the focus on our attention, we actually increase the depth of how well we can attend: when the mind is "released from elaborative thinking . . . [*about* our thoughts, sensations, or experiences] . . . more resources are made available to process information related to current experience" (Bishop et al. 2004, 233).

Analogously, we might apply ahimsa as a strategy of mindfulness-based microresistance for WPAs to use in their workplaces to keep purposefully directing attention back to emotional labor and wellness. Microresistances, or daily incremental efforts that challenge prejudice (Irey 2013, 36), provide a means of coping with microaggressions by labeling the aggression and reframing it in terms of our emotional needs, a counterstrategy of nonviolence. Cynthia Ganote, Floyd Cheung, and Tasha Souza propose a microresistance model called Opening the Front Door (OTFD) that clarifies the process and provides an achievable outcome that my readers may appreciate. The phrase "opening the front door" is a mnemonic device for their four steps:

Observe: State in clear, unambiguous language what you see happening.
Think: Express what you think or what you imagine others might be thinking.
Feel: Express your feelings about the situation.
Desire: State what you would like to have happen.

The authors developed this model originally to help recipients of microaggressions and their allied colleagues confront and resist microaggressions in the workplace, specifically those that arise from competing values and hierarchies, like the ones I describe. While their microresistance model is not indebted to mindfulness, it is striking how much more meaningful the model becomes when we approach it through mindfulness completed in the spirit of nonviolence toward our emotional health. Their model illustrates how, like the breath, when we focus on emotional well-being in the face of conflict or violence, we can better attend to our experiences and consequently can articulate our emotional needs. Their model also becomes another example of how restorative practices, like those Mwenja discusses as well as those I discuss in these pages, that stem from mindfulness, can attune us to our feelings, which can be a powerful means of building conversations that validate well-being.

To apply their model to the WPA, we can see how WPAs who practice mindfulness—even only metaphorically within the context of administration and not through a formal contemplative act like yoga or meditation—will be prepared to "observe" their emotional geographies. Centered focus through mindfulness expands the purview of ahimsa as we learn to better sustain our attention and therefore understand our feelings and experiences, so that we are not tugged along the current without understanding or, in turn, any sense of power or control over what is happening to us. It's the difference, to return to my opening examples, of reactively jumping up into a headstand even if that pose may be harmful to our current abilities just because the teacher calls out the pose, as opposed to being fully aware of the moment and our bodies within it to pause and honor our boundaries and presence in the moment to respond with intention by moving into a safer alternative like legs up the wall. It's the difference of recognizing the emotional labor WPAs perform throughout the day, so we can identify, vocalize, and share our affective experiences—like I do in my last section—instead of walking around in a fog of disappointment, stress, and dejection. Ahimsa means we shift our reiterative and habitual performances of emotional labor for a more mindful understanding of our emotion work, enacting the model's first move, to *observe*. For me, it means outlining, as I do above, the injustice at work in my department as my upper-level writing course was erased when all other courses were left untouched; it means seeing this deletion as a microaggression that shows prejudice against my field and me as a harbinger of new ways of thinking about our literature-centric curriculum; it means reflectively drawing connections between these systemic factors and my personal well-being as a WPA.

But to practice ahimsa through the OTFD strategy, I cannot stop there; I must act through my thoughts and feelings, which become agentive. Ahimsa is not passive or meek; it means we *actively* employ mindfulness to attend to the realities of our situations. This attention leads to increasing awareness that translates into renewed agency: "*Ahimsa* faces the opponent with kindness and sympathy but with the sure determination that whatever the opposition, it will hold its ground" (Easwaran 2011, 192). To "hold my ground," I have requested meetings to explain clearly my thoughts about the course deletion and have articulated my feelings of frustration and dejection. I have explained that I feel unfairly treated and that I would like to find a sustainable way to continue to offer my course and negotiate the lower enrollments we face. In reframing the conversation through these terms, I enact mindfulness by approaching my response not as reactive but as asserting purposeful and motivated resistance and reflective understanding of the larger emotional geographies at play in my workspace. Because ahimsa is a means of enacting emotional agency through mindfulness, it actualizes the microresistance model's final step, *desire*, which helps us use our agency toward getting what we want.

Strategies like OTFD pursued mindfully through ahimsa are not guaranteed to eradicate prejudice. Indeed, I was told in response to my careful discussion that instead of my writing course, I could teach any literature course as a replacement, since "everyone else was also teaching outside their specialty," referring to other literature faculty who were teaching courses in historical ranges not typical of their research. Since I felt this offer was still unresponsive to my needs and resulted from prejudicial thinking used to evacuate writing of its disciplinary status, I used the space created to discuss the differences between a field, a discipline, and a subfield, which elevated the conversation from a momentary opportunity to change my immediate course problem to one that engages in a larger move toward social justice through clarification that might promote positive change toward greater inclusion of writing and greater equity among classes and faculty in the future. With mindfulness, I was able to reframe this problem as systemic and not only a personal slight, which hugely impacts how I understand my emotional work within my environment and how I position myself in relationships with others.

Both the yogi and the WPA can use ahimsa to practice emotional sustainability. I have been more interested in this chapter in decoding our emotional labor as WPAs than providing tidy solutions to it. Mapping the ways we labor to increase others' well-being and the ways our own well-being is compromised is akin to learning to follow the breath in mindfulness meditation. As Jon Kabat-Zinn suggests, mindfulness promotes the enactment of ahimsa by serving as a pair of "shoes" we can wear, "protecting us from the consequences of our own habits of emotional reaction, forgetfulness, and unconscious harming" (2005, 57). We cannot have power and control without awareness; mapping the boundaries of our well-being and the reactive emotions that arise in emotional encounters with others is necessary to develop mindfulness. This awareness is an active way to promote ahimsa in our workplaces.

Ahimsa helps WPAs identify and label the specifics of their local emotional geographies, making visible the emotional labor they already perform; it can also help us map the emotional labor required of our leadership in ways that promote awareness and well-being and decrease the emotional violence and mindlessness that too often serve as unquestioned scripts within our workplaces.

NOTES

1. The difference to press here is the intention behind the yoga practice. The kinds of practices I will discuss in these pages refer to ones completed with the intention of mindfulness and not only exercising or relaxing. While yoga practiced with the goal of developing mindfulness will certainly increase the practitioner's flexibility and decrease stress, these can be classified as effects of mindfulness and the consequences of changed ways of being and not simply an exercise regime. Understanding practice in this way allows us to see how we might apply the intention of mindfulness to other practices like academic administration, which I consider here.
2. In this way, yoga becomes a metaphor for life and ahimsa a metaphoric concept to live by, calling to mind the work of George Lakoff and Mark Johnson in *Metaphors We Live By* (2003).

REFERENCES

Ahmed, Sara. 2004. "Affective Economies." *Social Text* 79, no. 22 (2): 117–39.
Ahmed, Sara. 2015. *The Cultural Politics of Emotion.* 2nd ed. New York: Routledge.
Baime, Michael. 2011. "This Is Your Brain on Mindfulness." *Shambhala Sun.* 44–84.
Bishop, Scott, Mark Lau, Shauna Shapiro, Linda Carlson, Nicole D. Anderson, James Carmody, Zindel V. Segal, Susan Abbey, Michael Speca, Drew Velting, and Gerald Devins. 2004. "Mindfulness: A Proposed Operational Definition." *Clinical Psychology: Science and Practice* 11 (3): 230–41.
Bishop, Wendy. 1999. "What Interests Me Is What Interests You: The Writing of WPAs." Paper presented at the WPA Summer Conference, Purdue University, West Lafayette, Indiana.
Brannon, Lillian. 2016. "Afterword." In Welch and Scott. Logan: Utah State University Press. 3–17.
Brewer, Meaghan, and Kristen di Gennaro. 2018. "Naming What We Feel: Hierarchal Microagressions and the Relationship between Composition and English Studies." *Composition Studies* 46 (2): 15–34.
Code, Lorraine. 2006. *Ecological Thinking: The Politics of Epistemic Location.* Oxford, UK: Oxford University Press.
Easwaran, Eknath. 2011. *Gandhi the Man: How One Man Changed Himself to Change the World.* 4th ed. New York: Nilgiri Press.
Elder, Cristyn L., and Bethany Davila, eds. 2019. *Defining, Locating, and Addressing Bullying in the WPA Workplace.* Logan: Utah State University Press.
Ganote, Cynthia, Floyd Cheung, and Tasha Souza. 2013. "Don't Remain Silent! Strategies for Supporting Yourself and Your Colleagues via Microresistance and Ally Development." Paper presented at the POD Conference, San Francisco, CA. https://sites.google.com/a/podnetwork.org/wikipodia/past-pod-conferences/2015-pod-conference/presentations-2015/cganote.

Geno, Rita. 2017. "The Meaning of *Namaste*." April 21, 2017. https://www.yogajournal.com/practice/the-meaning-of-quot-namaste-quot.

Hargreaves, Andy. 2001. "The Emotional Geographies of Teaching." *Teachers College Record* 103 (6): 1056–80.

Harris, Michael S. 2019. "The Zero-Sum Game of Faculty Productivity." February 7, 2019. https://www.insidehighered.com/advice/2019/02/07/academics-should-make-trade-offs-faculty-work-more-explicit-opinion.

Hebb, Judith. 2005. "Reenvisioning WPAs in Small Colleges as 'Writing People Advocates." *WPA: Writing Program Administration* 29 (1–2): 97–110.

Hesse, Doug. 2015. "The WPA as Worker: What Would John Ruskin Say? What Would My Dad?" *WPA: Writing Program Administration* 38 (2): 129–40.

Hochschild, Arlie. 1983. *The Managed Heart: Commercialization of Human Feeling.* Berkeley: University of California Press.

Irey, S. 2013. "How Asian American Women Perceive and Move toward Leadership Roles in Community Colleges: A Study of Insider Counter Narratives," PhD diss., University of Washington.

Iyengar, B. K. S. 2002. *The Tree of Yoga.* Boston, MA: Shambhala.

Jaggar, Alison M. 1992. "Love and Knowledge: Emotions in Feminist Epistemology." In *Gender, Body, Knowledge,* edited by Alison M. Jaggar and Susan R. Bordo. New Brunswick, NJ: Rutgers University Press. 145-71.

Kabat-Zinn, Jon. 2005. *Coming to Our Senses: Healing Ourselves and the World through Mindfulness.* Hachette.

Lasater, Judith. 2000. *Living Your Yoga: Finding the Spiritual in Everyday Life.* Berkeley, CA: Rodmell Press.

Micciche, Laura. 2002. "More than a Feeling: Disappointment and WPA Work." *College English* 64 (4): 432–58.

Nhat Hanh, Thich. 1976. *Miracle of Mindfulness: An Introduction to the Practice of Meditation.* Boston: Beacon Press.

Satchidananda, Sri Swami, translator. 2011. *The Yoga Sutras of Patanjali.* Buckingham, VA: Integral Yoga.

Schell, Eileen E. 1998. "The Costs of Caring: 'Feminism' and Contingent Women Workers in Composition Studies." In *Feminism and Composition Studies: In Other Words,* edited by Susan Jarratt and Lynn Worsham. New York: Modern Language Association. 74–93.

Welch, Nancy, and Tony Scott, eds. 2016. *Composition in an Age of Austerity.* Logan: Utah State University Press.

8
REPRESENTING THE BASEMENT

Alexis Teagarden

What kinds of self-identity promote sustainable writing programs? In Laura Micciche's (2007) exploration of composition's self-conceptions, she finds that its preferred identity metaphors are often ones of subordinated location, like that of the basement. Previous reflections support her interpretation. Emily Isaacs and Melinda Knight (2014), for example, argue that "[l]ocation conveys psychological as well as physical power" (46) and describe their solution to the travails of writing program work as literally and metaphorically moving up and out. Micciche takes a more nuanced stance, recognizing that subordinated identity metaphors produce both good and ill effects. Such metaphors help the field identify with marginalized people: "Caring for those who regularly slip through the cracks or are viewed as minor, uninteresting, or troublesome—i.e., first-year writing students—is inextricably related to the field's own identity within English" (36). Yet Micciche ultimately questions their utility, arguing that such identities sustain rather than critique subordination, making it impossible to imagine, or enact, alternative ways of being.

In response, she suggests shifting identity metaphors from "location" to "space." Carolyn Calhoon-Dillahunt (2018) follows that recommendation, arguing for the importance of FYW by explaining: "I am not talking about a particular content, but rather a space in academia" (276), a view that grounds her eventual claim to the CCCC audience that FYW "is our space of power" (282). But I wonder how useful such a switch from location to space can be, given that Micciche partially grounds her concerns in George Lakoff and Mark Johnson's (1980) theory of conceptual metaphors. For their work also demonstrates how spatially based conceptual metaphors underwrite much of the English language's descriptions of social status. Shifting from location to space might not create the break from subordinated language that Micciche and Calhoon-Dillahunt seek.

In this chapter, I start with the same place as Micciche—the basement—but propose a different way of amending it. I argue that subterranean space is often given lowly status in the US popular imagination, yet domains as diverse as fantasy literature and contemporary engineering provide alternative views, ones that highlight the valuable affordances of spaces underground. Rather than claim writing programs should leave the basement—as Isaacs and Knight do—or remove it from our identity metaphors—like Micciche advocates—I suggest we embrace the idea of the basement as an inherently sustainable space, one standing in contrast to the wasteful, isolating, and traditionally exclusive nature of the above-ground Ivory Tower.

To consider the ways the basement metaphor shapes approaches to writing program administration, I first chart its use across the scholarly literature. I then show how that usage mostly conforms to conceptual metaphors, mainly drawn from spatial and orientational domains. I challenge those conceptual metaphors by providing alternative views of subterranean space, using examples from fantasy and contemporary engineering. I conclude by arguing that WPAs can embrace their metaphorical basement space as a way to reimagine their program's place in the academy, a space that can help minimize the traditional ills of isolation and hierarchy while also promoting the values of community and sustainability.

LITERAL AND FIGURATIVE "BASEMENT DAYS"

Locating first-year writing (FYW) in the basement has a history both literal and metaphorical. Reviewing the history of composition and writing programs reveals the basement as a common workplace. This appears as literal fact, as when Terry Dean's (1989) article directs correspondence to "The Learning Skills Center, Basement, South Hall." Career reflections find this setting worth reporting: Teresa Enos (1999) wryly notes her first tenure-line position with the writing faculty was "housed, of course, in basement cubicles" (82); Gail Stygall (2003) describes "prototypical basement offices" (8), and Wanda Martin (1988) calls her fledgling basic writing program a "basement band" given its location (30; see also Davies 2013; Rider and Broughton 1994). Writing classes banished below ground is another motif: Jim Porter (2002) describes his first experience with computer classrooms "in the basement of the math building" (380); Joy Ritchie and Kathleen Boardman (1999) locate the 1980s–1990s feminist conversations about composition not in the published literature but rather "in informal conversations, in basement classrooms" (589). Fred Johnson (2008) discusses issues with literal basement classrooms, then treats these specific classrooms as a metonym for all the issues attending "departmental disunity," arguing: "Problems in the basement, then, tend to be material results of a fractured community" (A10). For as literal as basement space can be for FYW programs, the basement as a metaphor is even more commonplace.

The basement, for example, often serves as the setting for the field's origin stories. Patrick Brantlinger's (1997) *PMLA* forum article provides such a narrative, telling how writing instruction was "relegated to the basement along with the graduate students and the part-timers who now ordinarily teach composition, while the tenured literature faculty levitated to the penthouse" (266). Winifred Horner's (1996) allegory runs the same: "Composition was a happy child, much beloved by his rich uncle, Administration, but despised by his mother and forced to go live in the basement" (198). The metaphor is so ingrained that Susan Miller's (1993) chapter title "The Sad Women in the Basement: Images of Composition Teachers" requires no further explication; the basement is mentioned only in the title.

By 2008, the anonymous Professor X could build his memoir and critique of college writing courses on two academic metaphors ("In the Basement of the Ivory Tower"), confident the architectural juxtaposition would make sense to readers of *The Atlantic*; these linked metaphors had already been noted in the literature by Rider and Broughton, among others. And Julie Schumacher's (2018) fictional send-up of a floundering English department renders the basement offices of lowly professors and grad students in painstaking, and painful, detail. Once in-house academic shorthand, the basement metaphor has gone mainstream.

However, rereading the scholarly literature shows that this metaphor has evolved along with writing program administration. Begun as a descriptor for all writing faculty, it now often focuses on contingent and part-time instructors—such as Professor X. Contrast Enos's (1999) first tenure-line job in the basement with Tony Scott's (2004) reflection on labor conditions at the turn of the millennium: "I often marvel at the difference between the portrait of writing instruction I see in our scholarship—where the teacher is assumed to be a full-time teacher with her own office—and the material reality I encounter in my everyday working life . . . I wonder how different our discipline and its scholarly conversations might look if we shined more of the light of our research on the basement offices of our contingent instructorate" (154–55). Here Scott, himself a tenured professor of Writing Studies, Rhetoric, and Composition, emphasizes how the twenty-first century saw tenure-line writing studies and composition scholars move up to the "penthouse" where Brantlinger (1997) earlier placed literature faculty, leaving the vast majority of fellow, but contingent, writing instructors below.

While I take the above examples from FYW programs, other writing programs root systematic issues in basement imagery as well. Steven North (1984) condemned the view of writing centers as a "proofreading-shop-in-the-basement" (444), and Lisa Ede (1989) reported a physical and figurative alignment in the early days of her writing center: "our second-class status is symbolized by our basement offices and inadequate staffs and budgets" (7). Rita Malenczyk (2007) answers a hypothetical question about the best place for a new writing center: "Depends on what kind of space is likely to become available—but never, oh never, in the basement" (149). Isaacs and Knight's (2014) study of writing centers does find progress in the centers' actual and symbol place. Reporting that only two writing centers defined themselves as housed in the actual basement, they "read these data on location as indicating an elevation of writing centers from the 'basement' days" (46). While their study suggests progress for writing centers' positions, the metaphor of basement persists, and not just in first-year writing.

Sister disciplines also recognize the metaphor as apt. Frank Dance's (2008) review of *The Economics of Attention* demonstrates that a similar feeling of marginalization exists among first-year speech/communication faculty. Coming across Lanham's line "Freshman composition has always lived in the basement," Dance responds "I couldn't help but wonder if he was friends with his next-door neighbors teaching the basic course in public speaking" (112). And Robert Root (2004) suggests a different hierarchy, but the same cellar, in "Putting Nonfiction in Its Place" when he wonders why nonfiction's place is always "the basement of the creative writing annex to the posh English multiplex" (294). Even student work is understood to occupy both actual and metaphorical basements. John Brereton (1995), for example, describes the sweep of possible spaces archiving student work: "Untold numbers of student papers sit in American college and university archives. These repositories vary widely, from the superb facilities at Harvard's Pusey Library, to a section of the library at Wellesley, to a dreary basement at the University of Minnesota" (xv). With so many disciplines dwelling below ground, perhaps these basement metaphors should emphasize the crowded space, the stuff of life that is not quite needed but also cannot be quite thrown out.

Curiously, though, Harvard's Pusey library is considered an underground space (Fuhlrott 1986; Hall 2004). So Brereton's divergent representations, from the "superb" to the "dreary," describe the same kind of architectural space—subterranean. It is not simply being underground that makes basements "dreary" but rather how such spaces are designed and symbolically understood. Thus, while basements are often dreary, dank, overcrowded, and underlit, they do not need to be. Attentive design can remedy many of these problems by building a "superb" space. This architectural reality can shift our metaphorical understanding of being placed in the basement. But imagining basements as important subterranean spaces can require overthrowing both lived experience and conceptual metaphors.

METAPHORS AT WORK

As a field, we can recognize "basement days" as a metaphor, one grounded in lived experience but now emblematic of a writing program's symbolic place. In naming it a metaphor, we can also see its constituent parts: our collective understanding of the basement operates as a source domain, elements from which people draw on to explain the target domain—here, writing programs (Johnstone 2008). When we think of basements as places where monsters lurk or servants dwell or forgotten objects pile up, then describing writing programs as basements ties them to all those negative cultural associations.

The spatial and orientational realities of basements also call up a host of possible conceptual metaphors, which further channel thinking. In *Metaphors We Live By*, Lakoff and Johnson (1980) define the idea of "conceptual metaphors," which they argue underwrite many English-language associations. Conceptual metaphors operate at the linguistic level; when explained, they sound more like clichés than literary or rhetorical figures. We often fail to see them as metaphors at all. For example, Lakoff and Johnson argue, "In some cases spatialization is so essential a part of a concept that it is difficult for us to imagine any alternative metaphor that might structure the concept. In our society 'high society' is such a concept" (18). This conceptual understanding of space, where *high* equates with power and prestige, correspondingly conditions English speakers to understand low spaces as representative of the other—lack of power, lack of position: the tower versus the basement.

Spatial conceptual metaphors limit our views of subterranean space, but so too do orientational ones. Lakoff and Johnson (1980) argue that, for English speakers, *up* is linked to positive values and *down* with negative: "High status is up; low status is down"; "Having control or force is up; being subject to control or force is down"; as well as "happy is up; sad is down" (15–16). They call this the "GOOD IS UP" category, explaining the association of good with up "gives an UP orientation to general well-being, and this orientation is coherent with special cases like HAPPY

IS UP, HEALTH IS UP, ALIVE IS UP, CONTROL IS UP. STATUS IS UP is coherent with CONTROL IS UP" (18). Similarly, they note, "MUNDANE REALITY IS DOWN" (19). And so the lived experience of basement space and the received wisdom of composition as dreary service work reinforce each other, giving the metaphor heft even if the material conditions of workspaces change, even if writing instructors continually try to reject the frame of composition as not real work (Brewer and di Gennaro 2018).

Conceptual metaphors channel our thinking. But considering alternative perspectives on subterranean design can help invent new ways of seeing the same space and new ways of framing WPA issues. Accepting the basement as our place, that is, need not mean capitulating to the view of composition as dreary toil by exploited faculty. By changing how we perceive basements, we can preserve the values that our field's history of subordination helped shape, while prioritizing work that supports others to overcome their socially stigmatized situations in sustainable ways.

ALTERNATIVE DOMAINS: SUBTERRANEAN SPACE'S VALUES

To reconsider the basement, let us first remember that the Ivory Tower has been an inhospitable place to many, including students in FYW classes (Haswell, Haswell, and Blalock 2004). But before determining how to change that, I think it also important to reconsider some of the more cherished representations of college. Take, for example, how Enos (1999) describes her "first academic misadventure" in terms of architecture: "I was studying literature (there were perhaps only three rhetoric and composition programs in the United States then), and all the literature professors were men. The department was housed in an impressive marble edifice that was also a research center for Victorian literature. Each professor's office opened into his very own classroom" (80). This image vividly contrasts with the description she provides of her own early workspaces. While Enos might not directly pine for the literature department's space, many of us could. Yet behind the gleaming marble and imagined tranquility, the structural design puts into stone the idea of teaching as isolated work—classrooms as owned rather than shared, blocked off from each other. What seems immediately pleasant—not just an office but a classroom of her own—becomes troubling when seen as a way of promoting isolation.

And overcoming isolationist tendencies can be understood as a core goal of WPA work, crossing classroom and program domains, or, as Ede

(1989) describes, "our effort to encourage collaboration and dialogue is inherently subversive—not just of our traditional educational institutions (we have always known that), but of one of the most important, because most hidden and commonsensical assumptions of our culture: that writing and thinking are inherently individual solitary activities" (9).

To raise our eyes to the lofty spaces of an idealized Ivory Tower can obstruct our inherent strengths and our foundational mission. And so rather than look to historical or popularly imagined views of college and attempt to make our programs over in their image, WPAs should seek alternative ways to see the space we already hold and learn how to work with its afforded strengths. Such work will likely mean our space develops differently. So it should; our recognition of student voices, our attention to labor conditions, our value of teaching is often very different from the traditional views of university work. But doing so requires ways of challenging prevailing basement metaphors. Both fantasy literature and contemporary engineering discourse provide examples.

Fantasy stories provide us alternative ways of thinking about underground space. Alice's tumble down a rabbit hole lands her in a strange and sometimes frightening place, where, among the course of other adventures, she is told lessons she once learned are wrong. Her attempt to recite the "How Doth the Little Busy Bee" poem, and its praise of diligent effort, is transformed into a new rhyme on the theme of how appearance deceives (Carroll and Gardner 23). I have often wondered if students in FYW see their instructors akin to the caterpillar, offering lessons that start off sounding similar to a high school English class but end with very different expectations. Might the adventures of Wonderland help first-year writing programs consider what they want students to experience as they navigate the new world of university life?

In contrast, J. R. R. Tolkien's fantasies ([1937] 1982; [1954] 1978) introduce the idea of hobbit holes as a domestic paradise—superior, in fact, to above-ground houses. For hobbits, life underground is preferred, because it is most comfortable (although it is only the rich hobbits that make their spaces luxuriously so). When underground options are not possible, homes are built to mirror tunnels. In Tolkien's telling, hobbits by necessity learned to build above ground, but did so in their own way: "They did not go in for towers." Instead, "[t]heir houses were usually long, low, and comfortable" ([1954] 1978, 27). The pairing of low and comfortable, with comfort as a central virtue for hobbits, provides us another option for viewing space. Certainly the constitutional dislike of adventure that characterizes most hobbits is in direct opposition to Alice's curious nature, but the contrast shows the copiousness inherent in the underground domain. Writing programs of all philosophies, from those stressing challenge and transformation to those privileging hospitality and comfort, can find a story to inspire.

And Terry Pratchett, playing with Tolkien and Carroll and seemingly every other writer to come before, imagines the conceptual metaphors that would govern a race that lived entirely underground—that of the dwarfs. The novel *Thud!* opens with a piece of the dwarfs' ancient writing explaining the origin of races, born in the mouth of a cave: "The first brother walked toward the light, and stood under the open sky. Thus he became too tall. He was the first Man. He found no Laws and he was enlightened. The second brother walked toward the darkness, and stood under a roof of stone. Thus he achieved the correct height. He was the first Dwarf. He found the Laws Tak had written, and he was endarkened" (n.p.). Such plays on language suffuse Pratchett's work, often turning Lakoff and Johnson's conceptual metaphors on their head; this example challenges the conception of light as understanding. Here as well is the idea that a roof of stone, not a view of the cosmos, inspires civilization and allows the dwarfs to find the written law. And while Pratchett's dwarfs, like all his characters, are a mix of good and ill traits (they are, for example, constitutionally bewildered by metaphors), their reverence for writing makes them appealing symbols for WPAs. Reading the world through the dwarfs' eyes provides new ways to think about assumptions buried in language, including those that limit how we value below-ground space.

While fantasy writing provides vivid reimagining of life underground, the domain of contemporary engineering gives us a practical set of virtues to consider, ones that emphasize how subterranean space aligns with sustainability goals. Dexter Hunt and coauthors (2016), for example, argue that the traditional "taller and denser" (8) design approach is unsustainable, whereas "greater use of [urban underground space] could allow for minimisation of above ground environmental and social impacts whilst improving access and service delivery for lasting economic viability" (19). Underground spaces, they show, "facilitate sustainable development, not least because they benefit from certain naturally embedded features" (12). Viewed this way, we can recognize basements become sustainable spaces, with their physical affordances prompting figurative ones.

For readers with basements of their own, expert discourse can be supported by lived experience; basements can be pleasantly cooler than above-ground floors in hot weather, and warmer, even without extensive heating, in cold seasons. Previous generations harnessed the way underground space moderates temperature when using cellars and below-ground buildings to store food, methods that are regaining popularity as people seek out more sustainable ways of living. Garden writer for *The Providence Journal* Henry Homeyer (2018) devoted an entire fall column to his methods of preserving his harvest. Among other strategies, he keeps "[p]otatoes, carrots, kohlrabi and rutabagas" fresh by storing them in his basement. Such methods prolonged the harvest in sustainable ways; unlike a refrigerator, cellars require no additional energy.

Of course, civil engineers and architects agree that a different kind of expertise is needed to make subterranean spaces safe and welcoming (Hunt et al. 2016). As in the imagined Shire, good underground living does not come easily or inexpensively. Yet, I see the call for new and differing expertise as supporting rather than weakening the value of the basement as metaphor. As Susan Miller-Cochran's 2018 CWPA conference plenary address demonstrated, WPAs take seriously Audre Lorde's warning that the master's tools will never dismantle the master's house. Rather than aiming to remake our house according to others' tools, we can reimagine the underground as a space of intellectual—even writing-centric—resistance. We can develop writing programs in ways that overthrow traditional models of academia, creating ones that better suit our goals and that prioritize responsible design instead of traditional status markers. For our task is not to replicate the old tower but build our own sustainable place.

Consider how the final report of a grant-sponsored Queens City College Freshman Year Initiative (FYI) linked success to both space and community, which both developed within a lovely basement space: "The best evidence for the success of the Freshman Year Initiative is that—to borrow E. M. Forster's title for his 1910 novel—we have a room with a view. . . . It is a large spacious room, 30 × 60, in the basement of a recently renovated building. There are three windows fitted at the top of the ten foot high ceiling, so that while we can't quite look out at the campus, the room benefits from natural light" (Summerfield 1996, 14). While praising her program's new subterranean space, Summerfield (1996) also identifies its cause, pushing against the idea that by succeeding in the university, the program must have replicated the preexisting structure: "(FYI) has been 'institutionalized.' . . . But the word, institutionalized, denies the character of FYI. The program seeks to humanize the system, change the ways in which we bring students into the university" (1). And she describes the program's work to change the system, how it links the power of dedicated collaboration with a place to engage in it: "The program gains its strength from its grassrootedness—faculty working together in teaching freshmen, observing, experimenting, talking to each other, comparing notes, making changes, and including the administration in their conversations. The administration, in turn, has created a crucial protected space in which faculty can do their work" (6). Internal papers have a different audience than scholarly publications, of course, and Summerfield's report may be read as a savvy WPA managing stakeholders and funding agencies rather than as a generalizable description of program success. As WPAs constantly negotiate campus and field arguments, however, I see this report as providing a model for how to recognize the importance of our working space while also reminding us that the quality of space comes from design, not location, and that good design supports the central goals of a program—here, collaborative work among students, faculty, and upper administration. I compare this basement-based program to Enos's (1999) marble halls of individually owned offices and classrooms. Aesthetically pleasing as they sound, it is in Summerfield's space that I see vital work happening, work which aims to change the entire university.

Summerfield's depiction of a spacious, well-lit basement room aligns with engineering discussions of what makes subterranean space work: natural light from cleverly placed windows, for example. Here is a real example of basement space shrugging off its reputation and writing program faculty intending to change the entire institution—a grand rather than sad role. It speaks to the metaphorical opportunities possible in embracing our place as in the basement, within the institution's foundation. Doing so does mean jettisoning cultural (and, at least in my case, personal) experience with terrible basements, replacing them with ideas of subterranean space from other peoples and from engineering possibilities. The larger metaphor is perhaps simpler—WPAs should accept that, since we dwell in a symbolic basement, we will need different design principles and program stories to make our space habitable, let alone hospitable.

Material inequalities will not be solved with new metaphors alone, but new metaphorical understanding can help us imagine different ways of solving old problems. Rebuilding our understanding of space and place might open up new ways of supporting writing faculty and students. It might help shift discourse away from the legacy of subordinate identity metaphors, with "literature in the penthouse" and "sad women in the basement." Representing our place as something like a snug hobbit hole can help us imagine writing programs as something less hierarchical, less adversarial, a program like Summerfield describes. After all,

WPAs who pull their programs into an upper-level room inevitably cast someone else down into a basement spot and perpetuate the issues of the original house.

Writing programs deserve a special set of design principles. Our task is not to replicate the old tower but build our own responsible, sustainable place. Let us represent the basement, while working to make sure our space measures down to what it can be—a place of community, welcome, and even adventure, a design foregrounding sustainability, resilience, and local harmony. In this way, working from the basement can counter some of the worst issues of the Ivory Tower while also building the foundations of a more just and more responsible university.

REFERENCES

Brantlinger, Patrick. 1997. "Forum." *PMLA* 112, no. 2 (March): 265–66.
Brereton, John. 1995. "Preface." In *The Origins of Composition Studies in the American College, 1875–1925: A Documentary History*. Pittsburgh, PA: University of Pittsburgh Press. xi–xvii.
Brewer, Meaghan, and Kristin di Gennaro. 2018. "Naming What We Feel: Hierarchical Microaggressions and the Relationship between Composition and English Studies." *Composition Studies* 46 (2): 15–34.
Calhoon-Dillahunt, Carolyn. 2018. "2018 CCCC Chair's Address." *College Composition and Communication* 70 (2): 273–93. https://library.ncte.org/journals/ccc/issues/v70-2/29927.
Carroll, Lewis, and Martin Gardner. 1999. *The Annotated Alice: The Definitive Edition*. New York: W. W. Norton & Company.
Dance, Frank E. X. 2008. "*Oscillatio.*" *The Review of Communication* 8 (2): 110–14.
Davies, Laura. 2013. "Taking the Long View: Investigating the History of a Writing Program's Teacher Evaluation System." *WPA: Writing Program Administration* 37 (1): 81–111. wpacouncil.org/archives/37n1/37n1davies.pdf.
Dean, Terry. 1989. "Multicultural Classrooms, Monocultural Teachers." *College Composition and Communication* 40 (1): 23–37.
Ede, Lisa. 1989. "Writing as a Social Process: A Theoretical Foundation for Writing Centers?" *The Writing Center Journal* 9 (2): 3–13.
Enos, Theresa. 1999. "Road Rhetoric—Recollecting, Recomposing, Remaneuvering." In *Living Rhetoric and Composition: Stories of the Discipline*, edited by Duane H. Roen, Stuart C. Brown, Theresa Enos, 70–86. Mahwah, NJ: Lawrence Erlbaum.
Fuhlrott, Rolf. 1986. "Underground Libraries." *College & Research Libraries* 47 (3): 238–62.
Hall, Loretta. 2004. *Underground Buildings: More than Meets the Eye*. Sanger, CA: Quill Driver Books.
Haswell, Janis, Richard Haswell, and Glenn Blalock. 2004. "Hospitality in College Composition Courses." *College Composition and Communication* 60 (4): 707–27.
Homeyer, Henry. 2018. "Gardening: You Can Eat from the Garden Every Day of the Year." *The Providence Journal*, November 23, 2018. https://www.providencejournal.com/entertainmentlife/20181123/gardening-you-can-eat-from-garden-every-day-of-year.
Horner, Winifred Bryan. 2010. "Kneupper Memorial Address: An Allegory." In *Making and Unmaking the Prospects for Rhetoric: Selected Papers From the 1996 Rhetoric Society of America Conference*, edited by Theresa Enos, 197–200. New York: Routledge.
Hunt, D. V. L., L. O. Makana, I. Jefferson, and C. D. F. Rogers. 2016. "Liveable Cities And Urban Underground Space." *Tunnelling and Underground Space Technology* 55: 8–20. doi .org/10.1016/j.tust.2015.11.015.

Isaacs, Emily, and Melinda Knight. 2014. "A Bird's Eye View of Writing Centers: Institutional Infrastructure, Scope and Programmatic Issues, Reported Practices." *WPA: Writing Program Administration* 37 (2): 36–67. wpacouncil.org/archives/37n2/37n2isaacs-knight.pdf.

Johnson, Fred. 2008. "Weak Ties and Academic Community." *Forum: Newsletter for Issues about Part-Time and Adjunct Faculty* 12 (1): A9–A11. ncte.org/library/NCTEFiles/Groups/CCCC/Forum/Fall2008FORUM.pdf.

Johnstone, Barbara. 2008. "Discourse and World." In *Discourse Analysis*, 2nd ed., 32–75. Hoboken, NJ: Wiley-Blackwell.

Lakoff, George, and Mark Johnson. 1980. *Metaphors We Live By*. Chicago, IL: University of Chicago Press.

Malenczyk, Rita. 2007. Review of *Discourse and Direction: The Postmodern Writing Program Administrator*, by Sharon James McGee and Carolyn Handa. *WPA: Writing Program Administration* 30 (3): 149–53.

Martin, Wanda. 1988. "Dancing on the Interface: Leadership and Politics of Collaboration." *WPA: Writing Program Administration* 11 (3): 29–40.

Micciche, Laura. 2007. *Doing Emotion: Rhetoric, Writing, Teaching*. Portsmouth, NH: Boynton/Cook Publishers.

Miller, Susan. 1993. *Textual Carnivals: The Politics of Composition*. Carbondale: Southern Illinois University Press.

North, Stephen M. 1984. "The Idea of a Writing Center." *College English* 46 (5): 433–46.

Porter, James. 2002. "Why Technology Matters to Writing: A Cyber-writer's Tale." *Computers and Composition* 20:375–94.

Pratchett, Terry. 2005. *Thud!* New York: HarperTorch.

Professor X. 2008. "In the Basement of the Ivory Tower." *The Atlantic*. https://www.theatlantic.com/magazine/archive/2008/06/in-the-basement-of-the-ivory-tower/306810/.

Rider, Janine, and Ester Broughton. 1994. "Moving Out, Moving Up: Beyond the Basement and the Ivory Tower." *Journal of Advanced Composition* 14 (1): 239–55.

Ritchie, Joy, and Kathleen Boardman. 1999. "Feminism in Composition: Inclusion, Metonymy, and Disruption." *College Composition and Communication* 50 (4): 585–606.

Root, Robert L. 2004. "Variations on a Theme: Putting Nonfiction in Its Place." *Pedagogy* 4 (2): 289–95.

Schumacher, Julie. 2018. *The Shakespeare Requirement*. New York: Doubleday.

Scott, Tony. 2004. "Managing Labor and Literacy in the Future." In *Tenured Bosses and Disposable Teachers*, edited by Marc Bousquet, Tony Scott, and Leo Parascondola, 153–64. Carbondale: Southern Illinois University Press.

Stygall, Gail. 2003. "A Report from a Writing Program Director in the Trenches: TAs and Unionization." *Pedagogy* 3 (1): 7–19.

Summerfield, Judith. 1996. *The Freshman Year Initiative: Creating Academic Communities for Students and Faculty at a Commuter College*. Washington, DC: Fund for the Improvement of Postsecondary Education. eric.ed.gov/?id=ED416774.

Tolkien, J. R. R. (1937) 1982. *The Hobbit*. Revised edition. New York: Ballantine Books.

Tolkien, J. R. R. (1954) 1978. *The Fellowship of the Ring*. Reprint. New York: Ballantine Books.

9
INTERLOCKING CIRCLES

Cynthia D. Mwenja

At the small public liberal arts university where I currently serve as first-year composition program administrator and writing center director, the student population uses circle metaphors to govern their group relationships and dynamics. Each year, the entire school divides into two teams for intramural competitions. When one of the teams forms a circle—linking arms with each other around the performance hall—they leave a small break because "there is always room for one more!" By contrast, the other team forms an unbroken circle because "a united circle is a united side!" These ideas aren't just expressed at the annual campus-wide competition between the sides; I often hear members of each side draw on these ideas as foundational principles for viewing the yearly rivalry and the values each side holds.

In a completely different arena—the field of restorative practices—the circle metaphor provides both a physical form and a mental model. Drawing on the work of restorative activists and scholars such as Howard Zehr and Ted Wachtel, restorative practitioners seek to create inclusive, respectful, and egalitarian communities, to restore individuals and the community when needed, and to transform individuals and their communities when possible—and they often conduct their work with people sitting in circles. This physical arrangement reinforces a mental construct that everyone is working together in a nonhierarchical way to solve problems and improve situations. Wachtel (2019) identifies the foundations of restorative practices in this way: "The fundamental premise of restorative practices is that people are happier, more cooperative and productive, and more likely to make positive changes when those in authority do things *with* them, rather than *to* them or *for* them." Thus—though the word "restorative" implies the existence of harms done that need to be restored—much of the work of restorative practices lies in creating relationships to minimize both conflict and the ensuing need for restoration within a given community. The circle—as metaphor and form—can remind us to sustain those relationships using egalitarian and inclusive ideals.

Having grown out of the restorative justice movement—which is chiefly concerned with responding to criminal acts—the field of restorative practices focuses on creating strong communities to support their members. For those of us doing writing program administration work, these communities can be created in individual classrooms, in the groups of people overseeing the composition program, in our departments, and beyond. Once a community is established, *if and when* conflict occurs, a restorative group responds to those conflicts with dialogue and restorative action. Within the current dominant US culture, people most often respond to wrongdoing and even accidental harms with blame, usually desiring punishment and ostracism for wrongdoers. In a restorative *justice* model, wrongdoers are asked to take responsibility to "put [things] right," as Howard Zehr (2002, 20) states. Within restorative *practices*, the community as a whole—or any member of it—can take the responsibility of "putting right." In doing their community-building work, restorative practitioners highlight expectations of inclusiveness and egalitarianism, often using a circle model. Thus—though the intramural teams at our university do not use the same words as a restorative practitioner might—the side with a circle that leaves "room for one more" enacts the inclusive nature of restorative practices, and the side with the completed circle enacts their egalitarian ideals.

In addition to providing opportunities for participants to work together, restorative practices offer a set of proactive and responsive conflict-resolution tools that can be used as the need arises, as restorative scholars Bob Costello, Joshua Wachtel, and Ted Wachtel articulate in *Restorative Circles in Schools*. The *proactive* aspect consists of creating a community that welcomes and supports every individual as equally valuable and respect-worthy. Groups who have learned to work together in community are often able to avoid or at least minimize conflict, due to the strength of the relationships they have developed. Situating such work in the classroom, feminist scholar and activist bell hooks (1994, 8) puts it another way, saying, "Seeing the classroom as always a communal place enhances the likelihood of collective effort in creating and sustaining a learning community." The *responsive* aspect of restorative practices arises in addressing harms done or conflict within the community when they occur. Rather than focusing on blame or punishment, restorative practices ask people to engage in dialogue and take action to restore individuals and their communities. Dialogue is clearly also a feminist strategy. For one example, as Kathleen Ryan (2012, 82) states, "dialogic negotiation is feminist pragmatic rhetoric's primary discursive method." The circle provides an ideal construct for engaging in inclusive, community-building—or community-repairing—dialogue.

As part of departmental and university-wide communities, writing program administrators (WPAs) are well positioned to engage in dialogue to nurture ideals of inclusivity and egalitarianism within the interlocking circles of stakeholders. Restorative justice pioneer Howard Zehr (2002, 13) defines stakeholders as community members and entities "with a stake or standing in [an] event or [a] case." WPAs work with students, fellow faculty members within and outside of the department, administrators from chair to dean to provost, librarians, other campus groups, parents, and community members. Elsewhere in this volume, Babb calls our work "fundamentally relational." Similarly to Babb's "rhizomatic," "forest and trees" conceptions, I understand these groups as overlapping and interconnected circles, both metaphorically and literally. Though these communities—and the individuals within them—clearly can and do experience harms that restorative practices address, the potential for restorative work lies predominately within developing more inclusive and egalitarian interactions within these communities. Kathleen Ryan (2012, 91), in her articulation of a "rhetorical ecological feminist agency," says that such a focus on supporting multiple stakeholders can "guide program decision-making towards flourishing for all of those involved, including teachers, students, and colleagues." If, as restorative scholars Margaret Thorsborne and Peta Blood (2013, 43) state, restorative practices begin by creating community for all interested stakeholders, then WPAs can increase the support for our programs and the strength of our work by inviting all of these stakeholders into our circles of inclusive and egalitarian practice.

Because I have long implemented the ideas of restorative practices in my composition classrooms, I was eager in establishing the WPA position at my university to explore the potential of using restorative practices in working with other stakeholders at the university. This project details how the composition committee—drawing on English faculty input and with the support of our chair, dean, and provost—has used the ideas of restorative practices and the circle metaphor and model to develop a new standard first-year composition (FYC) curriculum for the English department. We have found that, while the circle metaphor helps to guide our thinking, it also gets expressed in actual, literal circles of people interacting within our department and across campus. This dual understanding of circles—as metaphor and literal enactment—resonates with Andrew Hollinger and Manny Piña's conceptions of WPA work as quantum physics (in this volume)—as "both/and." Just as light is both wave and particle, the circle is both metaphor and literal construct for my WPA work. In this article, I first discuss the ideals underpinning what I term "restorative composition pedagogy," then I detail our composition curriculum committee's experiences in using the metaphor and model of interlocking circles of stakeholders to sustain us in our work. In this essay, I argue that writing program administrators (WPAs) can use restorative practices to draw on these interlocking circles of support—both metaphorical and literal—within our institutions, even when these circles fluctuate and evolve.

THE CIRCLE OF THE CLASSROOM: RESTORATIVE COMPOSITION PEDAGOGY

Our work as WPAs allows us to see the many approaches to writing instruction represented in our departments. Many FYC instructors do support their students in a variety of ways, but blame and punishment are still present in many FYC classrooms, despite Mina Shaughnessy's (1976) work exhorting FYC instructors to more deeply understand where students are coming from and the challenges students face. Some FYC instructors still blame students for a lack of knowledge; I often hear FYC instructors saying some variation of "the students should know this already." Additionally, when students make mistakes or cause trouble in some way for the instructor, the first response for many instructors is to penalize the student with a poor grade or punitive consequence. A restorative classroom moves away from blame and punishment to help students learn what they need to know to succeed in the writing classroom and to address writing tasks generally. A restorative writing program supports its instructors in similar ways, helping them to succeed and thrive through a circle of care.

Our WPA work, along with our work within individual composition classrooms, also lets us see how many students have been harmed by previous experiences with English and composition. Many of our students have stories of being shamed or denigrated for their weaknesses in expressing themselves in writing. When they have not performed up to a certain standard, our students have often been blamed for their failures rather than having more effective writing strategies modeled and explained. Many instructors are steeped in this model, as well, and we WPAs, in drawing on the circle paradigm, can guide instructors toward learning new attitudes, welcoming students of all experience levels to our writing programs. A restorative composition pedagogy can help students revise their opinions of their shortcomings by reframing the conceptions from a model of "right" and "wrong" to a model of "more effective" and "less effective." In thinking in terms of inclusive circles, instructors can learn to help students see themselves as competent rhetors who can make effective choices in specific rhetorical situations.

Restorative practices can provide specific strategies for WPAs and composition instructors to use in addressing the harms that students have perceived that have been done to them and in creating more inclusive and equitable composition classrooms. Many composition scholars already work in ways that fit within a restorative construct. I term the melding of current best practices in composition pedagogy with restorative theory "restorative composition pedagogy," or RCP. The hallmarks of RCP are to create inclusive and egalitarian composition classrooms designed, as far as possible, to meet the needs of all stakeholders—students, instructors, WPAs, departments, universities, and communities. Restorative composition pedagogy isn't just for the classroom, however; its values can and do drive practice and decision-making throughout the writing program at our institution.

RCP posits that, in order to meet the goals of the writing program, instructors must develop classroom settings in which as many students as possible can meet the program's standards. In providing a space in which all students are able to learn and thrive in a cooperative setting, this pedagogy imagines that teachers can better help a wider variety of students to meet the outcomes standards for the writing program, thereby addressing the expectations of all stakeholders. An inclusive class aims to include all sorts of people by providing assignments and activities to appeal to and welcome people from as many backgrounds as possible, and a restorative pedagogy seeks to include and engage the full spectrum of students in the classroom community. A restorative WPA can use these same strategies to create an inclusive setting for instructors in the writing program, too.

RCP clearly aligns with feminist pedagogies. As Laura Micciche (2014, 128) highlights, feminist pedagogies have, among other hallmarks, "distributed agency through collaborative practices and alternative classroom arrangements." RCP embodies these principles with continual collaboration between students and instructor and by employing a variety of classroom strategies, from individual to pair to small-group and whole-class work. Additionally, Carolyn Shrewsbury (1987) says that a feminist pedagogy addresses "empowerment," "community," and "leadership." RCP empowers students by giving them agency within the classroom to participate in examining how specific writings are effective and ineffective. Each student has the opportunity to participate in the classroom community, and students are mentored in learning how to help each other develop stronger compositions. Similarly, WPAs can create departmental circles of practice in which instructors feel empowered, included, and mentored in their work.

Likewise, many composition pedagogy scholars focus on the ideas of inclusiveness and egalitarianism in the writing classroom. For example, in "Composition Studies Saves the World!," Patricia Bizzell (2009, 178) says that, in reimagining composition studies as student demographics changed, "[i]nstructor and students alike found that what was needed was not a one-way acculturation process, but a two-way, indeed a multidirectional process of collaboration and change." In Bizzell's description, everyone in the class, including the instructor, works together and learns from one another to create something better; these ideas absolutely match a restorative approach, both at the classroom level and in the writing program as a whole. In showing their willingness to learn from students—as well as facilitating discussions where students learn from each other—instructors disrupt the hierarchical classroom models that imply instructors are the only source of knowledge in the classroom. The circle metaphor can guide instructors as they shift the classroom model from hierarchical to egalitarian practices, and it can guide WPAs to make similar changes at the program level.

A restorative composition framework helps faculty and students to interrogate an idea that many still hold, the misconception that some people are naturally good writers and that such people write strong drafts by themselves on the first try. Collin Brooke and Allison Carr (2015, 63) frame this idea by saying that in instilling the norm of poor first drafts, we improve their understanding of the writing process, "treating failure as something all writers work through, rather than as a symptom of inadequacy or stupidity." Within the RCP practice at our institution, our instructors go a step further, reframing a bad first draft as a success, not a failure. Because we require three drafts total—a first draft to focus on revision, a second to focus on editing and proofreading, and the final draft to polish and pull all feedback together—each draft submitted is successful when it meets the goals for the specific draft. As I explore below, our writing program has also embraced the idea that drafts are successes on which we can build; this is another way in which our writing program reflects the restorative model.

Another major idea of restorative composition pedagogy is the idea of "preventing issues from occurring [by] building healthy relationships" described by Thorsborne and Blood (2013, 43). By concentrating on building relationships in the classroom, they say, restorative teachers will decrease the amount of time needed to address classroom challenges. One of these strategies is in explicitly setting the ground rules for respectful interactions. As Costello, Wachtel, and Wachtel (2010, 26) point out, instructors must "present clear guidelines and goals for discussions," so that students understand they "are expected to participate" and be respectful and that everyone "need[s] to feel safe to share their ideas." By addressing these ideas "proactively," these authors say, instructors can "dispel many potential problems" (43). The circle—literal or metaphorical—provides a safe space for these relationships to be built and flourish.

One more crucial restorative strategy beneficial for composition classes is the use of the circle as a site for discussion and reflection. In restorative circles, everyone in the group sits in a circle and has equal opportunity to participate in the discussion (Costello, Wachtel, and Wachtel 2010, 22). The ideas driving restorative circles—everyone has the opportunity to participate in the discussion as equally as possible—permeate a restorative composition pedagogy. Whether the students write individually or discuss a given subject in a small group or with the whole class, every student can, if they choose, voice an opinion and be heard. As the class continues, students who may have been more reticent to speak up in the beginning often become more confident in exchanging ideas with their peers, whether in pairs, small groups, or with the class as a whole. As WPAs, we can use the same strategies to include all of our composition instructors in the creation and unfolding of the writing programs on our campuses.

While much of the focus in restorative settings is on proactive work that creates community—thereby sidestepping some conflicts—the restorative approach also provides a model for response to challenges; this model can be used within any of the stakeholder communities interacting with our work. Rather than focusing on blame or punishment for wrongdoers, a restorative approach focuses on using dialogue and repair of harms to restore the community—and individuals to their places within it. As Zehr (2002, 20) states, a restorative "view of wrongdoing emphasizes the importance of making amends or 'putting [things] right'" in responding to "harms done." Continuing, Zehr (2002, 36) says, "one basic value is supremely important: respect." In restorative spaces, instructors show respect for students even when working through challenges—and the instructors ask for respect in return. Common "harms" that can be addressed in such restorative ways are "errors" in student work, plagiarism, and classroom rudeness. When we approach students respectfully to discuss issues as they arise, we open a space for them to respond rather than react. I envision "repairing harms done" as both responding to interpersonal difficulties and as helping students improve their writing and their ideas about themselves as writers. RCP focuses on improvement rather than faultfinding, both interpersonally and in composition assignments. Likewise, restorative WPAs can focus on mentoring instructors for continual improvement of instruction.

While most theories of composition pedagogy focus solely on the teaching of composition, RCP also covers the everyday interactions professors have with their students, both online and in person. This tactic aligns with Nancy Sommers's (2012) observation that we are teaching students, not writing. She says, "Everything shifts when we transfer the focus of our comments from the writing to the writer, from monologue to dialogue, and from instructor-centered commands to instructor-student partnerships" (xiv). Such a shift in attitude can help to improve the relationships between instructors and their students, and these improved relationships can provide an atmosphere in which students feel more supported. Thorsborne and Blood (2013, 57) frame this approach as "seeing others as people," and they say that the teacher's "way of being" will contribute to the success of the students. In her discussion of *ahimsa* in this collection, Christy I. Wenger calls such an approach "mindful consideration for oneself and for others" that results in "cultivating well-being." We WPAs can draw on such mindful consideration for all of our stakeholders, from classroom, to campus, to community at large.

Restorative composition pedagogy can be differentiated from other pedagogical approaches in that every aspect of the class, from content to the style of social interactions, is chosen to communicate inclusiveness, egalitarianism, and respect for every member of the group. This approach builds on Mina Shaughnessy's (1976) ideas that composition teachers must embrace a new way of teaching writing in order to understand, include, and reach students from a variety of backgrounds. Additionally, by contrast with "student-centered" pedagogical models, RCP explicitly includes other stakeholders, particularly the instructor, within the circle of respect and restoration. Currently in the US, college composition instructors are often overwhelmed with grading demands from overly large class sizes and best practices that seem to mandate individualized substantive feedback on every draft. Many of these instructors are adjuncts or other non-tenure-track employees, so they have little job security and are also often poorly compensated. Restorative WPAs include instructors in the circle of care in as many ways as possible, including providing support and advice for streamlining grading and advocating for better and more secure working conditions for these classroom stakeholders.

Some readers may fear that restorative composition pedagogy may be too soft on students in some way; however, a restorative approach asks instructors to be both supportive and demanding. As Thorsborne and Blood (2013, 34) state, "if we are working successfully with young people . . . three things need to be present: support (teaching explicitly what is needed), high expectations (pressure that comes from a relationship of mutual respect) and insistence (the motivation and persistence that comes from a relationship of mutual respect)." The mutual respect engendered in restorative spaces allows instructors to demand—and receive—quality work from their students.

My classroom case study of RCP at another institution indicates that RCP is an effective strategy for teaching composition and rhetorical analysis; students also appreciated the restorative aspects of the class. The FYC program at my current institution will begin ongoing assessment of our RCP course design beginning soon, so further results will be available in the future.

THE CIRCLE OF FACULTY

With this background in collaborative relationship-building and problem-solving, I consider myself lucky to have joined a faculty that has agency to make institutional decisions, both at the departmental and university-wide levels. When I joined the English faculty, there were thirteen faculty members who were tenured or tenure-track and three adjuncts. Two of the tenure-track folks focused on creative writing, two of us were composition and rhetoric specialists, and the rest were literature professors spanning time periods and geographic ranges for a traditional coverage model. Of the adjuncts, one had earned his bachelor's and master's degrees from our English department, while the other two had worked with the department for several years.

When I joined the faculty, these faculty members were all free to develop their own FYC curricula. Faculty members had been asked to use the Council of Writing Program Administrators guidelines for course outcomes, but otherwise, all faculty—tenure-track and adjunct—could decide how to best meet those outcomes with their individual course designs. Although the majority of the tenured and tenure-track faculty had developed solid FYC syllabi, there were several problems with the situation. First, we as a department did not have a shared set of expectations for first-year composition, and we did not have shared language about writing as a discipline. As a result, students were often unable to see the continuity between FYC 101 and 102 if they took the courses from different professors. The biggest issue, however, was that the adjuncts did not have a standard course to follow, so each one had created syllabi from their own past experiences, and these syllabi often did not reflect current best practices in composition pedagogy. As a department, we needed to articulate a vision of composition pedagogy for ourselves, and we needed a standard curriculum in place to communicate our vision to our adjunct instructors. We needed to create a circle, a community to guide the creation of the needed standard curriculum.

Many of these issues related to the fact that the department did not have a writing program administrator (WPA) position. As one of two composition and rhetoric specialists (at the time) and a member of the composition committee, I resolved to act, as far as possible, as unofficial WPA, tracking my time and efforts, then to make the case to the administration that the position was needed. To act as unofficial WPA, I decided to do two major things. First, I interviewed everyone teaching FYC to determine the instructional commonalities already present in the department. In gathering this information, I acted as a "cartographer," in Katherine Daily O'Meara's conception of the WPA in this volume. Second, I set up monthly support meetings for interested FYC instructors, in which we discussed challenges and shared solutions for FYC instruction. These monthly meetings established a community that supported both individual members and the continuing refinement of the standard curriculum to better meet student and instructor needs.

Previously, in acting as research assistant for the WPA during my master's program, I had seen how that WPA had created consensus for a revised FYC curriculum by talking with all FYC instructors: graduate students, adjuncts, and teaching-track as well as tenure-track professors. This approach matched my vision of creating a revised curriculum at my current institution by working collaboratively and inclusively with interested stakeholders. While I did not explicitly invoke the circle metaphor in my conversations with FYC instructors of all stripes, I did let each person know that I was talking to everyone who taught FYC, so they knew I was gathering information from each member of that "circle." In "Grounding WPA Work" (elsewhere in this collection), Ryan Dippre discusses a similar process in which programs are driven by principles grounded in the concerns of their specific campuses. In interviews with all FYC instructors, both tenure-track faculty members and adjuncts, I asked three open-ended questions: "For you, what is the goal of First-Year Composition?" "What do you think should be included in First-Year Composition?" and "What do you want students to know when they come to your sophomore literature and upper-division English classes?"

In coding the information, the composition committee quickly realized that our faculty had collectively recreated the standards from the WPA Outcomes Statement (Council of Writing Program Administrators 2014). Our first reaction was one of wry amusement—I had conducted multiple hours of interviews and we had spent several hours together coding the data, only to realize that we had recreated our existing guidelines. After our amusement died down, we became heartened because the department, as a group, was aligned with current best composition pedagogy practices. The faculty had answered questions extemporaneously; most folks generally did not refer to their syllabi or course outcomes in our conversations. The biggest result of this spontaneous regeneration of the WPA Outcomes was that we could tell the faculty that the guidelines were not imposed by some outside authority but that they had emerged from our own departmental circle of practice. We had created the sort of "artisanal production," molded to our institution's and department's needs, that Robyn Tasaka discusses in this collection.

The members of the composition committee (all junior, untenured professors) did, however, have to continually reassure the other tenured and tenure-track (TT) professors that they would be completely free to use the curricula each had already developed for themselves. Professors teaching FYC would need to meet the WPA outcomes as was already required by the department, but professors would be free to use none, part, or all of the new standard as they saw fit for their individual classes. The composition committee does not and will not have the authority to impose the standard curriculum on TT professors. Since we have put the standard into place, about half of the TT FYC professors have chosen to adopt it, and several others have taken advantage of the standard handbook and various instructor resources—ranging from peer-review strategies to model student texts—we have made available in a password-protected space online. It is interesting to note anecdotally that one professor learned just before the semester started that she would need to teach an FYC class. At the end of the semester, this professor stated in a faculty meeting that, while she had experienced doubts before beginning the semester, the course was far better than any other FYC course she had ever taught, and the curriculum committee provided ongoing, helpful support when challenges arose. This professor continues to use our new standard curriculum to teach both semesters of first-year composition.

Within the Faculty Circle: Composition Committee

The composition committee wholeheartedly supported a push to develop a standard curriculum. This group formed the first and most important circle supporting a better articulation of first-year composition at our university. Once we gained the blessing of the departmental faculty and department chair, we established a three-member subcommittee with the task of creating a standard FYC curriculum. As this committee began discussing various theories to drive the FYC practice on our campus, I asked if we might consider using restorative practices to do our own work—to work collaboratively and as equals in creating the curriculum. When the other two members agreed, I asked if we might also use restorative practices as a guiding idea for the curriculum itself—in other words, to write a curriculum that, at every turn, asks students to work collaboratively and inclusively, then to meet challenges with dialogue and restorative action. In agreeing to move forward by using restorative principles as a guideline, we created the first of the interlocking circles that supported the process.

ADMINISTRATIVE CIRCLES: CHAIR, DEAN, PROVOST—AND GRADUATE STUDIES COORDINATOR

While restorative practices can facilitate dynamic learning communities within individual classrooms and FYC programs, they can be much more effective if their entire departments and institutions support their work. As the FYC curriculum committee continued our discussions, we realized we needed support outside of our circle; while we had approval to move forward from the department and chair, we needed financial support beyond the department to complete the course design in time for implementation the following semester. We first applied for monies from a specific grant pool related to teaching initiatives. When our application was rejected, we were not sure how to move forward. The department desperately needed a standard curriculum rooted in current best composition pedagogy practices, but the members of the committee were not able to invest the time needed if they were not going to be compensated for their work. The circle surrounding the FYC program could have easily fallen apart at this point, and I could have found myself reduced to a circle of one. One of the other FYC committee members, however, approached the dean of our college directly to ask for funding. This committee member had been part of the department longer than I had and, as director of the campus writing center, she had developed strong working relationships with our chair and dean. Because of her request, our department chair and the college dean quickly committed to contributing to our efforts, and the university provost followed suit. Because of this support, we were able pool resources from three campus entities to fund our grant application. Our circle, interlocked with several larger circles of support, was able to move forward with our work.

As we developed the curriculum, the members of the FYC curriculum committee worked as equals—each of us offered our tried and true assignments and classroom activities, and we included those from other folks in the department as well. We used the RCP guidelines articulated above to drive decisions about what to include in the course design, and we used restorative strategies to address disagreements during the process: we listened to each other, and we strove to find solutions that honored everyone's points of view. One example of this happened in setting up our standard online course. Two committee members disagreed about how to best display daily class activities—by having every detail constantly visible, or by organizing the information under links that could appear in several places in the course shell. At first, it seemed as if the choice was to go with one format or the other. After a great deal of discussion, however, we realized that we could actually arrange the standard format so that both people could have the design they preferred. Our commitment to finding such solutions came from having established restorative practices as the foundation of our work.

Another member of the faculty circle emerged as a supporter of our efforts. Once I voiced my desire to take on WPA responsibilities, the graduate student program coordinator saw an opportunity to shuffle responsibilities. If a WPA position could be officially established, the person in that position could take some of the graduate student coordinator's responsibilities; he could then expand his activities in program and student development. Because we were able to discuss our situation, he had the information he needed to propose a new structure within the department: an expanded set of responsibilities for him, and a new position for a WPA. The chair and dean agreed with his proposal and established the WPA position, slated to begin the following academic year. The circle of the composition committee was supported by the interlocking circles of the graduate committee and the administration.

While the members of the composition committee were compensated in part for the work of creating a new standard FYC course, the individuals involved definitely supported each other and our work beyond a level that might normally be expected. We definitely felt the "abiding sense of mutual responsibility" that Lydia Wilkes addresses in this volume. On one hand, I do think that I was incredibly lucky to have such hardworking, dedicated compatriots join me in doing this work. On the other, I also think that we all took joy in being part of an egalitarian, respectful, and collaborative group that was filling a real need in the department. As we did our work together, we continually created and strengthened this foundational circle for our work.

THE CIRCLES IN ACTION: WORKING TOGETHER DURING THE FIRST ACADEMIC YEAR

Once the FYC curriculum committee developed the standard curriculum, the two other committee members committed to using it, as did our department chair. The adjuncts—a different group of folks by this time—were required to follow the new course design. While this requirement may seem to contradict restorative practices by hierarchically imposing constraints on the adjuncts, we knew we also needed to consider our responsibilities to the other stakeholders—students, the department, the university, our accrediting body, and the governing bodies in our state. To meet the expectations of the multiple stakeholders, we must provide a reliable course design that enacts current best practices in the field and meets the requirements of the various entities overseeing FYC instruction at our institution. We balanced this hierarchical requirement of adjuncts with an inclusive, egalitarian, and collaborative working style for our composition instructor community throughout the semester. The members of the curriculum committee continually solicited feedback and implemented changes to the curriculum based on input from everyone who participated in our monthly meetings. We made no hierarchical distinctions between adjuncts and TT folks; we accepted suggestions for revision, refinement, and improvement from everyone. In the pre-semester training for the new curriculum, we highlighted the idea that our course design was not just a series of assignments; it was also a plan to support students by scaffolding strong writing practices and to include students by making expectations transparent. We also continually reminded the participating FYC instructors that the course design was not perfect; we made a commitment to improving the course based on everyone's experiences and feedback. Both in training and throughout the semesters that followed, the adjuncts particularly have said how much they appreciate this opportunity to share ideas and participate in improving the courses we are all teaching.

Restorative scholarship offers a road map for individual and group restorative conversations. The first and most simple way of initiating a restorative conversation, according to Costello, Wachtel, and Wachtel

(2010, 12), is by making an "affective statement," which is "an expression of personal feelings." The authors continue, saying that such statements "help clarify boundaries, provide feedback, and build empathy." These affective statements lie at one end of a spectrum of restorative responses, with formal circle conferences with all stakeholders on the other end of the spectrum. I have not yet needed to draw on the most formal, prescribed circle conference structure as a WPA, but several of us teaching FYC have used private conferencing to address serious classroom behaviors ranging from plagiarism to habitual disruptions.

While restorative practices do provide more formal options for very serious behavior, the other more casual strategy is the use of "small impromptu conferences" in which "a few people meet briefly to address and resolve a problem" (Costello, Wachtel, and Wachtel 2010, 13). Within these meetings, people talk about what happened, consider who may have been affected by the event, and offer solutions for making things right (Costello, Wachtel, and Wachtel 2010, 10). These sorts of conversations can help stakeholders change problematic behaviors and restore the community. In our monthly FYC meetings, we engaged in just these sorts of conversations. Everyone present asked for and offered advice, both for their own approaches to teaching—correcting their own behavior—and for addressing classroom challenges—improving student participation in class. We discussed subjects such as whether and how much to limit student use of electronic devices in class, how to help students overcome their internalized ideas of themselves as poor writers, and how to better teach specific genres and concepts. The group consists and consisted of adjuncts, nontenured instructors, and tenure-track folks, and while we may not have reached the level of "radical collectivity" that Belk explores in "The WPA as Labor Activist" in this collection, we have definitely expanded the "scope of labor . . . beyond disciplinary boundaries and tenure status," as Belk outlines. These monthly meetings worked as restorative circles to address all of the things that concerned us throughout the semester, and we all learned from each other in a nonhierarchical way.

One sign of the strength of the relationships in our circle of practice is that the people who teach the standard FYC curriculum engage in "small, impromptu conferences" on a near-daily basis. While our work isn't relegated to Alexis Teagarden's "basement," as discussed in this collection, we have definitely developed a less hierarchical relationship that provides "places of community," as Teagarden describes. Our instinct is to turn to each other to collaborate on solutions to pedagogical and classroom issues as they arise, and we respect the viewpoints of the other instructors, whether tenure-track or adjunct. I was not sure, however, if the other FYC instructors were tying our work to restorative practices or if they simply enjoyed collaboration. Within just a few weeks, the answer became clear. Multiple instructors began conversations by asking, "What is the restorative response to this situation?" We have created a circle of restorative practice to support our FYC program, and that circle interweaves with other circles of support on our campus.

These circles of support also interlock with related campus entities. Our campus librarians worked with us to establish standard content for FYC library visits in FYC 101 and 102; they also helped us to identify an open educational resource for the course handbook. The director of the writing center at the time—then a member of the composition committee—made sure to use the same language to discuss the writing process in the writing center as we use in the standard curriculum so that we could begin to develop a shared language about writing in the department. Our campus academic success center is available to help students better plan their time, so we can send our students there to consult when we see them getting off-track in time management. We have also established a page in our online learning system for all faculty members to post helpful assignments, classroom activities, and model texts. Even faculty members who are not using the standard curriculum are using these resources. The various circles interpenetrate and support each other in multiple ways.

To be clear, we have faced challenges along the way. As Thorsborne and Blood (2013, 45) point out, people who begin to use restorative practices in their classrooms need a restorative place to discuss their own challenges in using the new paradigm. We used our monthly meetings as that place to talk about restorative strategies. Many of us struggled with balancing punitive measures and more restorative ones. For example, I had a policy of "absolutely no late papers for any reason" prior to developing this curriculum, and other instructors pointed out that this policy did not seem to fit the restorative paradigm. They shared a variety of strategies that allowed students to recover from the mistake of submitting a paper late. One instructor allows students to turn in one paper late during the semester, with no questions asked; students can invoke the "one late paper rule" when they need to. If more than one student submits a paper late, several FYC instructors extend the deadline for all students by a few days, provided that the course calendar allows for such an adjustment. Because I offer an optional revision opportunity for each paper, I now allow students who miss a paper deadline to submit the final draft during the revision period; they waive the opportunity for revision when doing so. All of these strategies allow students to "put things right" and continue to be part of the classroom community.

We also want to continue to develop our reach to people within our classrooms and our department. As a group, the committee recognizes the value of embedding and continuing to expand Universal Design for Learning so that we include all students to the greatest extent possible. Within the department, we would like to expand the instructor circle to include all TT people teaching FYC. One faculty member has chosen to use the handbook we chose, and another has joined us in implementing the standard curriculum in her FYC 101 class, but most tenure-track FYC professors beyond the curriculum committee have not yet used the standard curriculum. Many professors, however, have come to RCP workshops I have offered covering subjects such as how to grade more equitably with a rubric and how to better meet the needs of students whose first language is not English.

Our circles have definitely changed over the course of the last year and a half. The provost who took part in funding our work has stepped down, and the supportive dean is now provost. The writing center director who formed an integral part of the Curriculum Committee and secured our original funding has left the department, so I am now directing the writing center as well as the composition program. Both tenure-track and adjunct personnel have shifted, and we've been lucky to add a full-time instructor to our department. These changes certainly resonate with the ideas Rona Kaufman and Scott Rogers cover in "Building the Plane as We Fly It" in the present volume.

Despite these challenges, limitations, and changing circumstances, we have made strides. We have collected feedback throughout the semester from those who have taught each course, and we made major revisions to both courses after every semester. These improvements demonstrate our commitment to collaboratively creating a strong FYC curriculum, and they embody Kim Gunter's understanding of WPA work as improv (elsewhere in this volume), where our work is "context-dependent, dialogic, and collaborative." Individual instructors have created valuable handouts, and we plan to revise the course handbook to include this material during upcoming semesters.

CONCLUSION

The inclusive and egalitarian circle metaphor and model has encouraged those of us creating the new curriculum to value each other's points of view and to solve problems collaboratively. Inspired by the metaphor and actuality of interlocking, supportive circles, we continually engage in the same process we ask of our students: in dialogue with peers, we are creating, revising, and editing our FYC courses. These ideas spill over to our course design and to our interactions with all instructors, including adjuncts. Whether in the composition classroom, FYC monthly meetings, or committee work sessions, the idea of an inclusive circle continually reminds us to value all voices in each community and include their perspectives as we revise our course design. This way of thinking disrupts hierarchies within the classroom and the FYC program. In creating this work together and communicating the vision that everyone who instructs FYC at our university is part of a circle of practice, we have found that we can help each other address classroom challenges in helpful, nonjudgmental, and supportive ways; we creatively problem-solve together. The metaphor and model of interlocking circles has allowed my job as WPA to be created and my work as WPA to be sustained within the communities of the composition committee, our department, and our university. Instead of feeling alone or embattled, I feel supported by layers of interwoven community. Our students—those with the open and with the closed circles—would be proud.

REFERENCES

Bizzell, Patricia. 2009. "Composition Studies Saves the World!" *College English* 72 (2): 174–88.

Brooke, Collin, and Allison Carr. 2015. "Failure Can Be an Important Part of Writing Development." In *Naming What We Know: Threshold Concepts of Writing Studies*, edited by Linda Adler-Kassner and Elizabeth Wardle, 62–64. Logan: Utah State University Press.

Costello, Bob, Joshua Wachtel, and Ted Wachtel. 2010. *Restorative Circles in Schools: Building Community and Enhancing Learning*. Bethlehem, PA: International Institute of Restorative Practices.

Council of Writing Program Administrators. 2014. "WPA Outcomes Statement for First-Year Composition (3.0)." WPA Council. Last modified July 17, 2014. wpacouncil.org/positions/outcomes.html.

hooks, bell. 1994. *Teaching to Transgress: Education as the Practice of Freedom*. New York: Routledge.

Micciche, Laura R. 2014. "Feminist Pedagogies." In *A Guide to Composition Pedagogies*, 2nd ed., edited by Gary Tate, Amy Rupiper Taggart, Kurt Schick, and H. Brooke Hessler, 128–45. Oxford: Oxford University Press.

Ryan, Kathleen. 2012. "Thinking Ecologically: Rhetorical Ecological Feminist Agency and Writing Program Administration." *WPA: Writing Program Administration* 36 (1): 74–92.

Shaughnessy, Mina P. 1976. "Diving In: An Introduction to Basic Writing." *College Composition and Communication* 27 (3): 234–39.

Shrewsbury, Carolyn M. 1987. "What Is Feminist Pedagogy?" *Women's Studies Quarterly* 15 (3/4): 6–14. http://www.jstor.org/stable/40003432.

Sommers, Nancy. 2012. *Responding to Student Writers*. New York: Bedford/St. Martin's.

Thorsborne, Margaret, and Peta Blood. 2013. *Implementing Restorative Practices in Schools: A Practical Guide to Transforming School Communities*. London: Jessica Kingsley.

Wachtel, Ted. 2019. "Defining Restorative." IIRP. https://www.iirp.edu/images/pdf/Defining-Restorative_Nov-2016.pdf.

Zehr, Howard. 2002. *The Little Book of Restorative Justice*. Intercourse, PA: Good Books.

SECTION III

Performance Crafts

10
THE AFFORDANCES AND RISKS OF ARTISANAL PRODUCTION AS A METAPHOR FOR WRITING PROGRAM ADMINISTRATION

Robyn Tasaka

In *The Omnivore's Dilemma*, Michael Pollan (2006) researches three meals: one factory-farmed, the second organic, and the third foraged. He examines the living conditions and slaughtering of the animals, management of costs, and challenges and benefits of each mode of food production. Pollan discusses artisanal products as the opposite of factory-farmed, mass-produced items, stating that the artisanal model "should not strive for uniformity in its products but rather make a virtue of variation and seasonality; it shouldn't invest capital to reach national markets, relying on reputation and word of mouth rather than on advertising" (249). Defining the work of writing programs and WPAs as artisanal offers several affordances to different stakeholders—to students, writing instructors and tutors, higher-level administrators, faculty in other departments, and ourselves as WPAs. In this chapter, I explore these affordances alongside the risks of embracing the metaphor of artisanal production.

AFFORDANCE: EACH PRODUCT IS UNIQUE

Framing WPA work as artisanal sends the message that each product is unique, whether the "product" is a tutoring session, a course section, a tutor, or an instructor. Defining these as artisanal conveys that variation is fine and even valuable, that every tutoring session or iteration of a course will be unique, that tutors do not need to provide the same type of feedback in the same way, and that instructors do not need to teach the same way.

I see a need for such messaging at the learning center where I work as tutor coordinator. At my current institution, a public four-year university where the most popular major is business (University of Hawai'i 2021), we often feel pressure from faculty and students to deliver a uniform product. Students and faculty may fault a tutor for providing incorrect information (for example about how to format a citation) or for not drawing the student's attention to a particular issue. Similarly, variation in first-year writing programs is often criticized. This desire for uniformity resonates with what Donna Strickland (2011) describes as "the normalizing quest" of "traditional systematic management" (106).

In contrast, the artisanal model frames variation as an asset. While consumers expect uniformity in mass-produced items, for example pre-sliced bread from the grocery store, we do not have the same expectation for bread from a farmer's market or specialty bakery. Both products are essentially the same, made of the same ingredients through similar processes and with similar nutritional value. Yet we have different perceptions and expectations of mass-produced versus artisanal products. When purchasing bread marketed as artisanal, we expect loaves to differ in shape or to be unevenly colored. We expect French bread to have smaller end slices, for example, as part of the character of the bread. We value these features highly enough to pay a premium, because artisanal products are perceived as the result of "exceptional skill" (Clegg 2007). The term "artisan" also captures the idea of "doing the best work for the community which also implies a pride in one's work" and "a sense of agency and conscientiousness in responding in ways that contribute to the good of the whole" (Brew et al. 2018, 119). Along these lines, presenting tutoring and teaching as artisanal can help us value both variations in "products" and the skill and conscientious effort behind the work.

Communicating the Value of Variation

Drawing on the artisanal metaphor in communications can encourage students and faculty to value variation in tutoring and writing instruction. Each tutoring session and class is different, and each tutor and instructor brings different strengths, such as patience, energy, empathy, or special skills. We shouldn't expect uniformity from tutors, teaching, or writing instruction; variation is an asset because it allows each person to draw on their unique strengths.

This metaphor can also be used to oppose the use of canned courses such as those produced by publishing companies and instead support the need for quality instructors. Increasingly, I have seen software that seems designed to function by itself, as if to eliminate the need for instructors. These programs incorporate instructional and assessment materials, and while they seem to be more common in subjects like math and business, similar software focuses on grammar, mechanics, and other writing skills. In my experience, software in no way replaces quality instruction, yet in some subject areas it is used in this way.

In one online class, virtually 100 percent of the course was delivered through a publisher-produced program, while the instructor only selected modules. Some courses rely heavily on this type of software; on one public campus I am familiar with, an instructor who "taught" one of these classes said he felt he was essentially a lab monitor. He was only paid for half the course's credits (presumably because the software performed the remainder of the labor). While I am not privy to how these staffing and wage decisions were made, I imagine administrators supporting publisher-produced programs as a cost-savings.[1]

From a big-picture administrative perspective, the appeal may extend beyond the financial. When instruction is mass-produced, courses can be taught uniformly and, presumably, all students in FYW sections will come out with the same skill set, which in theory could make it easier to design the courses students take after completing FYW. Experienced writing instructors, however, know that it's not this simple. Any uniform skill set that students would have upon completing a set of computer-delivered modules would be highly limited. I cannot imagine effective, mass-produced writing instruction.

My experience with publisher-developed online curricula has shown me that this form of mass production is ill-suited to education. The program's attempt to customize curriculum per student through a pretest is a meaningless gesture compared to the genuine customization a quality instructor can provide. Even if they are not able to customize a semester-long course to the needs of each individual student, strong teachers tailor each iteration of a course to that term's students as a group, moving through material more slowly or quickly as needed. In highlighting the value of individual variation, the artisanal metaphor opposes the use of canned curricula.

Drawing on the artisanal metaphor, I envision a public relations campaign—perhaps a writing center window display or flyers around campus—that advertises "Fresh Artisanal Tutoring" and features tutors and their unique approaches on loaves of bread. One might say, "Sabrina uses humor during her tutoring sessions to help you destress."[2] Another: "Nick shares his experiences as a student and what works for him." Yet another: "Jamie always brings a positive attitude to her tutoring sessions." A similar approach might work for instructional faculty assigned to different sections of writing, to highlight perhaps one instructor's background working with second-language learners, another's experience as a technical writer, a third's experience teaching in the Education department.

Writing programs do try to publicize information about variation among courses to students, for example, through department websites, but perhaps faculty in other disciplines, advisors, and upper administration are neglected (or more challenging) audiences for this information. Kimball (1998) describes the apparently timeless challenge of working with faculty in other disciplines on writing instruction, saying that her WAC committee faced "distrust and cynicism" from these faculty (65). She talks about the importance of "establish[ing] an atmosphere of trust and goodwill in our dealings with faculty" and how "[t]he writing center and Division have also worked hard to establish themselves as visible and respected entities on campus" (65).

How can we address the challenge of helping faculty in other disciplines understand and value variation in the ways writing courses are taught? Perhaps more importantly, how do we help upper-level administrators understand and value this variation? One start is to draw on the artisanal metaphor to help all stakeholders value the various strengths of faculty. The Council of Writing Program Administrators (1998) supports these types of efforts in its recommendation that evaluation of WPAs can include how we "communicate curricular goals, methodologies, and overall programmatic philosophy in such a way as to lead to positive and productive results for students, instructors, and school," for instance by visiting department or class meetings, presenting at semester convocation, creating and distributing flyers or brochures, sending mass emails, posting information on campus or online, hosting open houses or other events where visitors are welcomed, or through one-on-one conversations.

Besides helping outside audiences like faculty and administrators appreciate variation in tutoring and teaching, a campaign marketing the work of writing programs as artisanal also reminds tutors and instructors of the value of their unique approaches. This can happen through language we use on a daily basis and formal training. In trainings and meetings with tutors or instructors, we might encourage them to reflect on their individual strengths and differences in response to questions like:

- What do you do to help students feel welcome in the center or in your classroom?
- How do you help students feel connected to you?
- What do you do to encourage students to return to the center and make another appointment (or to ask questions in class or attend office hours)?

- How do you help students hear critical comments?
- How do you help students acclimate to college culture?
- What helpful information can you share with students from your experiences as a college student and/or employee?
- What do students gain from a session with you (or by enrolling in your section) versus with one of your colleagues?

As WPAs and WCDs, this artisanal product framing reminds us to value each of our tutors and instructors for the individual strengths they bring and to be gracious when offering corrections. It's a reminder to us to provide feedback using the compliment sandwich, which can be hard to remember in the daily (and semesterly) chaos.

AFFORDANCE: AVOIDING THE GLORIFICATION OF EFFICIENCY

While efficiency is prized in mass production in ways that are often unsustainable, the artisanal model supports sustainability by reminding us that efficiency is not the highest goal. This model can address Strickland's (2011) call that scholarship in writing program administration "go beyond the instrumental questions of how to 'get things done' to include questions of the ethical and political consequences of doing so" (121). The artisanal model, when contrasted with mass production, provides a frame for reflecting on the values that guide our work as WPAs. If we believe mass production is unsustainable, as Pollan and others have argued, and that artisanal production is more sustainable, we can ask ourselves, what does an artisanal model of WPA work look like?

One aspect of a sustainable, artisanal model of writing program administration is the valuing of quality over efficiency. This valuation works in slightly different ways for tutors paid hourly and instructors on salary or a contract.

Tutoring

Framing tutoring as artisanal communicates that efficiency is not as important as quality. Emailed feedback from tutors is a popular option for students (and some faculty) on my campus, where over 50 percent of courses are online. Because a few faculty require students to work with tutors, during some weeks our center has seventy drafts in the inbox and only a handful of writing tutors with varying availability. We limit tutors to one hour on each draft for pedagogical and practical reasons but we appreciate tutors who are able to work more efficiently, needing just thirty minutes to provide feedback. Knowing there are so many students waiting for feedback, it's hard not to feel pressure to be efficient, which can sometimes lead to lower-quality work, such as reusing previously drafted comments with less customization or skimming through a draft rather than reading closely. When this happens it is crucial for tutors and WPAs to remember the value of providing quality feedback even if it takes a little longer.

We can encourage ourselves and tutors to value quality over quantity by posting reminders to ourselves and passing those reminders on to our tutors. Tutors shouldn't feel pressured to limit themselves to thirty minutes per draft if spending more time would lead to higher-quality feedback. And as WPAs, we should be gracious with those tutors who take a little longer.

We must also consider the competing values of efficiency and quality in tutors' work experiences. To support the overall sustainability of the center as well as individual tutors, we may be tempted to prioritize efficiency and sacrifice quality not just of work but also of life in the short term. For example, I have had a tutor be extremely frustrated with a particular student but also the only tutor available at the time the student prefers to visit. While it is important for this tutor to face challenges and grow tutoring and interpersonal skills, I also must be aware that she may quit if pushed too far. We face similar challenges when balancing tutors' requests for time off. While we appreciate having all the help we can, we sometimes have to sacrifice in a particular week for the tutor to maintain their academic standing and mental health. The metaphor of artisanal production reminds us to prioritize quality rather than short-term efficiency, which contributes to long-term sustainability through caring not only for the efficient completion of work but peer tutors' quality of life.

Instructors

Though this approach works slightly differently with salaried or contracted instructors, the artisanal metaphor also encourages WPAs to be patient with instructors, and instructors to be patient with themselves and their students. If I imagine myself as an artisanal baker, I might manage my resources by focusing on perfecting one particular bread or pastry rather than trying to make twenty different products well. This focus of energy encourages sustainability by taking measures to avoid burnout, an issue that Babb and Wilkes also discuss in this volume. I hope this is something that WPAs consider when assigning sections. If it is impossible to minimize the new course preps an instructor has, then like the artisanal baker, WPAs and instructors can consider how instructors can focus their energy in other ways, perhaps by developing one skill per term rather than trying to excel in all areas at once. When I was a developing instructor, I focused on one thing at a time, like being more purposeful in using course readings in one term, on improving presentation slides I used in class in another, on improving one major assignment in yet another, and so on.

The artisanal metaphor can help instructors be patient with students as well. The artisanal metaphor reminds us that our goal is not to mass-produce writers. Individual variation is valuable in student writers, who bring varied strengths and pursue careers and lives that require different skill sets. Valuing variation comes into play especially when grading writing. Working against the common focus on deficits—missing thesis statements, weak support, lack of citations—the artisanal metaphor reminds us that we should shift our focus to what student writers are doing rather than what they are neglecting to do. As Asao Inoue (2014) says, "Teachers miss a lot when they only look for evidence of outcomes in drafts" (343).

The artisanal metaphor also reminds us that growing as a writer takes time. For students to do their best, we must allow them the time to write, whether this means setting aside class time or being realistic about what they are able to accomplish outside of class. We must remember that students will rarely make tremendous leaps in a single writing assignment or even a single semester. Instead, revisiting and reinforcing skills over multiple assignments, semesters, and years will best enable students to develop their craft. The artisanal metaphor can also help students to understand how writing continuously supports development and improvement, just as a recipe may change over time ("I find that if you knead it this way . . ." or "I find that if I add the salt after . . .") and can always be improved.

The artisanal metaphor reminds WPAs, tutors, instructors, and students that efficiency should not necessarily be our highest goal. In some instances, this means prizing quality over efficiency in ways that support long-term sustainability; in others it means being patient with ourselves and others as we complete our tasks and develop our skills. In supporting tutors and instructors in their development rather than insisting on efficiency, the artisanal metaphor also responds to the perception that "management" is linked to exploitation of employees (Strickland 2011, 15), which leads WPAs to prefer the term "administrator" to "manager." Along these lines, the artisanal model has the potential to divert us from a model of exploitation, but only if we as WPAs keep in mind and support the ideals of artisanal production, such as the time required for quality work, and if we support in tutors and instructors the development of "agency and conscientiousness" in carrying out their work (Brew et al. 2018). We must take care, however, to truly support these ideals rather than unethically benefitting from perceptions that artisanal products are of higher quality and humanely produced. The point is not only to market and support writing instruction as artisanal to allow the freedom to teach and tutor in different ways and on flexible schedules, but also to support the development of instructors and tutors as artisans who are conscientious in their work.

AFFORDANCES: EFFECTS OF ARTISANAL THINKING ON PERCEPTIONS OF TUTORING AND TEACHING PROCESSES

Defining tutoring and teaching as artisanal can also shape how tutors and teachers think about their work. Factory farming reminds me of an assembly line, specifically of the thoughtless production of a worker who is a cog in the machine and may not feel much connection to the outcome of his labor, and of an unsustainable process that uses up workers and natural resources. In contrast, when I think of the creation of an artisanal product, I think of taking pride in one's work, of finding value and fulfillment, of being a nerd of whatever is being produced—a bread nerd, a pickle nerd, a beer nerd—a person who will talk about fermentation or various ingredients endlessly. These bread/pickle/beer nerds may think about their work the way I think about writing or teaching: I am always interested in learning more and improving my understanding. This aligns with the idea of "academic artisans" described by Brew and coauthors (2018) in that they are focused not simply on doing their jobs but on doing them well, "on providing a service to the institution by going beyond necessary tasks and contributing to a bigger whole . . . demonstrat[ing] a sense of responsibility and agency . . . a commitment to the institution [and] a conscientiousness about fixing the things that need fixing" (123). I hope that all instructors view teaching this way. And when I think about the tutors I have trained and supervised for the past few years, I see that there are some who view tutoring from the perspective of an artisan and others who don't.

Tutors

My hope is that an artisanal view can help tutors to take pride and interest in developing their skills. As Rebecca Rickly (1998) says, "This is the goal that most of us have for our peer tutors: to become reflective practitioners as they learn, observe, and practice their skill" (44). I hope that the artisanal metaphor will help tutors improve their practice, talk about tutoring in different ways, and see the value of their labor, which in turn helps instructional faculty also see the value of the services peer tutors provide. I think instructional faculty notice and respect tutors who are thoughtful and reflective about their tutoring practice.

How do students who come to the center as tutees, though, feel about tutors who take a more reflective approach? What does this look like to a tutee? Students sometimes take a more transactional view of tutoring. At the extreme end, Peter Carino (2003) says, "students sometimes come to the center expecting work to be done for them in exchange for the time they sacrifice" (102). Virtually all students want tutors who can help them; they may not care so much what is behind this help. I think students benefit from tutors who take pride in their work and continuously improve strategies through an interest in their work. Perhaps students need help to understand the value of reflection the way WPAs do. When a student can't get an appointment because the center is closed for training, they need to be persuaded that this training will positively impact their tutoring session the next week.

How do we encourage tutors to approach their work from the perspective of an artisan who takes pride in their craft and is always looking to improve? According to Langer, seeing oneself as part of a professional community encourages this perspective in K–12 instructors (in Penrose 2012, 110). Reading scholarship on tutoring or connecting tutors to a professional community, whether through interactions with other student leaders on campus or tutors on other campuses, might foster this artisanal perspective. I have also seen evidence that observations, training, feedback from students, and prompts for self-reflection encourage tutors to see themselves this way. These activities show tutors that they should celebrate their strengths, but that there is always room to grow and improve. In a self-assessment, asking tutors to identify areas for improvement or set goals for the semester prompts them to consider their continual development and growth. Within this self-assessment, asking tutors to rate themselves on different criteria like "I behave in a friendly manner toward tutees" or "I help students develop as independent learners" draws their attention to areas of strength or weakness they might focus on. Feedback from supervisors or other tutors who conduct observations and from tutees who complete surveys provides tutors both the space to revel in their successes and recognize areas for improvement.

Training also is a place for tutors to realize their strengths and weaknesses, which can come through simply attending training, participating in discussions and group activities, and leading portions of the training when they are an experienced tutor. Supporting peer tutors' growth and learning builds our reputation as an on-campus employer. This encourages sustainability by supporting recruitment of future tutors, whether informally through word of mouth or through feedback specifically solicited from peer tutors and used in recruitment documents. There is also the perspective from Total Quality Management, a management style that originated in Japan in companies like Toyota and gained popularity outside Japan in the 1980s, that quality increases productivity and "brings . . . increases in the responsibility of each employee and an emphasis on teamwork" (Strickland 2011, 113). While Total Quality Management has its critics and we must approach it with an eye toward ethics and politics as Strickland recommends, I find value in the idea that supporting and growing tutors pays off in multiple ways.

Instructors

Previous sections of this chapter discussed the artisanal metaphor's affordances for instructors in terms of valuing individual variation and devaluing efficiency. When it comes to harnessing one's inner beer nerd, my tendency is to assume that instructors already do this—that writing and the teaching of writing are the things they nerd out on.

In this respect, the artisanal model serves as a reminder that our work should feel artisanal; we should nerd out on writing and teaching the same way the baker nerds out on bread. When this is not the case, when we feel like machines, squashed by the pressures of efficiency and mass production and forced to teach too many students in too many sections, we often despise our work. These elements negatively impact sustainability by lessening the quality of teaching, leading to burnout, and ultimately driving instructors away. So how can these moments be minimized, whether by instructors or administrators? As instructors, maybe it's by doing what we can to manage our workload. Maybe it's by doing our best without killing ourselves. Maybe it's by letting good enough be good enough—again keeping an eye on the long-term goal of sustainability.

As administrators, we might start by asking, What (or where) is the administrator in the artisanal model? According to Strickland (2011), if we look at Latin roots, "to direct or manage a group of people . . . can suggest either that one dominates them or that one provides guidance" (59). I assume our intent is not to dominate, but we might look at what guidance we are able to provide. We might also think of administrators as facilitators, as those who help others do their jobs and grow. Along these lines, in the artisanal model, the administrator is the person who organizes the farmer's market, the landlord who leases the land or space to the producer, or perhaps an experienced mentor-producer who can offer tips. Following this line of thinking, the role of administrators in supporting an artisanal model of instruction is to provide resources—from supplies to advice to appropriate spaces for the different tasks of teaching, research, professional development, collaboration, and so on.

Ideally, of course, administrators can also help instructors to work as artisans through enrollment caps and humane course loads as CCCC recommends (Conference 2015) and with the goal of increasing the quality of teaching and long-term sustainability of instructors and programs. When financial constraints make ideals difficult to reach, perhaps instructors can be at least treated as artisans, as experts in our fields, for example by being provided space in campus talks to share our areas of expertise or even simply asking after instructors' areas of interest (though, to be fair, these are poor replacements for appropriate resources and humane workloads).

One thing for instructors to remember is that the artisanal model does not mean withdrawing as a scholar. The artisan I envision is engrossed in their labor, with an eye toward community demand. She is not pushed and pressured by constant consumer need, though she does consider community engagement as she develops new flavors and products and reworks recipes. The model balances engagement with one's content and with the community one serves. The artisan engages in mutual conversation and shares caring relationships with members of the community. The idealized farmer's market transaction is more than financial, intermixed with personal greetings ("How are you? How's the family?") and knowledge-sharing ("How would you recommend preparing these?"). With mutual regard between them, the community values the artisan as well—the valuable services or products she provides, the knowledge she has about her product, and the role she plays in the community. Discussions of sustainability often argue that the concept must go beyond the economic and also be concerned with people and the environment. Similarly, the market transaction we imagine artisans taking part in encourages sustainability in that the buyer and seller value one another beyond the financial transaction itself.

When applied to the classroom, the "community" is in large part the students, and we have only a certain degree of control over how students regard their instructors. But instructors can foster a relationship with students that goes beyond the minimum transactions by getting to know members of the community through small talk, sharing aspects of their lives beyond the classroom, and being frank in ways that reveal their personalities. Instructors can also demonstrate their valuable knowledge just as a farmer or producer might. We should not allow the artisanal metaphor to be conflated with the Ivory Tower; instead we should take the artisan engaged in her community as our model.

Heavy reliance on contingent faculty to teach writing courses challenges the artisanal ideal. Underpaid and overworked contingent faculty are apt to feel less like artisans and more like mass producers. When employed under these circumstances myself, I definitely felt like a "grading machine." And I had to celebrate those days when I was able to grade like a machine because they allowed me to take time off in evenings or on weekends. If artisanal labor entails nerding out on one's content, contingent labor conditions make it hard to remember what one may have at one point loved about writing or teaching. The conditions of contingent labor often require maximizing efficiency, in order to maintain or increase employment, take on a heavier course load or additional employment, or search for one's next job. When contingent faculty are underemployed, stretched for time and money, and literally disposable, the artisanal metaphor is foreign to their experience. They cannot be blamed for "striv[ing] for uniformity" to streamline grading or other teaching tasks. This can affect quality of teaching and quality of life—and thus threaten the sustainability of this model.

The artisanal metaphor provides a reflective way of thinking about one's labor and an ideal that can be used to grow community-engaged professionals and create the conditions that enable tutors and instructors to do their jobs well, both of which encourage the sustainability of individual tutors and instructors, which in turn contributes to the sustainability of writing centers and programs.

THE VALUE OF REPUTATION AND WORD-OF-MOUTH ADVERTISING

Returning to Pollan (2006), he also says, "the artisanal model . . . shouldn't invest capital to reach national markets, relying on reputation and word of mouth rather than on advertising" (249). Drawing inspiration from this part of the quote, WPAs should not deify growth—especially not above the quality of the program's reputation and service. When Pollan (2006) says the artisanal model "shouldn't invest capital to reach national markets," I think again of artisanal products found at farmer's markets. These vendors focus on doing what they do well and aim to grow in that way rather than aiming to be in every Walmart and Safeway. As a result, they grow slowly and maintain their quality; they may not have a huge market, but they always do quality work.

Tutoring

For tutoring services, to some extent, we already know the value of reputation and word-of-mouth advertising, such as when a student shares a positive tutoring experience with their friends and classmates or when an instructor promotes our services. Are there ways, though, that we can intentionally promote our reputation and encourage word-of-mouth advertising? I attempted a promotion that encouraged current tutees to bring a friend, incentivizing this with an entry in a monthly drawing for a ten-dollar Amazon gift card. (We also use this same drawing to incentivize tutees to provide feedback on tutoring sessions.) We publicized this promotion primarily through flyers, our tutors, and online. Unfortunately we had zero takers.

This promotion was created not just due to Pollan's assertions but also in response to a decrease in requests for tutoring in some subjects. In brainstorming with our tutors in this area, they said that in the past they often worked with small groups—two to three students who would come to the center together. These tutors also talked about their and their tutees' observations that in classes, it's not just one student who needs tutoring support, but the whole row of students. This was another reason I thought it would help for current tutees who value tutoring to bring a friend. I imagined them engaging their classmates in conversations about their assignments or exams and suggesting tutoring support. However this didn't pan out.

We considered that tutees may hesitate because they feel uncomfortable having someone witness their academic struggles. Perhaps this is a unique challenge in using word-of-mouth advertising for tutoring services, which leads to the next question: How can we encourage word-of-mouth advertising in ways that do not ask tutees to expose their vulnerabilities? One option might be to focus on nontraditional students, who sometimes (but not always) seem less sensitive about exposing their shortcomings. Some nontraditional students are comfortable admitting and even publicizing the tutoring support they receive, confident in their strengths and honest about their weaknesses. We can help provide these students the language to talk about tutoring experiences, such as, "I'm great at math, but writing is a huge struggle for me. I always enjoy working with a tutor when writing—they help me to know what I'm doing well when I get stuck on a draft."

Another way to encourage word-of-mouth advertising without highlighting students' vulnerabilities might be to aim the promotion toward other aspects of center services such as it being a hang-out-and-study space or a place to get snacks or borrow a stapler.

We also hope that instructional faculty provide word-of-mouth advertising for tutoring by including information in their syllabi and course websites and discussing and promoting these services in class, something we can encourage them to do by providing services appealing to faculty. For example, we've developed an online video orientation to the center aimed at online students that instructors can share on class websites. We also promote a research and writing workshop series to instructors, some of whom require students to attend, or offer extra credit for attendance. We've also piloted a scavenger hunt of our center website that instructors can assign as another way for students, including distance students, to familiarize themselves with our services. Lastly, we are working on an online course orientation that could be assigned in online classes where students have traditionally struggled to fulfill online course expectations. By creating activities where instructors see a need, I hope they will promote these activities and incentivize completion. I hope that this encourages instructors to provide word-of-mouth advertising for our center so that students are encouraged to use our services.

Marketing and WPA Work beyond the Writing Center

Instructors too, if they are worried about classes or sections being cut, understand the value of reputation and word-of-mouth advertising. Beyond particular sections or classes, perhaps marketing comes into play for the writing program as a whole in response to myths about writing held by faculty. We know that myths about writing abound. Complaints about the shortcomings of writing programs in preparing students for the writing tasks they face in various disciplines at various levels across the university are common. The artisanal metaphor highlights the value of personal connection in managing perceptions of and complaints about writing programs and, perhaps in turn, myths about writing.

When we talk about farmer's markets, we often talk about knowing the producers of your food. The relationships and interactions intermix discussions of personal life and the farmer's expertise and provide a model for interactions between WPAs and faculty in other disciplines.

Like the farmer (or baker or other producer), the WPA must build these relationships with those who consume our products. It's admittedly weird to think of our students as the products that go on to write in other classes, or our tutoring services or writing instruction as the product that an instructor might have an opinion about. Nevertheless, these relationships, which Babb (this volume) also discusses, are beneficial. This is because we do depend to some extent on instructional faculty to promote tutoring services. And we do have to sustain ourselves in these universities in which everyone has an opinion about how writing should be taught. Building these connections with faculty in other disciplines through events like brown-bags, division meetings, and convocations or through informal interactions can help these faculty to understand what is being done in writing courses and why, along with what skills and experiences students are (and are not) bringing with them.

OVERCOMING RISKS

While the artisanal metaphor can help us value variation and quality over quantity, envision ideal working conditions, and communicate these values to various stakeholders, the metaphor comes with definite risks. As I show, artisanal products are often classified as luxury items rather than necessities, the artisanal metaphor can be used to justify abuse of WPA labor, and artisanal production has inequitable associations with race and class.

Artisanal Products as Luxury Items

Because artisanal products tend to be expensive, during times of belt-tightening we may choose cheaper, mass-produced items. As Carino (2003) says, writing centers are already "vulnerable to budget cuts and seen as expensive peripherals for remediating students considered unprepared" (97). On the other hand, we might decide that artisanal products are worth the cost—even during times when we are having trouble making ends meet. We can similarly argue that tutoring and other writing programs are still worth funding because of the value of the product(s) and the value this spending brings to our community.

In this way, the artisanal metaphor prepares us to make these arguments when we know we are in danger of losing funding. We need to be able to talk about the quality of our product, including the impact tutors have on students, the impact the tutoring experience has on tutors themselves, the way campus employment provides tutors a home on campus, and the way the learning center provides a valuable space for students on campus.

There is also a risk in presenting classroom instruction as artisanal. As Marc Bousquet (2008) says, within the university, "managers are continuously being asked to improve efficiency: that is, to continuously produce more with lower labor costs" (104). With constant efforts to cut costs, upper-level administrators may decide that we can only afford mass-produced education. Yet again, the artisanal metaphor provides a way to argue that quality instruction is worth the cost, an argument supported by CCCC documents arguing that working conditions must be equitable to produce "sound writing instruction" (Conference 2015). Acknowledging increased reliance on contingent faculty, CCCC's *Statement on Working Conditions* (Conference 2016) says, "departments and programs need to provide equitable working conditions for all faculty, including reasonable workloads," "access to . . . curricular decisions," and access to resources and professional development.

Despite concerns with working conditions, a standardized curriculum may have pedagogical benefits, such as logically building other courses on a common foundation. It's not clear exactly where CCCC stands on standardized curriculum, but the recommendation that all instructors have "the opportunity to contribute to the development of writing curriculum and instruction" (CCCC 2016) suggests that any standardization should still allow individual instructors opportunities to make the curriculum their own. CCCC also states that "[w]riting instructors perform most effectively—and student writers learn best—when instructors are treated as professionals" who know how to design courses. The idea that "sound writing instruction" requires professionals who are appropriately supported aligns with the working conditions envisioned through the artisanal metaphor.

Artisanal Labor as Fulfilling

The artisanal metaphor also risks making WPAs vulnerable to the abuse of labor. We already see this in education, where teachers at all levels are expected to labor beyond the workday out of love. Artisanal production feeds into this same idea of working for the love of a craft rather than for monetary compensation. Doug Hesse (2013) has written about these pressures for WPAs, driven by the sense that there is always more work to be done, that one's work identity defines one's self-worth, and a sense of responsibility for one's colleagues and program (410). This can lead to burnout, because there is always "the impulse to make something bigger or better." While many WPAs (like many in academia) find satisfaction in their work and want to perform beyond minimum expectations, this path is dangerous and unsustainable.

According to a *Chronicle of Higher Education* article, "devotion to our work makes us prime candidates for exploitation" (Gooblar 2018). Drawing on a psychology study, Gooblar (2018) says, "the more committed [non-tenure-track faculty] were to their institutions, the more likely they were to experience high levels of workplace stress, and to experience depression, anxiety, and stress more generally." Gooblar links the work of teaching specifically to burnout, attributing this to the nature of teaching as "emotional work, requiring reserves of patience and ingenuity." He provides recommendations for avoiding faculty burnout, including "[t]ak[ing] time off, if only for an evening." It's quite worrisome that so many of us apparently need to be told to take time off. Hesse (2013) has also talked about the need for WPAs to schedule personal time, for example to commit to "[t]hree nights a week and one day each weekend when no work comes home" (412), which seems like too little when considering the traditional forty-hour work week. When using the artisanal metaphor, we should be aware that it risks feeding into the expectation of overwork.

CLASS AND RACE CRITIQUES OF ARTISANAL CULTURE

Artisanal culture has additionally been critiqued for hiding the labor of people of color. Jackson (2017) in "The White Lies of Craft Culture" describes the way artisanal culture "elevates" and "legitimizes" products which have previously been devalued due to associations with Black, Brown, or hip-hop culture. In addition, the producers and consumers of craft culture are primarily white, and craft culture "consistently engages in the erasure or exploitation of people of color whose intellectual and manual labor are often the foundation of the practices that transform so many of these small pleasures into something artful" (Jackson 2017).

It is important to note that Jackson's critique is not of artisanal production itself but of the erasure of the labor of people of color. Drawing from her critique and Strickland's (2011) encouragement to attend to ethical and political concerns in WPA work, we might instead consider how to use the metaphor of artisanal production ethically. The raced, classed nature of artisanal production—the sense that these products are produced by and for whites and elites—might be taken as a warning that we must not reserve quality education only for these groups. Contrasted with the predominately white, wealthy flagship and Big Ten institutions I attended, the community colleges and smaller public universities where I have worked target traditionally underserved communities. While mass-produced education is often seen as "good enough" for students from lower socioeconomic backgrounds, as seen in the use of publisher-produced online courses, we must argue that all students deserve quality education.

One of the biggest barriers might be the constant pressure to cut costs. The idea of "mass customization" might be helpful for thinking through how quality, customized writing instruction can be provided for all when money is tight. Gooley (1998) defines "mass customization" as customized products delivered on a mass-production timeline and at a mass-produced price point (49). While the details of Gooley's work are dated, mass customization has only grown. Think of CafePress, for example, which allows customers to print custom designs cheaply and quickly. Even the US Postal Service allows customers to design custom postage stamps.

From the perspective of the producer, the demand for mass customization is a bit terrifying—is it even possible to meet such demands? According to Gooley (1998), mass customization of products like cars and computers is possible through careful coordination and technological advances; while education is not a car, computer, or T-shirt, perhaps coordination and technology can provide clues to make mass customization sustainable in WPA work as well. Gooley (1998) describes, for example, different levels of customization that are more or less possible to mass-produce. While a custom-made suit resists mass production, we are able to select different features when purchasing a car because various parts are produced and assembled into a semicustomized product. Similarly, I have heard new teachers be encouraged to think in terms of twenty-minute modules that can be reassembled differently in future semesters. Gooley (1998) also describes a strategy called "postponement of assembly," in which parts are available but not assembled until an order is received. Along the continuum of customization and standardization, this strategy can promote quality instruction rooted in the agency and conscientiousness of a highly skilled instructor while also helping them prevent burnout.

Jackson's critique of artisanal culture, however, focuses on production, on the covering over of the labor of workers of color. How might this criticism inflect the ethical use of the artisanal metaphor when applied to WPA work? I don't think there is necessarily the same danger with applying the artisanal metaphor to WPA work—outside of the covering-over of the work of people of color that is unfortunately common in many areas of academia and beyond. Perhaps the key power relationship to consider in applying the artisanal metaphor to WPA work is that between the administrator and the employees. Does the artisanal metaphor risk covering over the labor of the less powerful here? By attending to the ways in which the labor of students, tutors, instructors, and WPAs can be artisanal, I hope that I have avoided recreating the unjust representation that Jackson critiques.

SO WHAT?

Attending a recent demonstration of an online proctoring service, I found myself in awe of what mass production can accomplish. The number of exams this company proctors is astounding. It enabled the company to train artificial intelligence to act as automated proctors that learn every day by working with human proctors. This company has big data as a result and provides an average of cheating instances, which then allows them to identify problems. With proctors in different countries, this company can provide extensive tech support and higher-level proctors in emergency situations. My jaw literally dropped multiple times during the presentation at the undeniable appeal of this type of mass production.

The benefits of mass production were again clear in a demonstration of an online tutoring service. In a way that our campus never could, this corporation provides round-the-clock tutoring on demand. With students around the world requesting tutoring, the company, which boasts thousands of employees globally, can give its tutors flexibility to work when they want. With tutors always needed in any given time zone, it is highly likely that there is student demand somewhere at the same time the tutor wants to work. Tutors can even log in whenever they want to try to pick up a tutoring session. This is not possible on a campus of three thousand where I try to provide fifteen tutors enough hours to make employment worth their time but not so many that they aren't able to attend to their own responsibilities.

This too, however, points to the artisanal metaphor's value. Just as small on-campus centers cannot compete with international corporations, the artisanal metaphor provides a way to counter mass production by "selling" our products on our own terms and interrogating our roles in preventing unsustainable practices.

The value of the artisanal metaphor likely varies based on campus size. When I worked at a writing center on a residential campus serving over thirty thousand students, the center was staffed differently. In some ways, though, institutional size may not correlate with mass production. Larger schools, for example, can often offer more customization, as did my former campus, where first-year writing courses focused on different topics and provided students multiple options. In contrast, at smaller institutions, too few sections exist for this to make sense, and with few alternatives students are likely to choose sections based on time-slot alone.

However, smaller schools often pride themselves on offering a personal touch. I felt lost in the shuffle as an undergraduate at a university of twenty thousand.[3] In contrast, my current institution prides itself on being a "family." One custom-built experience students have at our campus is that in some divisions, senior capstone courses are essentially one-on-one directed studies between student and faculty member, something not possible at larger institutions.

The appropriateness of the artisanal metaphor may also vary by campus mission. My current campus's mission (University of Hawai'i 2018) claims we are "student-centered" and offer an "environment where students of all backgrounds are supported," as well as one that "fosters excellence in teaching [and] learning." Instructors who draw on the artisanal metaphor can capitalize on their strengths and adapt to students' needs seem a good fit for this campus mission and any institution that prioritizes teaching.

Regardless of institutional size and mission, the pressures to mass-produce and increase efficiency seem never-ending. Public campuses are asked to do more with less government funding, all while trying not to raise tuition *and* while increasing services to provide what each student needs. Even in the push for mass production, though, the human touch and individualization still have value. There is still a desire for individualized learning and an understanding that education cannot be fully mass-produced. Furthermore, people always want "items that are tailormade for individual needs" (Gooley 1998, 49). This is the way in.

Mass-produced curricula cannot (yet) meet the desire for individualized learning. The artisanal model still has sway. The artisanal metaphor can still be used, to an extent, to persuade students, tutors, instructors of writing and other disciplines, WPAs, and upper-level administrators of what writing programs and writing instruction need to be.

NOTES

1. To be fair, this is perhaps not an entirely new problem. It may be exacerbated by digital technologies that enable online learning, but instructors can also rely on paper textbooks in equally problematic ways, letting the text dictate the focus of the course, reducing their job to simply selecting chapters for students to focus on

each week. I recently had a conversation with an instructor who was exhilarated by the idea of developing course topics independent of a textbook, as if she had always assumed that her only option was to choose a textbook and follow it.
2. While my examples here draw on real names of past tutors I have worked with, the qualities assigned to tutors are hypothetical.
3. This is definitely not everyone's experience. I have seen and heard stories of students who received strong mentoring and guidance from faculty at institutions of twenty to thirty thousand students.

REFERENCES

Bousquet, Marc. 2008. *How the University Works: Higher Education and the Low-Wage Nation.* New York: New York University Press.

Brew, Angela, David Boud, Lisa Lucas, and Karin Crawford. 2018. "Academic Artisans in the Research University." *Higher Education* 76, no. 1 (7): 115–27.

Carino, Peter. 2003. "Power and Authority in Peer Tutoring." In *The Center Will Hold: Critical Perspectives on Writing Centers*, edited by Michael A. Pemberton and Joyce Kinkead, 96–113. Logan: Utah State University Press.

Clegg, Alicia. 2007. "Ways to Make Excellence Pay: Founders of Three UK Artisan Businesses Tell Alicia Clegg of Their Search for a Business Model That Allows Superb Craftsmanship to Make Money." *Financial Times*, October 17, 2007.

Conference on College Composition and Communication. 2015. *Principles for the Postsecondary Teaching of Writing.* https://cccc.ncte.org/cccc/resources/positions/postsecondarywriting.

Conference on College Composition and Communication. 2016. *CCCC Statement on Working Conditions for Non-Tenure Track Faculty.* https://cccc.ncte.org/cccc/resources/positions/working-conditions-ntt.

Council of Writing Program Administrators. 1998. *Evaluating the Intellectual Work of Writing Program Administrators.* http://wpacouncil.org/positions/intellectualwork.html.

Gooblar, David. 2018. "4 Ideas for Avoiding Faculty Burnout." *Chronicle of Higher Education*, April 4, 2018.

Gooley, Toby B. 1998. "Mass Customization: How Logistics Makes It Happen." *Logistics Management and Distribution Report* 37 (4): 49–54.

Hesse, Douglas. 2013. "What Is a Personal Life?" In *A Rhetoric for Writing Program Administrators*, edited by Rita Malenczyk, 407–14. Anderson, SC: Parlor Press.

Inoue, Asao. 2014. "Theorizing Failure in US Writing Assessments." *Research in the Teaching of English* 48 (3): 330–52.

Jackson, Lauren Michele. 2017. "The White Lies of Craft Culture." *Eater*, August 17, 2017.

Kimball, Sara. 1998. "WAC on the Web: Writing Center Outreach to Teachers of Writing Intensive Courses." In *Wiring the Writing Center*, edited by Eric Hobson, 62–74. Logan: Utah State University Press. doi:10.2307/j.ctt46nzf8.8.

Langer, Judith. 2000. "Excellence in English in Middle and High School: How Teachers' Professional Lives Support Student Achievement." *American Educational Research Journal* 37 (2): 397–439.

Penrose, Ann M. 2012. "Professional Identity in a Contingent-Labor Profession: Expertise, Autonomy, Community in Composition Teaching." *WPA: Writing Program Administration* 35 (2): 108–26.

Pollan, Michael. 2006. *The Omnivore's Dilemma.* London: Penguin.

Rickly, Rebecca. 1998. "Reflection and Responsibility in (Cyber) Tutor Training: Seeing Ourselves Clearly on and off the Screen." In *Wiring The Writing Center*, edited by Eric Hobson, 44–61. Logan: Utah State University Press. doi:10.2307/j.ctt46nzf8.7.

Strickland, Donna. 2011. *The Managerial Unconscious in the History of Composition Studies.* Carbondale: Southern Illinois University Press.
University of Hawai'i. 2018. *Strategic Action Plan.* University of Hawai'i—West O'ahu. https://westoahu.hawaii.edu/strategicplan/.
University of Hawai'i. 2021. "Distribution of Majors by Education Level." Institutional Research, Analysis & Planning Office. https://data.hawaii.edu/#/reports/ENRT08A?IRO_INST_AND_UHCC=WOA&SEM_YR_IRO=2021-8&MAJOR_TOGGLE=ALL_MAJORS&ETHNICITY_TOGGLE=ALL_ETHNICITY.

11

"BUILDING THE PLANE AS WE FLY IT"
Revising Our Thinking about Our First-Year Experience Program

Rona Kaufman and Scott Rogers

The study of program design is the study of program failure and revision. WPAs must be skilled in accommodating change, even as, as engineer Henry Petroski (1992) explains, "constant change means there are many more ways in which something can go wrong" (2). Of course, failure in our line of work comes with material, emotional, and political cost. We're perpetually asking ourselves: How do we leverage change to make our programs more sustainable? How do we innovate and iterate without risking too much for ourselves and those invested in or implicated by our programming? And how do we accommodate changes requested or demanded by others without sacrificing (too much) of our core commitments and values?

Our associate provost, with whom we work closely in leading our university's First-Year Experience Program, often says that "we are building the plane as we fly it." This metaphor, usually uttered in moments of structural upheaval or policy change, reveals the improvisational nature of our work,[1] as well as our nonautonomous location at a nexus of curricular and co-curricular campus units. The metaphor reveals the limitations and the risks of our work: fail to build or repair the plane safely, and the plane will crash, taking us with it and harming the people on the ground below. And how sustainable is a plane, perpetually reconstructed in mid-air? Airplanes are damaging to the environment, uncomfortable, and insensitive to both the employees who staff and support them and the passengers who reluctantly board them. At the same time, the metaphor is appealing, even hopeful. We are the organic builders of an organic plane. We are agentive, energetic parts of an interconnected landscape linking people and places and with a birds-eye view of how our campus learning ecology operates. It is thrilling to build the plane in the air, even if there is an urgency to hold things together.

https://doi.org/10.7330/9781646423064.c011

In this chapter, we weave together institutional histories with interviews of colleagues to offer an account of our program and to articulate the ways in which our central metaphor remains necessarily sustainable within our specific working context. We argue that the unfinished airplane captures the dynamic, protean nature of writing programs, particularly at institutions like ours that are largely off the rhetoric and composition map. We suggest that the plane functions, for us, as an "operative" metaphor by which we can use uncertainty to effect change in our program. The operative metaphor, following Donna Strickland (2011), provides the WPA with language for thinking broadly about writing program design and administration, in order to track moments and opportunities for agency within contexts that may appear or feel disempowering. Amidst falling enrollments and a declining faith in the value of a liberal arts education, the plane perpetually under construction heightens our understanding of dangerous pressure points. Finally, the metaphor helps us identify the range of interests that shape how writing is delivered and valued within the institution. Seeing and understanding these interests and the ideological systems that drive them helps us make decisions that can serve the best interests of our students and faculty.

DRAWING UP THE BLUEPRINTS: OUR PROGRAM ORIGINS

Pacific Lutheran University (PLU) was founded in 1890 by Norwegian Lutherans motivated in part by the Norwegian Synod's "academy movement," which encouraged the establishment of schools that would help immigrants adapt to a new place and find jobs as well as serve the church and community. A Lutheran approach to education insists on free and open inquiry, on questioning, on considering multiple possibilities, on rationality informed by faith. PLU's mission is "educating for lives of thoughtful inquiry, service, leadership, and care—for other persons, for the community, and for the earth," and it's something that's invoked often.

Our First-Year Experience Program (FYEP), which is about thirty years old, requires students to complete a two-course sequence (a writing seminar and discipline-specific inquiry seminar) along with co-curricular components. Roughly six hundred students a year come through each of these courses, which are mostly taught by tenure-line or full-time visiting faculty from across campus.

The history of first-year writing at PLU fits largely into a national narrative of composition, which most scholars trace to Harvard in the 1870s: written entrance exams testing both knowledge of literary reading lists and command of grammar, spelling, and expression—and a belief in the power of remediation. Yet in 1975 and 1976, as institutions reconsidered their writing courses—who takes them and for what purpose—PLU faculty undertook a study of writing at PLU, surveying five hundred students and over a hundred faculty. Their subsequent report (Benton and Seeger 1976) called attention to a series of tensions involving English 101—that English faculty, for example, thought that their primary duty in teaching the course was to focus on development of thinking, while faculty outside the English Department thought, in general, that faculty *ought* to focus on development of expression. Benton and Seeger deem a placement exam "unwise," as it "tells a student only one of two things: 'You write well enough,' or 'You don't write well enough.'" The report calls for a move away from a deficit model and a focus on the senior year: "What should be done in the freshman year is to determine just what elements of the PLU curriculum would most likely help a student develop his writing skills most efficiently, so that his writing skills as a senior would be at the level of proficiency we would like to expect in college *graduates*—not in college freshmen" (Benton and Seeger 1976, 30; emphasis in original). They also note students' overall dissatisfaction with their English 101 courses, which they found to be difficult, irrelevant, boring, and unevenly delivered across sections.[2] Benton and Seeger make recommendations for the development of a comprehensive program with a lower enrollment cap for English 101 and the addition of a second course (English 102) that would be rooted in writing across the curriculum.

Following these recommendations, PLU became a WAC institution, although it would take over a decade for FYEP to be formally adopted by the faculty. Based on student and faculty response and resiliency in multiple General Education revisions, FYEP is recognized as successful. Writing 101, one of two required courses for first-year students, is often held up as one of PLU's marks of distinction. Over time, we have heard different rationales for its success. It could be that the Lutheran commitment to considering all ideas means that one person *can* start a program that the entire university will adopt. It could be that a commitment to service rather than to humanism—again, PLU has never been a strictly liberal arts institution—has always shaped writing pedagogy here. It could be that Lutherans have always valued language and believe, with Wittgenstein, that the limits of one's universe is language—a reason to care tremendously about writing. And it could be that its ability to build and rebuild in motion—its ability to respond to change on the fly and to pilot new ideas—gives it greater odds of pleasing many constituencies all at once.

First-Year Experience Programs as Ecological Systems

FYEP emerges from a national conversation about the importance of the first year in the undergraduate curriculum. According to Mamrick (2005), the origins of the first-year seminar (FYS) can be traced back to the transitions course of the 1970s, which was typically designed to provide opportunities for increasingly diverse student populations to build support networks on campus and to smooth the adaptation to college life. In various iterations, it has served as an extended orientation, an academic seminar course, a preprofessional or disciplinary introduction, or a study skills course (Mamrick 2005, 16). In any particular model, skills like writing may be emphasized or de-emphasized based on local need and instructor expertise. However, regardless of its form, the course typically carries a number of institutional goals, including retention, academic achievement, increased involvement or improved attitudes about higher education, and more meaningful interactions with faculty early in the academic career (Barton and Donahue 2010).

Writing studies has not had a great deal to say about the first-year-seminar model, likely because of the idiosyncrasies in how the seminar is constructed on different campuses. Zawacki and Williams (2001), for example, highlight the impact of campus culture on seminar design in their investigation of the linked learning community, one iteration of the first-year experience. They note how the dynamics of staffing courses, delivering curriculum, and assessing student learning are made more difficult in the learning community model, with many variables not present in a traditional FY composition classroom (Zawacki and Williams 2001, 135–36). The presence of so many different, simultaneous components in the FYS can obscure the focus on writing, both for those *in* the FYS and those who are assessing it. It is difficult to teach writing while also maintaining the spirit of transition and building a cohesive and generative learning community.

Ultimately, we have been able to secure the resources we *need* to build and fly the plane, while making everyone as comfortable and welcome *as possible*. At PLU, we have had two and a half tenure lines committed to rhetoric and composition faculty in our English department for more than a decade, a luxury that not all universities our size are willing or able to support. This certainly demonstrates a commitment on the part of the faculty to support writing pedagogy in our department and division, as well as across the entire university (searches are approved and hires are made by the provost, after all, not the chair or dean). Through our leadership in FYEP and the campus writing center, we are able to influence faculty, student, and administrator perspectives on writing in important ways. Specifically, we echo many of the conclusions drawn by Emily Isaacs (2018), who explains that schools with a full-time WPA tend to have more training for FYC faculty, more transparent or visible learning objectives, more emphasis on process and on instruction that is rhetorically framed and focused (with less emphasis on skill-and-drill pedagogy), and lower class sizes. And while we note that WPA work is different in FYE programs, these are elements of our program that our predecessors secured and we maintain through careful maintenance of our campus writing construct (White, Peckham, and Eliot 2015).

TAKING FLIGHT: NEGOTIATING CREW AND BAGGAGE CONCERNS DURING ASCENT

One of the recommendations of the 1976 report led to the hire of Chuck Bergman (by training, a scholar of Early Modern literature, but someone who had helped train graduate students to teach writing) to develop a more systematic writing program at PLU. Chuck applied for and won NEH Consultancy Grants three years in a row, bringing to campus esteemed scholars from rhetoric and composition to help begin the work of developing a writing across the curriculum program. Chuck says, "It was really kind of a heady time, because there were all these ideas about writing as process, not writing as product, and drafts, and collaboration, and that sort of thing. And it really transformed the way we talked about writing on campus." Additionally, Chuck worked with faculty at other universities in the region to offer regional conferences and joint training sessions. The result of this decade-long effort was the proposal of a writing program that would be based in seminars, have themes, and be taught by the faculty who had participated in the training. The English Department embraced this approach, in part because it meant they would teach fewer sections of first-year writing, and they were able to staff the other sections with volunteers from across campus because of their experience in learning about writing instruction. "That's what the workshops did," Chuck says: "They created a paradigm shift on campus about what writing is all about. . . . so when it came time to ask people to be part of the seminars and to teach them, we were able to say, 'You will bring more enthusiasm in your own scholarship, you will change your relationship to your scholarship as well as the way you teach. And I think you'll find it exhilarating.' And it was in fact the case that people really found themselves with a kind of enthusiasm for academic writing that they didn't formerly have."

After the creation of a writing center, after a series of experimental offerings, and alongside the development of a writing major in the English Department, English 101 became Writing 101. That four-credit course, along with a two-credit Critical Conversations and a January term (J-term) residency requirement, made up the Freshmen Year Program (renamed First-Year Experience Program in 2002), was voted on by the faculty in 1992 and fully implemented in 1995. The two courses were staffed by faculty across campus and had three goals: literacy, thinking, and community. According to a 1997 internal program review, students in the program "develop conceptual and rhetorical skills as they practice scholarship that is both active and reflective, critical and impassioned, personally committed and socially responsible." The review concludes with high marks for the program: "The Freshmen Year Program at PLU is distinctive, coherent, and pedagogically sound. It offers students a powerful introduction to college life and the life of an educated person, engaged and thoughtful." It notes the need for more institutional resources and for clarity in J-Term and the second course, but it celebrates the program's "competitive edge ... in attracting new students, and this is a program in which we can take genuine pride" (3).

While Writing 101 has flown remarkably steady for the past twenty-seven years, FYEP as a program has changed considerably since its implementation and has been asked to take on more and more work of the university—from registration to orientation to assessment to career connections to study skills to student satisfaction surveys to vocation to assessment to disciplines to mission. Some of these biggest changes include

1. **The second course.** A shift from a two-credit Critical Conversation to a four-credit, double-dipping disciplinary Inquiry Seminar has made the second course more susceptible to political battles about the size of General Education and departmental control over curriculum.

2. **Adding co-curricular components.** While the first commitment of FYEP is always academic, the program has increasingly recognized the role that community plays in intellectual development. As such, Student Life is deeply involved with the program with (1) the implementation of a two-day retreat (called Explore!) focused on vocation during J-Term, (2) a Common Reading Program initiated in 2006 that is tethered to Orientation, and (3) the implementation of Living Learning Communities. We began with a pilot program in which six WRIT 101 courses were linked with six residence hall wings. Now, we commonly offer sixteen to eighteen linked sections, a full half of our 101 offerings.

3. **Sequencing.** In 2015, in order to have a more scaffolded curriculum and a more common experience, we began offering WRIT 101 almost

exclusively in the fall term. This move has affected staffing in significant ways. On the one hand, English Department faculty cannot offer as many sections, as they also have to offer courses for the literature and writing majors, thereby requiring that more faculty from other units across campus teach in the program. On the other hand, faculty from some units that would like to participate cannot, or cannot as often as they'd like, as they have to contribute to their own majors and to other interdisciplinary programs.

4. **Assessment.** We have one of the few program-level assessments that operates with any level of success without the threat of an outside accreditor to dictate an assessment timetable (e.g., Nursing, Business, and Music). In fact, as we review these central documents in 2019, one of the things that strikes us the most is how the program was lauded in 1997 for being assessment-friendly: "It is an ability-based freshman curriculum, well designed for an institution increasingly interested in issues of assessment" (2).

As FYEP takes on more, or changes, parts—staffing, assessment, partnerships, curriculum—it becomes heavier and more cumbersome. This is particularly troubling when we encounter turbulence. Despite the fact that FYEP is respected on campus, it still can be hard to staff, in part because most departments prioritize staffing of discipline-based courses over interdisciplinary courses, but also because many faculty are daunted by the thought of teaching writing. And it can be very difficult, even when staffing is in place, to balance disciplinary interests with programmatic goals and learning outcomes. In addition, as FYEP develops increasingly intricate relationships with other programs on campus, relationships that require attention and care, we can lose our focus on teaching the courses. Callista Brown, a former director of FYEP, points to the ongoing nature of some of these concerns. She says, "Problems that plagued the program early remain. Departments are supportive of FYEP, but don't want their best teachers teaching in it. Advocates saw the value of writing in their majors, but didn't want to create space or time to prioritize it in their own curriculum."

Maintaining a sense of community of faculty who are devoted to teaching is a further challenge. Jim Albrecht, another former director, notes that the development of the program comes at the cost of faculty development: "I feel like when I came to PLU there was less administrative or institutional change going on . . . I feel like there was a real culture at that point where you had people who cared about their teaching, and who got together and worked on pedagogy. And that was the glue that held it together. And now I just don't know that there's that same kind of culture." In other words, coherence in the program isn't coming from attention to the daily, on-the-ground teaching of these courses; instead, it's coming from the nexus of relationships on campus, an understanding of how FYEP connects to other units on campus. For dedicated faculty who love teaching first-year writing and are always looking for new things to do or improve, that move away from classroom pedagogy is a loss.

BUILDING (AND REBUILDING) THE PLANE AS WE FLY IT

Our moment for change, for rebuilding this wing or engine in the air, arrives amidst major shifts in the university. We have just experienced a Faculty Joint Committee tasked with reducing expenditure (including faculty lines). We have had a warning from our regional accreditor, largely focused on widespread assessment failures. And we find ourselves overhauling the general education curriculum, with FYEP as a foundational piece. Anxiety on campus is high, even as faculty, staff, and administrators recognize a need for change.

We recognize the danger implied in our metaphor, and we recognize that our metaphor resonates not only in our local context but also in national and international ones. We do not take the metaphor lightly. On the day we proposed this chapter, an airport employee stole a passenger plane from Seattle-Tacoma International Airport, taking it for a reckless ride until crashing it on Ketron Island and killing himself. In the year we've spent writing this chapter, two Boeing 737 Max 8 jetliners have crashed, killing 346 people, including crew and passengers. Yet we are also inspired by another aviation news story from the past year: a Swedish student and activist used her standing body on an international flight to prevent an Afghan asylum-seeker from being deported. Despite (and because of) these life-and-death connotations, we value the metaphor for how it accounts for the social and emotional experience of WPA work, as well as the material constraints that shape how, where, and when that work might be done. We like how this metaphor captures the chaos of our work. It honors our labor at the same time it foregrounds the high-stakes nature of our work. The uncertainty of program design, implementation, and assessment. The precarious position of writing in the university and of contingent or nontenured writing teachers more specifically. The politics of academic discourse that weigh most heavily on diverse students.

We also like how the metaphor helps us recast our work as WPAs as a form of "operational management," which Strickland (2011) describes as an opportunity to "notice and investigate our emotional stances toward our work, our beliefs about what constitutes a successful program, our beliefs even about the very values we see in the teaching of writing and about what we think makes a good teacher of writing" (121). These aspects of WPA work exist in tension with economies operating within the institution that may reduce our work to budgets, student evaluations, and retention. However, these economies are not, according to Strickland, by nature exploitative or capitalistic. Rather, they represent a wide range of interests and investments and may be rerouted to serve our interests. Strickland describes her work as a WPA in terms of her efforts to "tweak" the system to balance sound assessment, program vision, and teacher autonomy.

In keeping with Strickland's vision of operative management, we look for those aspects of our program that we can manage or those institutional systems we can productively navigate. When we are at the mercy of powerful forces in the institution, we try to protect ourselves and others. In the best moments, we are empowered with the requisite tools to build programming that serves both students and colleagues. In the worst moments, we hold ourselves responsible for those same communities.

FYEP occupies a strange place in the writing ecology of our university. Departments champion FYEP for its important position in the general education curriculum, and we think it is fair to say that most of our colleagues understand its value. The administration champions FYEP because it serves as a model for assessment at a university bereft of viable models.[3] The English department champions FYEP because it reflects our larger service to the university and because many of us are dedicated to effective writing pedagogy. Student Life champions FYEP because it is the primary site of integration between the academic and engagement "sides" of the university curriculum. Admissions champions FYEP as a welcoming place where students will transition into the academic habits and cultural life of the university. Colleagues from other divisions and schools across campus champion WRIT 101, in particular, as a reliable place in the general education program that doesn't take up space in the major and where students may "learn to write." All of that is a lot of pressure on the sole required writing course and an inconsistent discipline-focused seminar.

In thinking about the many interests that contribute to the design and operation of our airplane, we turn to recent work by Ryan Skinnell (2016), who has attempted to rethink a narrative of composition studies as passively undervalued, by pointing to how our programs regularly serve to legitimize university mission generally and general education programming more specifically. In our own context, for example, FYEP is among the few programs with established systems for assessing and revising curricular goals and systems. We deliver on the university's mission through a commitment to diversity, justice, and sustainability, as well as innovative teaching. Notably, sustainability at PLU moves beyond traditional environmental concerns to emphasize intersections of the natural world with sustainable human systems. We work with the values of Lutheran higher education by emphasizing questions and inquiry and conversations that matter beyond the boundaries of campus. We serve as the bridge or gateway to the culture of the university and, in so doing, we are regularly held up as a model for success.

Operating at a nexus of institutional interests, Skinnell (2016) says composition programs like ours may serve as "concessions" (14) in that they are yielded to power, often in exchange for benefits. At Arizona State University, the focus of his study, Skinnell notes that the first-year writing program has regularly been used to "solve institutional problems." It has been "introduced, reformed, maintained, threatened, or eliminated" as part of "negotiations related to larger, non-disciplinary institutional exigencies" (14). While concessions can be viewed negatively—have they turned us into a budget airline? are we being merged with another airline that will ultimately swallow us?—they can also be agentive. Skinnell argues that composition endures as a requirement "because of its significant, positive value to institutions and to various stakeholders, which makes it available to concede" (15). It is a known quantity, a powerful language that everyone seems to speak. Because FYEP is the "language that everyone speaks," it may sometimes be leveraged to achieve our own goals.

Aided by Skinnell's framework, we're specifically interested in two concessions here.

CONCESSION #1: EMBRACING COMPROMISE TO ASSURE SUSTAINABILITY

Our first concession is that we accept a second-class status in practice for a favored rhetorical position that secures the resources we need to keep the plane aloft. Departments regularly assign our courses to visiting or contingent faculty, despite a spoken commitment to putting our best and most institutionally stable faculty in the first year. At the same time, the program seems to be understood as a place for innovation. Where departments and discipline-focused programs may be reluctant to modify their own curriculum, they seem to agree on (1) the value of the FYE program, (2) the importance of writing for first-year students, and (3) the opportunity provided by a coherent program largely staffed by someone else (e.g., not the faculty in their own programs). We find this interesting because it reflects confidence in our program at the same time it suggests we are positioned somehow outside the politics of traditional programming. The funding will arrive somehow, the staffing, the curriculum, and an assessment plan. All of it will happen, but someone else will need to do it.

Despite this, our administration uses the program as a calling card and model for what can be done when disciplines collaborate. For example, Jan Lewis, our Associate Provost for Undergraduate Programs, highlights how the program is distinctly mission-driven. She explains, "I think the whole idea of learning and community and the critical thinking piece, the broad program goals, are absolutely [mission-focused]. They're getting students started out on that pathway, absolutely. It absolutely reflects our overall mission." Other interviewees focused on how the program develops student aptitude for inquiry, collaboration, and care for community. Rose McKenney, a professor from Geosciences and Environmental Studies and regular teacher of Writing 101, notes the value of FYEP as a training ground for success in the university. She explained how students are "acculturated" into core PLU concerns, including the "questioning piece that's a common thread in Lutheran higher education [which] is embedded in the structure."

FYEP also serves an important recruiting function. In a fairly traditional general education curriculum, FYEP is distinctive, thematic, and interdisciplinary. Callista Brown explains that the program "has always been popular with prospective parents and prospective students" because "it was not only an English department class," as it might be at other universities.

While we are constantly aware of the danger, others seem excited to board the plane, excited for where they are going.

While a lack of independent institutional location means we have little authority to control how departments around campus support or value the program, our mission alignment means we remain essential to the university. In this way, our independence offers us some agency. A supportive associate provost means our funding stream, such as it is, is safe. It cannot be cannibalized by departmental interests. And while departments are reluctant to provide experienced faculty for courses that do not directly benefit their major, these faculty do occasionally find their way to the program. In such instances, they engage in a multidisciplinary, student-centered curriculum that defies disciplinary norms and standards. Skills and ways of knowing define the curriculum rather than departmental traditions. Callista Brown notes the organic nature of this faculty-development opportunity: "Our goal was, if we could establish a culture across the university, if there were a few people in every department who were beginning to understand writing from this perspective, that it would seep upward instead of trickle down." In other words, operating in interstitial spaces, we're able to model good pedagogical practice and to influence curricular revisions throughout campus. Specifically, we've seen how our outcomes statement and our assessment model have been adopted in some departments, most significantly in Biology, Geosciences, and Philosophy, where FYEP pedagogical innovations have been implemented formally and informally throughout the curriculum.

Other planes from the same airport are built more effectively in light of the blueprints we generate from ongoing change. As we compromise and struggle, we are making the rest of the fleet more safe, more sustainable.

CONCESSION #2: CREATING SPACE AND ADJUSTING COURSE WITH INCLUSIVITY IN MIND

Student Life also has a major stake in the success of the program. FYEP is the only institutional location where virtually every student has a similar experience. As a gateway to the academic and social life of the university, then, it is a valuable space for student life programming. Jes Takla, Assistant Dean for Campus Life, explains how 101, in particular, is a foundation for students adapting to the social and academic life of the university. She says, "There's so much that students need to know to be fully robust, contributing members of a community in a society, whether that's right here now in the residence hall, or there are multiple intersecting communities now and forever as they graduate from PLU. And, so, in many ways, this is the foundation for a life of being a functional, critically thinking, contributing community member. All that is wrapped up in this writing class." While Jes validates the work of writing instruction, she also articulates a vision of curricular and co-curricular integration that frames a particular understanding of what the program does. She suggests that, "at its best, a program like this with the linked courses is about play and collaboration and experimentation and fun." As the program's administrators, we agree and celebrate her vision. However, the challenge of aligning limited faculty time and program resources with the goals of Student Life results in our second concession: our seats aren't always built with our present passengers in mind. They too must be dismantled and rebuilt.

That we've been able to leverage our position in our program at the nexus of so many overlapping and conflicting institutional interests has allowed us to champion diversity-oriented pedagogy and ethical hiring practices. We're not always successful, but pedagogical practices rooted in concerns about diversity and access have long been commonplace in our program. Callista Brown describes how early visits from scholars like Susan Jarratt created a space for discussion about what would then have been called "women's studies" or "multiculturalism." She explains that "a central concern [of the program] has been helping teachers teach students who might be resistant to difficult conversations about race, gender, etc." This remains true today and becomes increasingly important as we find ourselves amidst a shift in student populations. Our Admissions division has engaged in a successful campaign to diversify a campus that has been historically white, privileged, and English-speaking. Last year, 2017–18, our incoming first-year class was over 40 percent first-generation and over 25 percent students of color (self-identified). This year, 2018–19, we welcomed closer to 50 percent first-in-the-family and 40 percent students of color.

However, differences in student background and experience, including academic preparation, pose significant challenges for FYEP. Prominent among these challenges is building a sustainable culture of inclusivity in our program. Linguistic diversity is a particular challenge for the 101 course, as faculty who were not trained in graduate school to teach writing often feel unequipped to teach students with diverse linguistic backgrounds and often believe that they must privilege Standard English over all other Englishes, creating a destructive feedback loop. Bamberg (1997) notes that the first-year seminar, because it wears so many hats, may disadvantage "students at the lower end of the admissions pool [who] may need the additional emphasis on writing and rhetoric provided by a general skills writing course even at these institutions" (13). Understood this way, FYEP may have worked so well for so long because we had a largely homogenous student population. Even though the 1970s report shows that faculty have long been decrying students' lack of sufficient preparation for college-level writing, we could expect that students arrived with similar backgrounds, experiences, and language.

For underprepared students and students who arrive with diverse linguistic practices (or expectations), the "catchall" nature of the program may be more troublesome. These students may be navigating a university context that is hostile to people who look or sound different, at the same time they are learning new content, new practice, and so on.

Or, if they are international students, they may be learning English, US Academic English, and US academic social and political conventions at the same time they're doing the other work of the course (Cox 2011). Students who identify as first-generation also face challenges in navigating classroom culture and seeking out support resources. Like most institutions, we pride ourselves on high standards, but these standards are often obscure and poorly explained. Of course, all of these identities often overlap on or with racialized bodies.

In our interview with Jes Takla, she described the illusion of teaching as a low-stakes affair. Suggesting the extent to which our alliance with Student Life has borne fruit, she explains, "When you think about the implications, this is about validating or invalidating certain ways of knowing," and it's about helping students find "a sense of belonging through this gateway program." In many ways, the stakes couldn't be higher. Jes adds, "For someone to get here, spend two semesters, but not find that sense of belonging and then drop out and leave with that debt but no degree—I mean, . . . some people . . . are now starting to verge on crisis . . . a more life-or-death situation."

What can we do from our position as directors of FYEP? We can embrace inclusive practices through strategic partnerships on campus. We can encourage faculty to teach themes and topics aligned with our mission—care for others and the earth, diversity, and social justice. We can support transparent teaching and assessment. Further, we can engage with deeper ethical questions about the purpose and value of higher education and more specifically of very expensive private institutions like ours.

Revising our General Education Program—as laborious, tense, and divisive as that work has been over the last year and a half—provides opportunities to improve conditions on the plane for everyone. Our new FYEP 102 course (a replacement for the Inquiry Seminar) will serve as a foundation for critical inquiry and diversity education at PLU. This will be a location from which to train faculty to decolonize their teaching practice. There's a lot at stake, as Jes Takla described to us: "If you're under-resourced and you're expected to provide this service, and you have to think about regulations, and you have to think about the staff delivering that experience and the structure that's guiding that experience—*what is the ethical responsibility you have to ensure that they have a non-detrimental, positive-learning experience when you don't feel like you have the full Cadillac structure in place?*" This is a question that guides us.

We assume that we will continue to staff both FYEP courses with a combination of tenure-line and contingent faculty, and we will continue to use FYEP sections to get contingent faculty to full-time or at least to half-time in order to receive benefits and higher pay per section and to avoid having NTT faculty be what Mike Rings, a contingent faculty member in Philosophy and regular teacher in FYEP, calls "freeway faculty," piecing together courses from universities and community colleges along Interstate-5. We will also provide faculty development and opportunities that help non-tenure-line faculty stay (because they are desirable as returning teachers) or secure work elsewhere because they have substantive training and experience in valuable teaching strategies.

CONCLUSION: KEEPING OUR METAPHOR ALOFT

Ultimately, we recognize the risks and challenges of our metaphor, but we feel compelled to stick with it. In many ways, the metaphor is sustainable by necessity. We are flying an incomplete plane into uncertain airspace. To land now would almost certainly be catastrophic. Additionally, we are part of the plane. To imagine differently is to deny our role in the system. The plane is retooled while in motion, from spare parts. Every part is used and reused, imagined and reimagined. And with each failure or accident we come to understand better the limitations and opportunities presented by design, personnel, and weather. Facing stiff headwinds, we persevere because our institutional lives depend on it. Jan Lewis captures this state well when she says, "I think the Gen Ed conversation has opened this up. Writing and reading are still central to the proficiencies that people are talking about. And I think there's an opportunity to think about how we do that in the Gen Ed conversation, as well as in the assessment conversation that we're having. I'm not sure we're ready to have it now. But we're going to have it because we have to."

And so we carry on.

NOTES

1. For another view on the improvisational nature of WPA work, see Gunter, this volume.
2. For a recasting of "unevenness" as a form of valuable variation, see Robyn Tasaka's chapter, "The Affordances and Risks of Artisanal Production as a Metaphor for Writing Program Administration" in this volume.
3. Karen McConnell, now Dean of the School of Education and Kinesiology and former Director of Assessment, traces the history of (and resistance to) assessment at PLU, including a warning from accreditors ten years ago that necessitated a real change in how we do assessment, leading to the creation of her position. Noting that FYEP was chosen by the provost as a place to begin—because of what was happening nationally with writing assessment, because FYEP teaches writing well, and

because focusing on assessment in a general education, non-discipline-specific program was "politically, more a more doable thing"—Karen says, "I would credit the FYEP with the [changed] culture [of assessment] immensely, because people were from all over. And so they were coming together. They were doing assessment together. It was going well, so it was no longer demonized in that setting. So then they go back to their home unit, who might still be grumbling and grousing, but they've had this other experience. I think that bled out. I think it really helped the campus."

REFERENCES

Bamberg, Betty. 1997. "Alternative Models of First-Year Composition: Possibilities and Problems." *WPA: Writing Program Administration* 21 (1): 7–18.

Barton, Andrew, and Christiane Donahue. 2009. "Multiple Assessments of a First-Year Seminar Pilot." *The Journal of General Education* 58 (4): 259–78.

Benton, Paul, and Rick Seeger. 1976. *A Report on Student Writing Skills at PLU*. Pacific Lutheran University.

Cox, Michelle. 2011. "WAC: Closing Doors or Opening Doors for Second Language Writers?" *Across the Disciplines* 8 (4): 1–20.

Isaacs, Emily J. 2018. *Writing at the State U: Instruction and Administration at 106 Comprehensive Universities*. Logan: Utah State University Press.

Mamrick, Marla. 2005. "The First-Year Seminar: An Historical Perspective." In *The 2003 National Survey on First-Year Seminars: Continuing Innovations in the Collegiate Curriculum*, edited by B. F. Tobolowsky, 15–20. Columbia: University of South Carolina.

Petroski, Henry. 1992. *To Engineer Is Human: The Role of Failure in Successful Design*. New York: Vintage.

Skinnell, Ryan. 2016. *Conceding Composition: A Crooked History of Composition's Institutional Fortunes*. Logan: Utah State University Press.

Strickland, Donna. 2011. *The Managerial Unconscious in the History of Composition Studies*. Carbondale: Southern Illinois UP.

White, Edward M., Norbert Elliot, and Irvin Peckham. 2015. *Very Like a Whale: The Assessment of Writing Programs*. Logan: Utah State University Press.

Zawacki, Terry Myers, and Ashley Taliaferro Williams. 2001. "Is It Still WAC? Writing within Interdisciplinary Learning Communities." In *WAC for the New Millennium: Strategies for Continuing Writing-Across-the-Curriculum Programs*, edited by Susan H. McLeod, Eric Miraglia, Margot Soven, and Christopher Thaiss, 109–40. Urbana, IL: National Council of Teachers of English.

12
I'M JUST PLAYIN'
Directing Writing Programs as Improv

Kim Gunter

Cheryl Glenn, Keegan Michael Key, and an anonymous dean walk into a bar. The dean is wearing ear plugs, and Glenn chides, "That's not what I meant by silence." Key morphs into Luther, Obama's anger translator, and shouts, "She's sayin', 'You're so lost you couldn't find rhetoric and composition at a CCCC convention!'"
 Wait.
 That's not the way I want to start this essay.
 Let's change the scene.

* * *

I am reminded of Min-Zhan Lu's (2009) admonition that "Metaphors Matter" when I stumble upon Collie Fulford's (2011) "Hitting the Ground Listening: An Ethnographic Approach to New WPA Learning." Indeed.
 Nope. That's not quite it either.

* * *

In this piece, I want to "name what I know" to be the archetypal experience, or at least *my* archetypal experience, of WPA life. Like Donna Strickland (2011), as a PhD student, I never imagined being "interpellated into . . . the hierarchy of contingent teaching faculty and tenure-track administrators . . . endemic to writing programs" (1), yet I have directed or codirected writing programs at four different universities. Some of those programs were smaller (e.g., with one thousand students spread across two first-year composition courses at a small, private institution) while others were more complex (for example, one that contained basic writing, first- and second-year composition, undergraduate courses, a TA training program, and a graduate certificate, serving altogether some five thousand students a year). Regardless of location, writing program administration has always seemed to me to be in part conjuring the future, imagining what could go wrong, and preparing today to face those distant challenges. I'm not alone. I sat in a 2019 CCCC session and listened to another WPA during a Q&A describe her computer desktop: "I have all these files saved, just in case," she shared.

The problem, of course, is that we can never prepare for everything. Because next fall's schedule is due today and performance review of twenty-five adjuncts is due two weeks after and we have to file curriculum proposals early next month and then we must prepare for the summer WAC workshops and, oh, by the way, a FYC student just made an alarming statement in class that must be investigated, there is, first of all, not *time* enough to develop plans for every contingency. Plus, some crises are just plain unforeseeable—being called into Academic Affairs, on one day, to learn of private, right-wing money pressuring the state university system to dismantle basic writing programs or, on another, to learn of a tenure-stream colleague's accusation of founding a new secret society for the FYC program's non-tenure-track faculty. (I kid you not.) Yet meet these crises we must.

As my fellow authors in this volume and I consider metaphors for WPA work and, at our editors' behest, try to craft more sustainable ones, I waffle. On the one hand, I'm sympathetic to all those plate-twirlers (Pinard 1999), kitchen cooks (George 1999), and unappreciated wives (McLeod 2007), and I know that the only way that I feel more or less "caught up" on work is at the end of a breathless yet typical seventy-hour workweek. On the other hand, what those metaphors don't capture is the *fun* of this job. When I partner with FYC students on a curriculum-development project or mentor an adjunct in proposing her first conference paper or talk with a biology professor about how much she's enjoying reading her students' journals or brainstorm with student affairs professionals about developing a stretch FYC class that will start in the summer and end in December for our TRIO students, there are moments when I feel downright giddy. How, then, to describe what Janelle Monae might label the highs and lows of tipping on the tightrope—Every. Day.?

Improv, particularly *improv comedy*, seems to me to capture much of my experience of my own professional life. According to Mick Napier (2004), "Improvisation is getting on a stage and making stuff up as you go along" (1). Nicolas J. Zaunbrecher (2011) acknowledges the truth of Napier's description but adds his own caution: "while it's not as complicated as all that, it's not as simple as all that, either. Improvisation is getting on a stage and making stuff up as you go along. . . . But there's a lot more involved in clearing that little space where the spontaneous can happen than merely sweeping the dust from the floors" (57). What, then, does the WPA's improv look like? What improv company are we a part of? Who are our fellow players, what is our stage, what are the rules of the skit, and how do we train ourselves to perform effectively so that we succeed during what seems to be only an unpredictable, spontaneous moment?

In the essay that follows, I begin by describing the fundamental tenets of improv comedy, tracing how these apply just as readily to much of the work of writing program administration. I then go on to explain that improv and WPA work (both of which might look like chaotic art forms) are marked by rules, and it is negotiation of these rules that result in virtuoso performances. After expanding on the importance of rhetorical listening in both acting and administration, I acknowledge that much of improv theory assumes an ideal ensemble and audience, something that WPAs cannot always count on, particularly if we embody marginalized subject positions that are often ironically erased *and* made hypervisible in some programs and on some campuses. Ultimately, I argue that thinking of writing program administration as improv can be empowering for WPAs, for it allows us to see our work as ever evolving, beyond accomplishments but beyond mistakes, too, as our programs and careers unfold.

UNSCRIPTED TERRITORY, OR THIS WEEK AT WORK

A heightened yet playful suspense marks improv comedy. Untethered from traditional scripts, improv comics do not utter the well-rehearsed, sixty-minute HBO special or the scripted *Saturday Night Live* skit. Instead, improv is "a form of unscripted performance that [in Chicago-style improv] uses audience suggestions to initiate or shape scenes or plays created spontaneously and cooperatively" (Seham 2001, xvii). Popularized in the US through improv companies such as Second City, the Upright Citizens Brigade, and the Groundlings, perhaps the zenith of the form's exposure in America came on *Whose Line Is It Anyway?* An ABC revamp of the same-titled British series (itself a revamp of a radio show), game master Drew Carey hosted and articulated the rules of each scene to actors including Ryan Stiles, Colin Mochrie, Wayne Brady, Josie Lawrence, and high-profile celebrity guest stars (most notably, Robin Williams) (Stiles, Mochrie, and Brady 1998).

Improv may look chaotic to newcomers. For instance, prompted by actors, audience members might shout out suggestions for a scene to be played before them. However, there are rules to the form, and WPAs may identify with three fundamental tenets of improv. Matt Fotis and Siobhan

O'Hara (2016) tell us that "the main rule of improv, 'Yes, And,' means *play along and pull your weight*" (36). Fotis and O'Hara instruct, "By saying yes, we accept the reality created by our partners and begin the collaborative process" (36). Take, for instance, Tina Fey's short lesson in improv with interviewer and former Google chairperson Erick Schmidt. When Fey visited Google headquarters on the book tour for *Bossypants* (2011), Schmidt challenged Fey to engage in a spur-of-the-moment improv session, Schmidt launching without warning into the following:

> SCHMIDT: "Stop, I've got a gun!"
> FEY: "The gun. The gun I gave you for our wedding anniversary, Erick? How could you?"
> SCHMIDT: "We're not married."
> FEY [to the audience]: "Ah ha. 'We're not married' is a denial. We've learned our first improv lesson." (Hoang 2015)

Fey goes on to explain to the audience that saying "yes" is the first rule to improv, but her explanation is in many ways unnecessary. As soon as Schmidt disagrees with Fey, audience members can feel the improv-ed moment deflate and the possibilities of the scene fizzle.

Saying "Yes, And" has seemed to be a daily experience during my seventeen years as a WPA. Note that uttering "Yes, And" does *not* mean that we must always *agree* with fellow ensemble players. Instead, "Yes, And" suggests that we remain active players in the larger show. We can take a critical stance toward the content of the improv while remaining in relationship with the players in the ensemble. When a dean cuts full-time rhetoric and composition lines, for instance, saying "no" as a WPA would typically make little difference. Instead, employing "Yes, And" (*yes*, we will have fewer full-time faculty, *and* that reality means that we will have fewer office hours for students and fewer program initiatives) keeps the content of the conversation evolving.

According to Mike Birbiglia (2016), the second rule of improv is "It's all about the group." In *Don't Think Twice* (his feature film that centers on a group of improv actors, a film that is really a love letter to the form), Birbiglia describes improv thusly: "It's about a group working together in the moment to create something that never happened before or will never happen again." To expand upon the dynamic, Birbiglia's script contrasts improv with other kinds of performance: "It's not about *you* looking good and it's also not about looking funny . . . or showboating." Instead, improv relies on "Group Mind," with members of the troupe "harmoniously working with the others" and striving to remain "intellectually . . . in synch" (Fotis and O'Hara 41). No wonder that in this film, director and screenwriter Birbiglia has all members of this comedy troupe pat each others' back and reassure, "Got your back," before they begin each show.

"Group Mind" hails individual programs but also the discipline writ large. At a previous university within a then fractious English department, a few literary studies colleagues accused tenure-stream rhetoric and composition scholars (all of us administrators—of the rhetoric and composition program, the writing center, and a WAC program) of concocting "best practices." Understand, our colleagues were not debating any particular *example* of a best practice (portfolio evaluation, for example) but were instead suggesting that we fabricated the concept "best practices" altogether. "That doesn't even exist!" an Americanist-who-regularly-reads-*CCC* shouted. Clearly, we were playing in different ensembles. By sharing policy documents from the discipline (such as the criteria for the CCCC Writing Program Certificate of Excellence, which notes that programs should use "current best practices in the field"), we sought to remain in conversation with department colleagues. More effectively, by sharing resources with the rhetoric and composition faculty, we were able to lead programs based on disciplinarily recognized best practices—not to satisfy our own egos but to foster the best possible learning experiences for students.

Finally, the third rule of improv, again according to Birbiglia, is "Don't Think": "It's all about getting out of your head. It's about impulse. It's about living in the moment. It's about now." We might trace this tenet to Fotis and O'Hara's instruction that we "*React!*" Fotis and O'Hara qualify this advice by quoting improv comedy titan Del Close: "Honest discovery, observation, and reaction is better than contrived invention" (qtd. in Fotis and O'Hara 49). (Note, too, that Birbiglia cites Del Close as originating the metaphor of "watching people put the plane together when they're already in the sky," the metaphor Rona Kaufman and Scott Rogers explore in more depth elsewhere in this volume.) Even in this admonishment to react, of foremost concern remain the relationships among the players:

> Reacting gives weight to what is happening and instantly heightens the relationship in the scene. That means you have to be fully listening in a scene—and not just to the words. Remember, *what* is said in a scene is not nearly as important as *how* it is said. "It's supposed to rain today" can mean a million different things depending on how you say it. So stop reacting blindly to information and start reacting to the energy and intention—react to the *how*. (Fotis and O'Hara 2016, 49)

There is here, then, a Stanislavskian nod to the "the art of experiencing" (Benedetti 1999, 201), to taking "action in the given circumstances"

(Carnicke 1998, 156). WPAs know all too well that the "given circumstances" of our local contexts determine much about our programs, and we rely on campus partners who see horizons not available to us. Whether we alter our paradigm for accepting transfer credit based on conversations with staff in the admissions office, or agree to higher WID course caps in Nursing due to that program's staffing crunch and accreditation metrics, intent listening and reaction that is responsive to the local scene are vital.

As a genre, improv is always an indeterminant, emergent, and provisional form. Actors arrive to the improv stage not knowing the topics of the night's performance but knowing that they and their fellow players must rely on one another to produce an effective textual experience. The text itself is ever-evolving, as it is composed on the fly, and it is ethereal, as the same text will never be reproduced. Individual players' contributions are determined only once they are on the stage and in the actual *doing* of the performance. Thus, the emerging text is provisional, the final product deferred and subject to change upon the contributions of the next player, the audience's reaction, the limitations of the venue, and more. As such, improv as a form is inherently context-dependent, dialogic, and collaborative, and the improv-ed text will only succeed through an ethic of mutual responsibility.

This description mirrors how I might describe a rhetoric and composition program and a WPA's position therein. Whether the WPA's partners are first-year composition students, faculty, university deans and provosts, staff in a university registrar's office, members of boards of trustees, publishers' reps, general education committees, CCCC panelists, private donors, or published colleagues whom we've never met but whose dog-eared volumes litter our desk (and that's just this week!), dynamic negotiation marks the WPA experience. We must act. As we do, our own performance and the development of our programs emerge, yet they remain provisional, as everything from changes in upper administration to new admissions formulas to resignations of faculty to complaints from parents may change the landscape of any given scene. Our roles demand flexibility and the setting aside of our own egos so that we might genuinely consider the affordances and limitations that all of our partners face, and much of our learning, our success, and, yes, our failures emerge in the doing.

IT'S ALL IN THE GAME, OR WHEN MIGHT CHAOS BE *KAIROS*?

While these fundamental rules of improv traverse the form, limitations within each scene differ, often according to what game is being played.

According to Zaunbrecher, "a scene is a unit within a show, with rules distinguishing it from other scenes; a scene's game is the set of formative rules applying to that particular scene" (52). For example, one thirty-minute episode of *Whose Line Is It Anyway?* might include three or four scenes. One scene might be based on a ten-minute parody of *The Dating Game*, with one performer playing the contestant who must choose among three bachelors, each with a bizarre quirk that the contestant must ultimately identify (such as the bachelor who is actually the world's biggest glutton, another who is an announcer on a television game show, and a third who is a chicken having difficulty laying an egg). The hilarity of improv, then, is not dependent on absolute freedom but instead on successful negotiation of each game's limitations. In fact, players' creativity is heightened by the limitations they face and players' skillful negotiation of them. For instance, in *The Dating Game* example, audience members chuckle as *Whose Line*'s gluttonous Mochrie attempts to answer contestant Brady's questions even as Mochrie feigns peeling a banana and eating it, and they laugh as Stiles squawks his answers as the uncomfortable chicken; however, they are uproarious when Mochrie suddenly mimes grabbing Stiles' leg and simulates eating it as a drumstick, Stiles falling in mocked pain to the floor. As Zaunbrecher argues, "the values of spontaneity formally inherent to improv depend upon limitation for their generation. . . . Rather than try to free ourselves from limitation, we should recognize it and work with it" (56). The fixed boundaries of each scene are paradoxically the source of the possibilities that may emerge from it.

All improv shows and all writing programs occur in a given place with a specific company of players and with specific audience members, but performance is more complicated than simply leaving it as "we all operate in a local context," for the truth is, the scene changes with each new email or each new meeting. Both improv actors and WPAs can ask, what is the company of players in *this* room willing or capable of doing? What knowledge, values, desires, resources, skills, networks, time, and energy might each player in our program, department, college, and campus bring to bear to contribute to the successful performance of *this* writing program initiative (and, alternatively, what does one writing program administrator bring to the success of her campus partners' ventures)?

Limitations and possibilities might also be determined not just by players but by the venue itself. Every act is taking place *somewhere*, and we must attune ourselves to the cultural codes of place. Where is *this* scene in *this* show or in *this* writing program happening, in terms of "temporal location, spatial location, and socio-historical location"? (Zaunbrecher

51). What are the expectations, priorities, and dreams that reemerge in this place, and what are the policies recorded in handbooks *and* in lore? Jason Farman (2012) reminds us that this information is not "raw data" but instead "a lived social space experienced in a situated . . . way" (85). How do those raw facts play out within the contact zone not just of a given campus but of a given meeting?

Finally, limitations and possibilities will emerge from a program's audience members. We can ask: who is in the audience during any given act, and what will that "audience's sociocultural gaze" (Zaunbrecher 51) see? What are the audience's expectations, their knowledge about the scene before them, their *self-assessment* of their knowledge, and their role in the show? Put differently, will *these* donors complain if our program (housed in a death penalty state) cosponsors a lecture by a death penalty abolitionist? (Yep.) Will *these* administrators who have invited us to revise the long-standing placement process for new FYC students fold when the two senior literature professors running that program rage about the usurpation during a department meeting? (Oh yeah.) Will members of *this* student body write complaining letters to the student newspaper if we offer an LGBTQ-themed composition course? (Take a guess.) And are there times that we as WPAs embrace those meaningful risks despite threat or jeer? (Damn straight. So to speak.)

The sheer number of rules and actions that any WPA might negotiate in any given performance is dizzying, and adding to the vertigo is the fact that we must often improv quickly, making on-the-go decisions. All the desktop files in the world may not prepare us for the email from the department chair announcing that our program's budget has been cut by 85 percent, or another message from our provost that thanks us for the program's robust assessment plan, one that has been lauded by visiting accreditors (kernels that fell into my inbox the same week at a previous institution). However, if the predetermined features of improv are what create the space in which players act, and if brilliance in improv manifests in its moments of spontaneity, we might consider the systems in which we as WPAs work as well as the *kairotic* moments that we seize and, when possible, trigger. As Zaunbrecher warns, elements such as "communicative codes," "cultural values," and "relationships—spatial, social, and axiological," all "will be either explicitly addressed or they will address themselves" (52). It's WPAs' long practice, though—in previous performances on campus, on listservs, at conferences, in publications, in classrooms, in review meetings, on committees, and over more than one strong coffee and stiff drink—that prepares us to make the spontaneous look natural when the *kairotic* moment strikes.

That long practice may be our own, or it may be someone else's. Unlike many fields where administration remains untheorized, junior and graduate WPAs may lean on an archive and a disciplinary community for mentorship. Alice Horning (2016), for instance, reflects on her scholarship "about class size [written] in a way meant to give other WPAs a resource to use in discussions with administrators" (73). Junior WPAs may also organize to provide support to one another. (For example, the Carolinas affiliate of CWPA was vitally important to me when I became a WPA while still an untenured assistant professor. That local network enabled me to access information and advice from others in my state university system in fast and productive ways.) For that matter, the new knowledge that j- and gWPAs bring, to the discipline and to local contexts, revitalizes what can too often become staid truisms (e.g., "*Our* students can't . . ." or "This administration will *never* go for . . ."). Remember: WPAs don't just read campus codes and values; they help to create them too, and WPAs of all ranks play important roles.

TELL ME WHAT'D I SAY, OR RHETORICAL LISTENING AND THE IMPROV-ING WPA

Active, deep listening responds to immediacy, both that inherent in improv as a genre but also in writing program administration. Improv works only through a process marked by engagement and listening. To ensure the success of the team, Fotis and O'Hara advise, "*The best way to support your partner is to actively listen*—even when you are off stage or on the back line. If you are actively listening you will be highly responsive to what your partner needs and you won't miss anything he or she may be implicitly or explicitly asking you to provide" (37). Fotis and O'Hara continue: "Everything that happens on stage is important, and it is your job to be aware of everything because a good improviser knows that whatever happens on stage can and will be used again" (42). A tripartite dynamic emerges here: improv only works if relationships between the players in the scene succeed; those relationships only succeed if all players listen intently to one another; and, drilling down, my play as an individual is so interwoven with other players that I succeed only when the company succeeds. There is, then, a demand for a kind of presentness in every interaction. In this foregrounding of relationships, not only do we avoid what Frost and Yarrow (2007) label as the "First Cardinal Sin in improvisation" (142), abandoning a fellow player, but we underscore a value of collective responsibility and intentional listening that is necessary if a performance is to succeed.

This necessity of remaining ever attuned to every scene is a fact of WPA life. Moreover, we must remain attentive to multiple scenes that are all happening at the same time. Turns in what the discipline considers best practices keep us reading journals and attending conferences and participating in (or lurking on) listservs, but program faculty's potential resistance to new goals and outcomes sees us scanning body language in program meetings, conversations in copy rooms, and policies on program syllabi. Our programs can be affected by all kinds of scenes happening in all kinds of places—from university strategic plans to student government association memoranda. Moreover, in part due to typical WPA workloads, there often is not time to pause and reflect and consider a decision as slowly as we might like. When an adjunct faculty member lands a full-time position at another institution two days before fall semester begins, for instance, we need to find someone to take her classes, and quick. When an angry student shows up in our office doorway in tears and cries that her composition professor just humiliated her in front of her classmates, we typically cannot ask her to make an appointment.

In their collection *Silence and Listening as Rhetorical Arts*, Cheryl Glenn and Krista Ratcliffe (2011) advocate for the rhetorical importance of silence and listening. They argue, "the arts of silence and listening offer people multiple ways to negotiate and deliberate, whether with themselves or in dyadic, small-group, or large-scale situations" (3). Ratcliffe (1999) reminds us, though, that this listening is intentional. We must listen "with the intent to understand not just the claims, not just the cultural logics within which the claims function, but the rhetorical negotiations of understanding as well" (205). "Standing under the discourses of others," she continues, "means first acknowledging the existence of these discourses; second, listening for the (un)conscious presences, absences, unknowns; and third, consciously integrating this information into our world-views and decision-making" (205). And, I would add, for WPAs, listening in this manner allows us to accrue—accrue knowledge (about our disciplines, programs, campuses) and accrue an administrative philosophy that is ever tapped when we must employ that decision-making, often on the fly, simply because there is so damn much of it.

Ratcliffe's listening invites us to turn away from the kinds of iconic, individual improv-ed moments issued by comic virtuosos and instead to reflect on *listeners as active agents*. Relying on improv-ed jazz as a model for learning within organizations, Frank J. Barrett (1998) concludes, "Usually we think that great performances create attentive listeners. This notion suggests a reversal: attentive listening enables exceptional performance" (154). While Barrett refers to accompanying musicians' ability to hear an improv-ing soloist and anticipate and support her future progressions, both improv actors and WPAs might take note of the power of intentional listening. (Remember that Ratcliffe, too, invokes improv jazz, advising TAs, "teaching performances are best when teachers listen and respond to the other players in the room [the students]" [*Rhetorical* 2005, 141].) It is not always, or maybe even often, the virtuoso WPA who inspires attentive listening from upper administration and program faculty; instead, it is more likely that our own intentional listening over long stretches of time ultimately enables our own and our colleagues' exceptional performances.

Whether onstage at Improv Olympic or in an adjunct's annual review meeting, this kind of purposeful, meaning-making listening holds the possibility of transformation. In Julie Jung's (2005) discussion of the rhetorical listening espoused by Jacqueline Jones Royster, Min-Zhan Lu, and Ratcliffe, Jung proves that rhetorical listening is deeply active as it tasks listeners to answer questions like these: "Why am I so threatened by this speaker's argument? What is my personal/professional investment in defending that which this speaker challenges? In what ways are the speaker and I alike? In what ways are we different? How do these similarities and differences challenge my comfortable worldview?" (18). There is implicit here a demand for receptivity. When a fellow actor issues an utterance, there is a mandate that, because we share the collective responsibility for this performance to succeed, we pay attention, remain present, and participate as this scene evolves. Thus, Erick Schmidt might respond to Tina Fey, not "We're not married!" but "How dare you bring up our anniversary, you cheater!" If we have been called to a meeting in which an associate dean relays that the "decision has been made" to raise composition course caps by 25 percent, saying "You can't do that" is not only not persuasive; it's not even true. Saying, however, "Okay, just know that I'll advise composition faculty to assign 25 percent less writing to account for their rise in workload in the face of a stipend that remains stable" encourages this scene's evolution (though perhaps not its ease).

Collie Fulford's (2011) work at North Carolina Central University exemplifies this rhetorical listening. As a white, queer, northeastern, newly minted rhetoric and composition PhD at an HBCU in the South, Fulford describes her first instinct as a new WPA to be that of "listening and observing" (160). Persuaded by her methodological background in ethnography to model simply "being there" as an administrator (160), eventually Fulford worried about the "racist residue of ethnography's roots" and reframed her approach to one of "being *here*" (162), collaborating with non–rhetoric and composition specialist colleagues on initiatives that included assessment, placement, and curriculum design. These responses reflect listening carefully, not just in the moment but over time, and remaining in dialogue as we recognize our partners' contributions, even as we expand upon them.

The capacity to listen, though it may not ameliorate all of our obstacles, may allow us to remain in conversation and exert agency within the ensemble before us. In *Improv for Storytellers*, Kevin Johnstone (1999) complains that advising actors "that they must be good listeners . . . is confusing" (59). Instead, he advises we should urge improv actors to "[b]e altered by what's said" (59). As a WPA, sometimes it's downright impossible *not* to be altered by what we hear. We are often the first to hear of a medical diagnosis and the subsequent need for medical leave for a composition faculty member. We hear of those hikes in course caps, which will mean fewer sections for part-time faculty who already live in tight economic margins. We listen to a department colleague declare that ours is not a discipline at a campus-wide forum, or listen as a former dean explains that revision is the cause of the program's purported grade-inflation ("If you keep letting them revise, of course their grades are going to rise"). Just as improv actors negotiate all manner of contingencies that play out in real time before them, we as WPAs juggle within our local contexts the priorities and exigencies of the moment. Listening, though, even when it's hard to do (maybe *especially* when it's hard to do), holds the potentiality for "enriching of [the] performance" before us (Frost and Yarrow 183). Whether we are examining our own ability to guide our program toward its aims, the program's capacity to serve its students, the program's place on our campus, the campus's writing culture, or our relationships with all of those constituencies on campus who become our fellow players—from the writing faculty to staff in residence life to institutional research and so many more—the ensemble and our part in it are simply incapacitated without the ability to listen rhetorically. Engaging earnestly with campus partners can lead to what may look like spontaneous brilliance to outsiders who've no cognizance of the hours of training, practice, and collaboration we've already devoted.

BLOCK BY BLOCK, OR IMPROV AS KALEIDOSCOPIC AND RESTORATIVE

In some ways, the company that I have been describing as well as the WPA-as-improv-player acting within it are both idealized, marked by, first, an interdependent ethic of care for all participants and, second, a collective responsibility for the show at hand. Saying "Yes, And," valuing the group, and listening with intent, for example, serve as features of highly functional ensembles. Improv handbooks frequently assume that players within the ensemble act within a matrix that is marked by good faith and mutuality. Similarly, improv actors and WPAs rely on audience members who will meet our performances in a spirit of collaboration and earnest partnership. It is difficult for improv to work if a cynical audience sits, arms crossed, lip curled, and eyebrow arched, daring actors to "go ahead, try and entertain me." For transformative performance to occur, ensembles must work within venues that embrace inclusion, possibility, and mutuality. In other words, improv agents and WPAs need fellow players and audiences who are rooting for us. Therein, actors *and* administrators feel safe enough to take chances, be imaginative, and transgress. Such a milieu nurtures possibility and allows for moments of transformation.

WPAs know all too well that we may not work in such environments. WPAs may find our performances blocked by everything from redistributed budgets to shifting institutional priorities to a misunderstanding of our discipline to tenure guidelines. "Blocking" is a term from improv comedy and describes one type of failure of a scene. Instead of saying "Yes, And" to a fellow player's contribution, another actor rejects or ignores the contribution. Blocking may occur for lots of reasons, for instance because one actor was not listening to another, because an actor was so focused on her own first response to the game at hand that she did not remain responsive to other ensemble members, or simply because an actor hasn't yet practiced saying "Yes, And" enough. Modeling support and embracing mutability, after all, take practice.

Blocking may particularly occur in cross-cultural interactions. Consider, for instance, the timeless essay by Jacqueline Jones Royster (1996), "When the First Voice You Hear Is Not Your Own." Royster tells us therein that the "'subject' position really is everything" and often serves as a "terministic screen in cross-boundary discourse . . . permitting interpretation to be richly informed by the converging of dialectical perspectives" (29). This convergence, though, becomes viable only when players listen to and can hear one another, for only thereby can we "exchange perspectives, negotiate meaning, and create understanding with the intent of being in a good position to cooperate, when, like now, cooperation is absolutely necessary" (38). Conversely, the inability to listen rhetorically may form long before the start of any particular improv-ed game, and *at best,* folk who live in silos (be they ones marked by race, region, sexual orientation, discipline, role on campus, and more) are not primed to be bravura players.

As we contemplate blocking (intentional or not), the whiteness of improv can't be ignored. Take, for example, the pattern of contributions of African American improv actors not being picked up by white members of an ensemble. African American improv actor Frances Callier commented on her apprenticeship at Second City:

> My humor has modified. . . . You can almost say that at times I have whitewashed my humor. If we go to play together—to support me you have to know the references that I'm making. . . . And so if you don't find [my ideas] funny, then I'm gonna pull back on my own personal humor or humor from my culture. And that's what happens . . . you just play generalities. (Seham 189)

British comic Tai Campbell (2017) goes further and complains, "Black people don't exist in improv. Well, there are about five of us. In a world where talking unicorns are real and time travel is possible, we don't exist." Campbell points to the lack of Black characters, performers, teachers, and audience members in British improv circles and ultimately concludes that the form itself in the UK is white due to replication of this myopic segregation: "Whether conscious or not, the scenes we create as improvisers come from our experiences, our point of view of those experiences, and the context in which we experienced them. So the vast, vast majority of scenes on stage reflect the experiences of, that's right, white people."

The erasure of marginalized people on the improv stage is made obviously plain by the fact that, to perform improv and to witness it, you need a body, what Carolyn Marvin (2006) might call "the stubborn, ineradicable foundation of human communication" (2). However, some bodies are privileged on improv *and* academic stages. Zaunbrecher defines improv as "*the deliberate use of improvisational methods in a performance that manifests in the context of a dual matrix of immanence—that of the audience's gaze to the performers and of the performers' bodies to the audience*" (50). The improv-ing body—as it gestures, rolls its eyes, cocks an eyebrow, completes a pratfall, makes use of a prop, pitches its voice, mimes an action, sighs, flirts, and more—displays itself before us in performance. Bodies marked as aberrant, though, face the paradox of being concurrently unseen and highly visible. In addition to the absence of people of color, Campbell argues, "although black people have it bad in improv, people in the LGBTQ community have it worse, as do people whose first language isn't English and disabled people." And Campbell might have added women to his list of folks marginalized within the form. (Search for any episode of *Whose Line Is It Anyway?* on YouTube and count up the white guys compared to everyone else.) If majoritarian players—white, cisgendered, heterosexual, and often male—have not challenged (or been forced to challenge) their own privilege, the bodies of actors of color or trans actors, for instance, along with the larger cultures that these bodies activate, are either ignored, tokenized, or problematized.

When I write of "actors" and "stages" throughout this essay, I mean not just comics and black box theaters but WPAs and campus quads; however, it may be especially important that I pause here and make those connections more explicit in terms of the paradoxical experience—that is, of being simultaneously invisible and made hypervisible, specifically within the profession. Perhaps this contradiction has played out in recent years no more dramatically than on the WPA Listserv or, more precisely, many folks' exit from that listserv as part of #wpalistservfeministrevolution. In the face of whitemansplaining that *just.would.not.end*, even after it was explicitly and repeatedly called out (by junior scholars, graduate students, and leading researchers in the discipline, most of whom identified as women and some of whom discussed their identities as women of color), the discursive patterns that have been the norm in that digital forum (such the norm that, for some, they disappeared) were unveiled. And to be clear, the norm? One where an incredibly small minority of the profession (ostensibly white, cisgendered, heterosexual, full-time, tenured men, many with a cadre of research assistants) pontificates over O/others. Perhaps more alarming, though, are the ways that so much knowledge in the discipline more broadly is gendered and, particularly, raced (i.e., whitewashed). For instance, Royster in "Disciplinary Landscaping, or Contemporary Challenges in the History of Composition" (2003) challenges us to consider just how the field might change if we reflect upon how "we select, focus, and develop, bringing more clearly and vibrantly into view particular features that we frame and foreground, while simultaneously disregarding or minimizing other features and dimensions that we might have selected, developed, and showcased instead" (148). How might "truisms" in the field fall into doubt if we consider whose stories are being told and whose blocked?

Whole textual worlds have been created to normalize some bodies over others. Whether we point to grammar manuals and dictionaries that privilege one dialect over another or we observe glossy fashion magazines that privilege gendered hegemonies or we examine legal codes designed to pathologize and contain communities (whether those be sodomy laws that have jailed queers or redlining practices that keep Bridgeport residents out of Fairfield), the closer a body abides by these cultural texts (we might even say, the more textual the body), the more "natural" the body seems to a majoritarian audience. Even now, I can talk about bodies in this text because my medium so textualizes them; the excesses of bodies are elided here—their smells, their hair, their sounds, their fecund corporeality, all are contained. However, all of these excesses of bodies are needed in improv. Moments of hyperbole call for bulging eyes, exclamation calls for a fist pounded on a chest. And those excesses are needed in administration—deep breaths to calm nerves as we sit behind mahogany conference tables surrounded by trustees, fingers tapping calculator keys as we try to find funds for an adjunct to attend a conference. Yet the excesses represented by a Black body or a queer body may be unmanageable for the white or straight actors in some ensembles and on some campuses. The genres of improv *and* administration call for the medium of the body, yet many ensemble players do not know what to do with the spectacle of a fellow player's body when it is marked as deviant.

How useful, then, is improv as a metaphor for WPA work if, its theorization aside, the actual instantiations of this art form are frequently whitewashed? Three things come to mind. First, there are interventions into the improv scene. Monet Marshall, a founder of Improv Noir, a Black improv comedy ensemble in Durham, North Carolina, notes the whiteness of regional comedy scenes: "People of color are the other in those spaces. . . . I think they feel like visitors" (Woods 2018). However, performing at The Vault ("a Durham event space devoted to cultures of the African diaspora"), Improv Noir performers have not "had to deal with white colleagues or spectators misinterpreting or dominating the conversation" (Woods). On the contrary, Shaun Landry, founder of the black improv group Oui Be Negroes, enjoys the dissonance that her white audiences feel: "We're very un-PC and it makes the poor white liberal head spin. . . . They don't quite understand that we're about parody and homage" (Seham 192). Second, Royster (1996) can serve as a guide to us in our uses of improv, insisting that it "operate kaleidoscopically" (29) and that it pay attention to "context, ways of knowing, language abilities, and experience, and by doing so . . . [have] a consequent potential to deepen, broaden, and enrich our interpretive views in dynamic ways" (29). Third, improv can function like Glenn's silence and Ratcliffe's listening: "These arts have been conceptualized and employed in different times and places by many different people—some with power, some without—for purposes as diverse as showing reverence, gathering knowledge, planning action, buying time and attempting to survive" (Glenn and Ratcliffe 2001, 2). As such, improv can work as a tool of "restorative literacy," what Eric Darnell Pritchard (2017) defines as a practice that "remakes those emotional resources people need for living, especially love, and returns them to work in the best interest of the individual and others" (24).

CONCLUSION, OR THE SHOW *WILL* GO ON

Improv should not be misconstrued as actions that we take because we have failed to prepare. Nicolas Zaunbrecher reminds us that improv is intentional and consented to by the actors prior to the start of any performance: "Improv is deliberate and agreed-upon by its performers as a pre-given structure, not a fallback position enacted when a prescribed performance fails" (49). Thus, as WPAs, we don't simply improv in the face of failure (for instance, when we've forgotten our lines or the deadline for spring contracts). Instead, we improv every day, listening intently, remaining in hive-mind, building relationships, and honing the craft. It is this work that allows us to respond to and, as we are able, trigger *kairotic* moments, whether that means seizing the opportunities available in a new QEP or weaving around an attempted block.[1]

Not infrequently, of course, we become aware that many of our campus colleagues may not be playing with us, or at least not playing by the same rules. Zaunbrecher lays out a taxonomy of improv rules. Reading through them, it's easy to imagine a week on campus. Rules are meant to be generative, "creating a system for us to invent new exercises, games, and show formats, and to modify existing ones to meet new goals or explore new territory" (Zaunbrecher 49). However, as WPAs slide from one venue to another, rules shift. For example, *goal rules*, Zaunbrecher reminds us, "establish something performers should accomplish" and "draw action in certain directions" (53); however, when I as a WPA lead a program that reports directly to Academic Affairs but includes only courses housed in a single English department yet must get approval for new hires from the College, knowing *whose* goal rules to attempt to meet at any given moment can be difficult. Zaunbrecher stipulates that *information rules* "determine *who* gets to know *what*; some information about the scene or its rules is available to some individuals and not to others" (53) and *manipulation rules* "give power . . . to someone beyond the performers; an outside party affects the scene's action by adding, removing, or changing information" (53). Here, I remember personnel decisions. These decisions include ones where I was disallowed from rehiring seemingly talented composition faculty yet denied the rationale for nonrenewal—I knew I was missing information—but also instances where *I* chose not to rehire a composition faculty member for what I knew to be concrete and justified reasons yet reasons that I could not legally share with the larger, skeptical program faculty, realizing that, here, *I* was the one denying information to others. "Focus rules," Zaunbrecher continues, "tell you how to get somewhere. . . . [A] game's focus is what performers concentrate on in making spontaneous choices . . . [or] call[s] for emphasizing or deemphasizing aspects of behavior" (53). However, if one goal of my performance is to earn tenure, whose game am I playing when I spend this month chairing a search for two new full-time composition faculty, planning campus-wide WAC development institutes, scheduling classes for the fall, and teaching, watching my own writing grow digitally dusty on my hard drive? Some days, then, I'm improv-ing for all I'm worth but retain the nagging feeling that every audience member who observes but a slice of my performance can see me flailing. In negotiation of these strictures and so many others, the local and rule-bound nature of improv and writing program administration come to the fore.

Spending our days improv-ing across various scenes, when we find ourselves in early evening sitting in a now quiet building, looking out our office windows at an inky night, if we are not careful, it can suddenly feel as if we have no partners at all, as if we are an ensemble of one. Kevin Johnstone implores his improv students, "Unless you are willing to be changed you might as well be working alone!" (57). The thing is, sometimes it can feel as if we WPAs are doing just that. After particularly bad weeks, I sometimes feel that I have slid from improv into Augusto Boal's invisible theatre, where actors perform in public spaces, never letting audience members know that they are watching theater. Privileging oppressive societal conditions as his subject matter and encouraging theatre that breaks down the audience/actor dyad, Boal sought for audience members to take from the theatre experience the impetus to effect progressive change in their own lives and worlds. Even performances like these, however, remind me that the malleability of discourse is a fact that I can return to in my own work, regardless of the ensemble that I may be working with, or against.

In his application of Hannah Arendt's philosophies to musical improvisation, Panagiotis A. Kanellopoulos (2007) discusses Arendt's "forgiving" as an answer to irrevocable acts. In jazz, Kanellopoulos suggests that

> 'forgiving' might mean letting things go, weighing possibilities and problems *without allowing judgment to become an impediment of action.* Judgment-in-action has a special sense in improvisation, where evaluative perceptions of each moment are signals that influence the way forward . . . In fact, what at a certain moment may be perceived as a 'failure' often opens up new possibilities for continuation. (113)

We can extend Kanellopoulos to improv comedy and to writing program administration. In improv, transgression is necessary. The humor frequently comes, not in adherence to the rules, but in the ingenious negotiation of them, and the best improv ensembles embody onstage a kind of solidarity, a commitment to putting forth the best show possible. To keep the show going requires an openness, an embrace of variability, and an eye toward the success of the ensemble beyond the immediate scene and beyond the individual. Improv strategies allow us, first, to steer through the uncertainty that will always manifest if we direct writing programs for any length of time. Secondly, improv strategies allow us to stitch together coherency, for the programs that we lead and for ourselves as actors, agents of (by turn) change, compromise, creativity, collaboration, and challenge.

For most of us, the shows in which we perform began long before we arrived onstage, and they will continue once we've exited. The show will go on without us, and others will improv after us. As our own performance unfolds, process and product collapse into one, with careers and legacies and programs and educations emerging as we consider the institutional affordances and limitations that play out on our local stages. Not just improv (both as a "spontaneous" reaction to local developments but also as a proactive anticipation of the actions that we foresee) but metacognition of the need for improv can help us to build (cross-)campus relationships and sustainable programs that take seriously our collective responsibility for the scene at hand.

NOTE

1. QEP stands for Quality Enhancement Plan, an increasingly common university initiative designed to improve student learning, often incorporating assessment activities.

REFERENCES

Barrett, Frank J. 1998. "Coda: Creativity and Improvisation in Jazz and Organizations: Implications for Organizational Learning." *Organization Science* 9 (5): 605–22.
Benedetti, Jean. 1999. *Stanislavski: His Life and Art.* London: Methuen.
Birbiglia, Mike, dir. 2016. *Don't Think Twice.* Los Angeles, CA: Cold Iron Pictures.
Campbell, Tai. 2017. "Why Aren't There More Black People in Improv?" *The Stage*, April 13, 2017. https://www.thestage.co.uk/opinion/tai-campbell-why-arent-there-more-black-people-in-improv.
Carnicke, Sharon M. 1998. *Stanislavsky in Focus.* Amsterdam: Harwood.
Farman, Jason. 2012. "Information Cartography: Visualizations of Internet Spatiality and Information Flows." In *Composing(Media)=Composing(Embodiment)*, edited by Kristin L. Arola and Anne Frances Wysocki, 85–96. Logan: Utah State University Press.
Fey, Tina. 2011. *Bossypants.* New York: Reagan Arthur.

Fotis, Matt, and Siobhan O'Hara. 2016. *The Comedy Improv Handbook: A Comprehensive Guide to University Improvisational Comedy in Theatre and Performance*. New York: Focal Press.
Frost, Anthony, and Ralph Yarrow. 2007. *Improvisation in Drama*. 2nd ed. London: Palgrave Macmillan.
Fulford, Collie. 2011. "Hit the Ground Listening: An Ethnographic Approach to New WPA Learning." *WPA: Writing Program Administration* 35 (1): 159–62.
George, Diana, ed. 1999. *Kitchen Cooks, Plate Twirlers, and Troubadours: Writing Program Administrators Tell Their Stories*. Portsmouth, NH: Boynton/Cook.
Glenn, Cheryl, and Krista Ratcliffe. 2011. *Silence and Listening as Rhetorical Arts*. Carbondale: Southern Illinois University Press.
Hoang, Long. 2015. "Improv Lesson from Tina Fey." YouTube video. Posted August 2015. www.youtube.com/watch?v=NmafmRIeeto.
Horning, Alice. 2016. "Contingent Labor and the Impact on Teaching: Thoughts about the Indianapolis Resolution." *Composition Studies* 4 (1): 73–75.
Johnstone, Keith. 1999. *Impro for Storytellers*. London: Routledge.
Jung, Julie. 2005, *Revisionary Rhetoric, Feminist Pedagogy, and Multigenre Texts*. Carbondale: Southern Illinois University Press.
Kanellopoulos, Panagiotis. 2007. "Musical Improvisation as Action: An Arendtian Perspective." *Action, Criticism, and Theory for Music Education* 6 (3): 97–127. Accessed April 7, 2019. act.maydaygroup.org/articles/Kanellopoulos6_3.pdf.
Lu, Min-Zhan. 2009. "Metaphors Matter: Transcultural Literacy." *JAC: Journal of Advanced Composition* 29 (1–2): 285–93.
Marvin, Carolyn. 2006. "Communication as Embodiment." In *Communication as . . . : Perspectives on Theory*, edited by Gregory J. Shepherd, Jeffrey St. John, and Ted Striphas, 67–74. London: Sage Publications.
McLeod, Susan. 2007. *Writing Program Administration*. Anderson, SC: Parlor Press.
Napier, Mick. 2004. *Improvise: Scene from the Inside Out*. Portsmouth, NH: Heinemann.
Pinard, Mary. 1999. "Surviving the Honeymoon: Bliss and Anxiety in a WPA's First Year, or Appreciating the Plate Twirler's Art." In *Kitchen Cooks, Plate Twirlers, and Troubadours: Writing Program Administrators Tell Their Stories*, edited by Diana George, 56–62. Portsmouth, NH: Boynton/Cook.
Pritchard, Eric Darnell. 2017. *Fashioning Lives: Black Queers and the Politics of Literacy*. Carbondale: Southern Illinois University Press.
Ratcliffe, Krista. 1999. "Rhetorical Listening: A Trope for Interpretive Invention and a 'Code of Cross-Cultural Conduct.'" *College Composition and Communication* 51 (2): 205–6.
Ratcliffe, Krista. 2005. *Rhetorical Listening: Identification, Gender, Whiteness*. Carbondale, IL: Southern Illinois University Press.
Royster, Jacqueline Jones. 1996. "When the First Voice You Hear Is Not Your Own." *College Composition and Communication* 47 (1): 29–40.
Royster, Jacqueline Jones. 2003. "Disciplinary Landscaping, or Contemporary Challenges in the History of Composition." *Philosophy and Rhetoric* 36 (2): 148–67.
Seham, Amy E. 2001. *Whose Improv Is It Anyway? Beyond Second City*. Oxford: University Press of Mississippi.
Stiles, Ryan, Colin Mochrie, and Wayne Brady. 1998. *Whose Line Is It Anyway?* Season 1, episode 8. Aired October 17, 1998. Hat Trick Productions, ABC Television.
Strickland, Donna. 2011. *The Managerial Unconscious in the History of Composition Studies*. Carbondale: Southern Illinois University Press.
Woods, Byron. 2018. "Improv Noir Is an Oasis for Black Performers and Audiences in the Too-White World of Improv Comedy." *IndyWeek*, July 26, 2018. Accessed April 7, 2019. indyweek.com/culture/stage/improv-noir-oasis-black-performers-audiences-too-white-world-improv-comedy/.
Zaunbrecher, Nicholas J. 2011. "The Elements of Improvisation: Structural Tools for Spontaneous Theatre." *Theatre Topics* 21 (1): 49–59.

Afterword
SUSTAINING WHAT FOR WHY?

Douglas Hesse

I'm writing from the basement.

My location may portend another tale of writing program relegation: Susan Miller's sad woman, economically deprived and intellectually disparaged. However, this book's authors (and explicitly Alexis Teagarden) have rightly scrutinized the basement trope and others. Whatever use the metaphors once had, their future values dim. Moreover, they mightn't be apt. Although writing programs remain seriously undersupported, writing currently fares better than many other areas affiliated with the humanities.

Still, I'm writing from the basement, and that fact matters—albeit quite literally. At this moment, it's the basement of my house, a bungalow in north Denver: the kind of space, better than many, to which Covid-19 displaced higher education in March 2020. I work at a small table beneath naked pipes in a semifinished room, contrasting dramatically with my comfortable office in the fancy university library that houses our writing program. In 2020, I've become a WPA in exile, joining the American diaspora of compositionist colleagues.

Perhaps education's extraordinary adjustments will be short-lived and future readers might see this afterword as a curious footnote. I'd happily be read as anomaly. For now, however, everything's at stake, and I wonder what metaphors would have emerged if this book's authors had started drafting in summer 2020. Consider Andrew Hollinger and Manny Piña's intriguing invocation of particles and waves. A pandemic framework might have added "field," the larger context, from Young, Becker, and Pike's 1970s tagmemic theory. Writing's fields are variously programmatic, institutional, disciplinary, systemic (higher education as a whole), economic, and environmental. One could keep scaling up to the existential, but no metaphor rescues writing from planet-killing asteroids.

Whatever the future of colleges and writing programs, it's clear that metaphors forged in the fires (or leavened in the bread? stitched in the fabric? coded in the software?) of the past are inadequate for the future. In response, many writers here focus programmatically. Rona Kaufman and Scott Rogers follow the metaphor of building a plane in flight; Kim Gunter proposes analogues from improv comedy. Still, there are myriad unexplored program metaphors: toolshed, launchpad, arsenal, agora, assembly line, forum, gymnasium, fitness studio, training camp, laboratory, garden, clearinghouse, triathlon, stage, and so on. Most writers here focus on the WPA role itself, joining an ongoing tradition.

ORIGINARY IDENTITIES

I became a WPA in 1987, a year after finishing my PhD and only a decade after the founding of the Council of Writing Program Administrators. At my first WPA conference in the late 1980s, David Bartholomae summoned the metaphor of WPA as Batman, the Dark Knight high above the Gotham City of composition. I was a bystander in the room at the 1992 WPA where the Portland Resolution started. As a participant in WPA's adolescence, I perceived two related energies.

One of them, personal and interpersonal, promoted affiliation. People who coordinated writing efforts had common responsibilities that were sideways of the usual administrative roles like chair or dean. It was reassuring, even energizing, to know we had company: other parents on the swim-meet bleachers, other scrapbookers, band members, churchgoers, hang gliders.

Part of our adolescent affiliation came through sacrificial service, as the Martha in the composition kitchen while the Mary of literature or theory enjoyed The Teacher's attention. My analogy to religion, with overtones of calling and sacrifice, reflects how many WPAs were sustained by a sense of higher purpose. Not that these consolations universally sufficed. Tempering romantic idealism were things like Chuck Schuster's evocative image of the WPA as *Animal Farm's* Boxer the horse, faithfully laboring to the point of demise. But even self-deprecation could rally. In the 1981 comedy *Stripes*, Bill Murray and Harold Ramis preposterously get themselves into the army and find themselves organizing a platoon the night before basic training graduation. Wanting to avoid the alarming possibility that failure means repeating training, Murray rallies his comrades into shape with a collective ethos:

> We're Americans, with a capital 'A', huh? You know what that means? Do ya? That means that our forefathers were kicked out of every decent

country in the world. We are the wretched refuse. We're the underdog. We're mutts! . . . We're all very, very different, but there is one thing that we all have in common: we were all stupid enough to enlist in the Army. We're mutants. (Blum)

WPAs were part saints, part dupes, part noble misfits with gumption. Of course, all these rallying identities accompanied belief that writing should be taught by people who knew what they were doing and were supported in the enterprise. Various formative metaphors coalesced, most notably in Diana George's *Kitchen Cooks* volume, as Lydia, Lilian, and Patti point out.

Paralleling this affiliative internal energy was declarative external energy, which claimed expertise beyond the merely managerial, as signaled in an early gospel, "The Intellectual Work of Writing Administration." Rich Bullock paired his *CCC* review of *Kitchen Cooks* with another book published the same year, Shirley Rose and Bud Weiser's *The Writing Program Administrator as Researcher*. Bullock astutely characterizes the two books' worldviews, saying that "the overall mood of *Cooks* is dark, because of the sense it conveys that to be a WPA is to be out of control. In contrast, the essays in *The Writing Program Administrator as Researcher* show WPAs taking control of their situations by researching them" (674).

The contrast suggests two metaphorical frameworks available to WPAs: consolation and challenge. *Consolation* comes from those metaphors (firefighter, caretaker, confessor) that cast the role as so demanding that one might be pitied but also, crucially, *forgiven*. Perversely, even as you mourn courses not taught or books not written, there is the succor of mighty forces arrayed against you. Alas. In contrast, *challenge* figures the WPA role, when approached wisely, as enabling traditional scholarly life. You have agency. Diligent work can lead not only to promotion but also toward higher administrative roles; after all, a full professorship in English, once the embodiment of privilege, looks less sweet these days. Agency also carries *blame*; it was possible, so what's wrong with you?

PROFESSIONAL INTERESTS

Maybe what WPAs really want to sustain is the very construct of writing program administration. With all respect to Edward Norton's character, the first rule of WPA club is to sustain WPA club.

Professionalized writing administration had a remarkable rise over the past four decades. In a recent chapter, I characterized how writing administration transitioned from a more or less accidental role in the 1970s, frequently performed by skilled people with no rhet/comp coursework, to a credentialed role in the 1990s marked by formal expertise, to an intentional role by the 2010s, with dissertations and career goals as WPA. I was wistful about, even suspicious of, this evolution, worrying that it subordinates "writing" to "administration," but my wise respondent, Eliana Schonberg, noted that times had changed, and career pragmatism was reasonable.

With the rise of WPA as a professional identity, sustaining its necessity became fundamental. The shift is subtle but meaningful, paralleling interests that Paul Starr traced for physicians in his Pulitzer-winning *The Social Transformation of American Medicine*. Physicians haven't always or everywhere been venerated. Even as doctors developed expert skills, they also had to develop professional authority: the *idea*, if you will, of physician-ness. Certainly, credentialed doctors making peer-reviewed treatments benefit health care and patients. Likewise, professional WPAs enacting sound practices benefit writing and students. Of course, the ends of sustaining the construct of program administration potentially might supplant sustaining writers and writing. This is the outcome of neoliberal WPA orientations against which Donna Strickland cautions in *The Managerial Unconscious*.

Long before the term "WPA" concretized, the notion that college writing needed managing in a way that, say, Shakespeare or astronomy did not has been part of the enterprise. In a talk at the 2000 WPA conference, Richard Lloyd-Jones noted the CCCC officers' wariness at the formation of the Council of Writing Program Administrators as redundant and competitive. Indeed, among fourteen reports from the first CCCC conference is one from "Workshop 13: Administration of the Composition Course." The report noted that, "[t]he chairman of a mature, energetic, intelligent staff should make himself as inconspicuous as he can; the chairman of a slack, incompetent, bored staff should make himself as conspicuous as he can" (41). The image is good cop / bad cop. The report lists seven responsibilities: hiring good teachers, fostering professional development, connecting faculty to colleagues across campus, fighting for "a fair share of professional recognition," knowing practices at other schools, conducting research, and being a good teacher (42). In many respects, sustaining those responsibilities within the WPA role has been a professional concern ever since. By the way, there's a telling metaphor in the foreword to the collected reports, which calls them "the most extensive and concerted frontal attack ever made on the problems of teaching college freshman English" (3).

STEWARDS, ARTISANS, WRITERS

I've just finished my fourteenth year as Executive Director of Writing at the University of Denver, where I'd come to start a new program in 2006. That I'm still a WPA after three decades (albeit with excursions along the way) is a matter of lamentation, celebration, or indolence. I've been occasionally beleaguered and often wistful, but for the most part, the work has been doable and rewarding.

I've had two consistent challenges. First are emotional: supporting people dealing with illness, doubt, depression, personal and economic struggles, physical and psychological harm, the whole host of human challenges. These elements were clear from the outset; on my very first day as WPA, in 1988, a new TA came to my office wanting to quit because in front of his class, he'd thrown up in a trash can. (I talked him out of it and switched him to a different section.) The second challenge is worrying about the health of the program. Twenty years ago, I imagined myself as provider and partner in "WPA as Husband, Father, Ex." (Surely I can now critique the metaphors.) But even now, during a basement-inducing pandemic, I worry about jobs. Have I done enough, kept us on the knife-edge of innovation, remained vital to the university brand-makers?

In recent years, I've pressed the idea of WPAs as stewards, experts who care for property they don't own. I modify the metaphor to cast writing programs as not singularly owned by powerful landlords (the WPA as Joseph, tending a provost pharaoh's granary through seven years, thick and thin?) but, rather, collectively held by fiduciary faculty performing professional knowledge in the interests of students and of the civic sphere. Rather than being overseer icon, as Jeanne Gunner feared in critiquing the Portland Resolution, the WPA steward is lead collaborator for a collective enterprise. (Gunner would surely have embraced the addition of John Belk's idea of labor activist.) As much as I like the metaphor, *steward* has the taint of servant for some, reified capitalism for others. For WPAs who aspire to leadership and power, the metaphor isn't very appealing.

Among many new metaphors in this book, the one that appeals most is Robyn Tasaka's idea of WPA as artisan. The metaphor recognizes complex circumstances, prizes ingenuity, values craft, resists algorithms, abjures assembly lines. Most importantly, artisanship echoes the nature of writing and teaching as necessarily heuristic. The artisan metaphor scales. I'm not invoking the dead poet pedagogy of Robin Williams or the genius artist ideal of Toni Morrison. Being an artisan involves learning basic techniques, studying with mentors, conducting research, using the best materials at hand, seeking advice, understanding tradition. It means, further, that resulting artifacts, whether pot, poem, or program, require the exercise of craft, often in conditions that conspire otherwise: constraints of time, resources, or circumstances.

Beyond WPA as artisan is WPA as writer. Yes, this means literal WPA job-based writing: articles, curricula, reports, policies, communications, the whole shebang. I surely hope such efforts include not only the stuff of career-making but also the stuff of writerly life for extra-academic readers, friends, even oneself, a gamut of genres. After all, we're administrators not of accounting departments or ice cream shops, fitness centers or insurance firms but of writing programs. Beyond that, I also mean the WPA as writer, well, metaphorically. We ought to conceive of ourselves as drafting, revising, and performing programs, determining stasis, addressing and invoking audiences in kairotic moments, drawing on experience and techniques, sharing drafts, collaborating, all the while working on deadlines: the fall schedule, annual reviews, new WAC proposals, all the rest.

WHY SUSTAINABILITY?

We live in times harshly divided about what should be sustained. Consider our environment. Beyond climate change deniers are worse: people who concede, "Sure, it's happening, but so what?" Even the venerable response, "What kind of world are we leaving our children?" receives naive optimism ("I have faith we'll sort this out"), stoic resignation ("We'll just adapt"), or selfish presentism ("The permafrost may be gone tomorrow; we're living today").

We could join climate nihilists, embracing the fatalistic postmodern position that there's nothing ultimately necessary in sustaining either rain forests or writing programs. This misguided approach might conclude that the profession itself has constructed writing requirements and their administrators as necessary. It might conclude that both exist to serve disciplinary interests in curricular territory and personal interests in identity, economics, and ego. That's a cynical pretext for sustainability.

I understand preserving the guild. If that's all the writers here had aspired to do, I mightn't press the point. But they rightly want more, and so should all of us. Sustainability must be grounded in some good greater than professional well-being. Sustainability matters because writing matters, because citizens and societies benefit from writing done well and suffer from writing done poorly, and because, in current higher education, writing programs offer the best means toward those ends. Better metaphors shape those means. We should use them.

REFERENCES

"Administration of the Composition Course: The Report of Workshop 13." 1950. *College Composition and Communication* 1 (2): 40–42.

Blum, Len, Dan Goldberg, and Harold Ramis, screenwriters. 1981. *Stripes*. Directed by Ivan Reitman. Columbia Pictures.

Bullock, Richard. 2000. Review of *Kitchen Cooks, Plate Twirlers, and Troubadours: Writing Program Administrators Tell Their Stories* edited by Diana George and *The Writing Program Administrator as Researcher: Inquiry in Action and Reflection* edited by Shirley K Rose and Irwin Weiser. *College Composition and Communication* 51 (4), 672–76.

Gunner, Jeanne. 1997. "Politicizing the Portland Resolution." *WPA: Writing Program Administration* 20 (3): 23–30.

Hesse, Doug. 1999. "The WPA as Father, Husband, Ex." In *Kitchen Cooks, Plate Twirlers, and Troubadours: Writing Program Administrators Tell Their Stories*, edited by Diana George, 44–55. Portsmouth, NH: Boynton/Cook.

Hesse, Douglas. 2020. "Aging through the Thirty-Year Rise of Professionalized Writing Administration." In *Talking Back: Senior Scholars and Their Colleagues Deliberate the Past, Present, and Future of Writing Studies*, edited by Norbert Elliot and Alice S. Horning, 189–2013. Logan: Utah State University Press.

Schonberg, Eliana. 2020. "Response: Embracing the Accidental Trajectory." In *Talking Back: Senior Scholars and Their Colleagues Deliberate the Past, Present, and Future of Writing Studies*, edited by Norbert Elliot and Alice S. Horning, 204–9. Logan: Utah State University Press.

Schuster, Charles I. 1991. "The Politics of Promotion." In *The Politics of Writing Instruction: Postsecondary*, edited by Richard Bullock and John Trimbur, 85–95. Portsmouth, NH: Heinemann-Boynton/Cook.

Starr, Paul. 1982. *The Social Transformation of American Medicine: The Rise of a Sovereign Profession and the Making of a Vast Industry*. New York: Basic Books.

Young, Richard E., Alton L. Becker, and Kenneth Pike. 1970. *Rhetoric: Discovery and Change*. New York: Harcourt, Brace, & World.

INDEX

accountability, 9, 26; relational accountability, 20–21, 23, 31
action, collective, 85–86
activism, environmental, 8; labor, 83–84, 87–88, 90–93, 94n4, 94n7, 94n9
activist, 83, 93; identity, 4; labor, 4, 11, 83–84, 87–88, 90–93; restorative, 157; WPA as, 4
Adams Wooten, Courtney, Jacob Babb, and Brian Ray, 7
adjunctification, 88, 89
adjuncts, 88, 91, 107, 164–166, 170, 171, 174, 216. *See also* faculty, contingent; faculty, non-tenure track
Adler-Kassner, Linda, 66, 71
advisor, academic, 114, 116, 117
advocate, advocacy, 4, 90, 91, 94n9, 114, 126
affiliation, 236
affordances, 118, 146, 177, 184, 186, 220, 233
agency, 141, 165, 178, 184, 194, 200, 209, 226, 237; distributive, 161; emotional, 142; feminist, 159; individual, 29; WPA, 37
ahimsa, 11, 123–125, 127, 128–133, 134–136, 137, 138–143. *See also* mindfulness
Ahmed, Sara, 135
airplane, plane, 12, 199–200, 202, 206–210, 212–213, 219, 236
Airport, Seattle-Tacoma International, 206
Albrecht, Jim, 205
Alexander, Jonathan, Carl Whithaus, and Karen Lunsford, 5
American Federation of Labor (AFL), 84, 86
an/Other, 63, 64n6; WPA, 53
Animal Farm (Orwell), 236
anti-exploitation, 11, 83–88, 90–94; principles of, 91
antiracism, vii
Arbery, Ahmaud, vii
artisan, 4, 13, 178, 184–185, 187–188, 239–240. *See also* baker, artisanal; labor, artisanal; metaphors, artisanal; model, artisanal; production, artisanal; tutoring, artisanal

assessment, vii, 59–60, 63, 68–69, 87, 101, 110, 118, 136–137, 165, 178, 204–207, 209, 210, 212, 213, 222, 226, 233n1; self-assessment, 185, 222
Atlantic, The, 147
austerity, 3, 5, 19, 25–26, 29, 51; austerity politics, 134
awareness, mindful, 124–125. *See also* mindfulness

baker, artisanal, 182, 186, 191. *See also* artisan
Bamberg, Betty, 211
Barad, Karen, 49, 57, 61–63, 64n3, 64n5
bargaining, collective, 85–87
Barrett, Frank J., 224, 225
Bartholomae, David, 236
basement, 11–12, 145–150, 152–155, 171, 235
Batman, 236
Benton, Paul, and Rick Seeger, 201
Bergman, Chuck, 203
Birbiglia, Mike, 218
Bishop, Wendy, 125
Bizzell, Patricia, 162
blame, 158, 160, 163, 237
blocking (improv comedy), 227–228. *See also* "yes, and"
Boal, Augusto, 232
bodies, racialized, 212
Bohr, Niels, 53, 56, 58
Boquet, Elizabeth, 6
Bossypants (Fey), 218
boundaries, emotional, 125, 133, 136
Bousquet, Marc, 192
Boxer (the fictional horse), 236
Brady, Wayne, 217
Brannon, Lil, 134
Brantlinger, Patrick, 147
Brereton, John, 148
Brew, Angela, et al., 184
Brewer, Meghan, and Kristen di Gennero, 139
Brooke, Collin, and Allison Carr, 162
Brown, Callista, 205, 209, 210, 211
Bullock, Rich, 237
bullying, 5, 39, 139

Burke, Kenneth, 7, 52, 56; Burkean identification, 53, 56–57, 63n1
Burnes, Pat, 69, 78n2
burnout, 3, 28–30, 35, 38–39, 46, 93, 182, 186, 192–193, 194

Calhoon-Dillahunt, Carolyn, 145
Callier, Frances, 228
Campbell, Tai, 228
capitalism, 4, 8, 84, 239; democratic, 84
care, 9, 20, 24, 125, 126, 130, 200, 205, 209, 212; circle of, 160, 164; ethic of, 227
caregiver, 125
caretaker, 125, 237
Carey, Drew, 217
Carino, Peter, 185, 191
Carroll, Lewis, 152
cartographer, 97–101, 109, 117–119, 134, 166. *See also* mapping
cartography, 97–101, 109, 110, 111, 114, 116–119
CCCC Writing Program Certificate of Excellence, 77, 219
challenge, 237
change, institutional, 29, 99
chaos, 75–76, 181, 206, 220
Charlton, Colin, et al., 7, 35, 49. *See also GenAdmin: Theorizing WPA Identities in the Twenty-First Century*
Charlton, Jonnika, and Shirley Rose, 50–51
Chronicle of Higher Education, 193
circles, interlocking, 12, 159, 160, 168, 169, 174
Close, Del, 219
Code, Lorraine, 129
Colby, Richard, and Rebekah Schultz-Colby, 91
Cold War, 77
collectivity, radical, 11, 83–88, 90–93, 171
College Composition and Communication, 23
colleges, community, 40, 194, 213
colonization (risk of), 100
comedy, improvisational (improv), 216–217, 219, 227, 230, 233, 236
community, 92, 116, 137, 139, 147, 153, 155, 157–159, 163, 164, 166, 171, 174, 178, 187, 200; campus, 37; classroom, 161–162, 172, 187–188, 191, 209, 210; of composition instructors, 170; disciplinary, 223; as a goal, 204; learning, 202; LGBTQ, 228; professional, 185; sense of, 205; as a value, 12, 146; WPA, 10, 30, 40, 41, 44–46
complementarity, 10, 52–54, 56–58, 63n1
"Composition Studies Saves the World!" (Bizzell), 162

concession, 208–210. *See also* Skinnell, Ryan
conflict, 7, 136, 138, 140, 157–158, 163; and commitments, 30; among stakeholders, 12. *See also* resolution, conflict
consolation, 237
consubstantiality, 56
Costello, Bob, Joshua Wachtel, and Ted Wachtel, 158
Council of Writing Program Administrators (CWPA), vii–viii, 3, 45, 46, 83, 94n4, 165, 180, 236, 238; Carolinas affiliate, 223
craft, 183, 185, 192, 231, 239–240
credit, precollege, 20–22, 27
critique, institutional, 99
cycle, ecologically adaptive, 20, 25, 26, 27
CWPA Workshop, WPA Workshop, viii, 5, 7, 110

Dance, Frank, 148
Dating Game, The, 221
Davis, Diane, 64n6
days, basement, 148, 149
Dean, Terry, 136
Deshler, David, 94n1
despair, cycle of, 89, 90
diffraction, diffraction patterns, 49, 57–58
"Disciplinary Landscaping, or Contemporary Challenges in the History of Composition" (Royster), 229
Discovery of Grounded Theory, The (Glaser and Strauss), 69
dissensus, 49, 60
diversity, 11, 83–88, 90, 92–94, 211–212; commitment to, 208; linguistic, 211
Don't Think Twice (Birbiglia), 218
double-slit experiment, 50, 52–54, 62
Dryer, Dylan B., and Mary Plymale Larlee, 78n2
dual enrollment, 21, 26–27; programs, 26; students, 126, 127
duality, 10, 49, 61, 63n1
Dunbar-Ortiz, Roxanne, 23
dwarfs, 152

ecology, 8, 36–37, 40, 46, 50, 129–130, 136; environmental, 9; learning, 199; institutional, 9, 93; rhetorical, 50; writing, 207
Economics of Attention, The (Lanham), 148
ecosystem, 5, 8–9, 25, 27, 44; of FYC, 26; of higher education, 94n7; university, 118
Ede, Lisa, 148
Einstein, Albert, 50
Elder, Cristyn, and Bethany Davila, 139
embodiment, 237

emergence, 10, 50, 53, 57, 61
emotional labor. *See* labor, emotional
emotions, 124, 126–128, 131, 135, 142
empowerment, 161. *See also* agency
enculturation, 100–101, 110
English, Standard Edited American Academic, 30
Enos, Teresa, 146, 147, 150, 154
enrollment, dual. *See* dual enrollment
entanglement, 61
essence (philosophical), 53, 63*n*2
essences (phenomenology), 68, 77
Estrem, Heidi, Dawn Shepherd, and Lloyd Duman, 28
ethics, 62, 63, 186
ethos, caregiving, 125

faculty, contingent, 26, 29, 51, 66, 188, 192, 208, 212–213. *See also* adjuncts
faculty, non-tenure track (FTNTT, NTT), 51–52, 90–91, 94*n8*, 94*n9*, 101–102, 104, 106, 108, 164, 193, 213, 216. *See also* adjuncts
Farman, Jason, 222
farming, factory, 184
feedback, 181–182, 185
feminism, 7, 86
Fey, Tina, 218, 225
Feynman, Richard, 49
fire: American Indian management of, 23–25; antiracist and decolonial possibilities of, 30–31; and burnout, 28–30; as creative and transformative, 20, 25; inner and personal, 28–29; metaphorical, 19, 24–27; and motivation, 28; residential, 19; Tanzanian government's management of, 24, 25; as a threat, 24–25; types of, 20–21, 24–25; US Forest Service and, 24. *See also* firefighter; manager, fire
firefighter, 10, 237; metaphor, 20–22, 28. *See also* manager, fire
firefighting, metaphorical, 19–20, 28; residential, 19. *See also* manager, fire
flourishing, mutual, 9, 24, 31
Floyd, George, vii
forest, 20, 29, 37, 44, 46–47, 116, 119, 159
Forster, E.M., 153
Fotis, Mark, and Siobhan O'Hara, 217–218, 219, 223
Freire, Paulo, 94*n7*
Frost, Antony, and Ralph Yarrow, 223
Fulford, Collie, 225
funding, 168, 173, 209; cuts, 6, 29, 138, 191, 196; dependable, 137; sudden changes in, 19; underfunding, 20

Gadamer, Hans-Georg, 68
game, zero-sum, 133–134
Ganote, Cynthia, Floyd Cheung, and Tasha Souza, 140
Gebhardt, Richard C., 44
GenAdmin: Theorizing WPA Identities in the Twenty-First Century (Charlton et al.), 7, 19, 36
geographies, emotional, 11, 124–125, 134–136, 138, 139, 141–143
George, Diana, 3, 35, 237
Glaser, Barney, and Anselm Strauss, 69
Glenn, Cheryl, 215, 230; and Krista Ratcliffe, 224
Gooblar, David, 193
Google, 218
Gooley, Toby B., 194
Gould, Drusilla, 22, 32*n4*
grading, 164–165, 183, 188
Greenaway, Peter, 97
groundedness, 66, 68, 70, 77–78
Groundlings, 217
Gunner, Jeanne, 239

habitus, white racial, vii, 9
Hahn, Thich-Nhat, 132
Hargreaves, Andy, 125, 135–138
harm, 90, 239. *See also* violence
Harris, Michael S., 133, 134
Heckathorn, Amy, 39
Hesse, Doug, 29, 126, 192, 193
heuristic, 11, 84, 87–89, 90, 92, 93, 101, 110, 114, 119, 121
hierarchy, 12, 146, 148, 215
"Hitting the Ground Listening: An Ethnographic Approach to New WPA Learning" (Fulford), 215
hobbit, 151
Hochschild, Arlie, 126–127
hole, hobbit, 151, 154. *See also* basement
Homeyer, Henry, 153
hooks, bell, 158
Horner, Winifred, 147
Horning, Alice, 223
"How Doth the Little Busy Bee," 151
Hunt, Dexter, et al., 152
Husserl, Edmund, and Quentin Lauer, 67

Ianetta, Melissa, 36
Idaho, dual enrollment in, 27–28
identification, 56, 60. *See also* Burke, Kenneth
identity, identities, 3–6, 8, 10, 13, 13*n1*, 23, 36, 49–50, 53–54, 58, 61, 63*n1*, 98–100, 125, 127, 137, 145–146, 192, 212, 229, 236–238, 240

246   INDEX

Improv for Storytellers (Johnstone), 226
Improv Noir, 230
improvisation, 12, 13, 51, 216, 223, 232. *See also* comedy, improvisational
indeterminacy, 10, 51, 53–54
Indigenous Peoples' History of the United States, An (Dunbar-Ortiz), 23
Industrial Union Manifesto (IWW), 94*n*2
Industrial Workers of the World (IWW), 84, 86–87, 92, 94*n*2, 94*n*3, 94*n*6
Inoue, Asao, 5, 30, 183
institutional ethnography (IE), 98, 101, 119
Intensive English Program (IEP), 111, 113, 116
intra-action, 10, 54, 61, 64*n*2
invisibility, 9, 36
Isaacs, Emily, 203; and Melinda Knight, 145, 146, 148
isolation, 12, 27, 37, 59, 146, 150
Itchuaqiyaq, Cana Uluak, 32*n*4
Ivory Tower, 11, 146, 147, 150–151, 155, 188
Iyengar, B.K.S., 130

Jackson, Lauren Michele, 193, 194
Jarrett, Susan, 211
Johnson, Fred, 146
Johnstone, Kevin, 226, 232
Jung, Julie, 225
justice, restorative, 158–159

Kabat-Zinn, Jon, 131, 142
Kahn, Seth, 5, 8, 89
kairos, 220
Kanellopoulos, Panagiotis A., 232
Key, Keegan Michael, 215
Kimball, Sara, 180
Kimmerer, Robin Wall, 23, 24, 25, 28, 31*n*2
Kitchen Cooks, Plate Twirlers and Troubadours: Writing Program Administrators Tell Their Stories (George), 3, 35, 237
Kynard, Carmen, 8

L2. *See* second language writing
labor: activist, 4, 11, 83–84, 87–88, 90, 92; artisanal, 188, 192; casualized, 4; conditions, 4, 147, 151, 188; emotional, 11, 38, 39, 46, 94*n*9, 125–128; 131, 136–143; organized, 83–84, 87; unions, 3
LaFrance, Michelle, 119
Lakoff, George, and Mark Johnson, 143*n*2, 146, 149, 152. *See also Metaphors We Live By*
land: American Indian and Indigenous perspective on, 20–21, 23–24, 30–32; as commodity, 19, 23; ecological orientation toward, 21; settler colonialist perspective on, 19, 23–25, 31; value of, 10
Landry, Shaun, 230
Langer, Judith, 185
Lanham, Richard, 148
Lasater, Judith, 123
Lauer, Quentin, 68
Lawrence, Josie, 217
Learning, Universal Design for, 173
Leverenz, Carrie, 29
Lewis, Jan, 209, 213
light, 10, 49–50, 52–54, 55–56, 57, 58–63, 152, 153, 154, 160; WPA as, 53–54, 62–63
liminal WPA. *See* writing program administrators, liminal
listening, rhetorical, 217, 223, 225. *See also* Ratcliffe, Krista
lived experience, 4, 67, 68–69, 70, 74, 77, 149, 150, 152
Lloyd-Jones, Richard, 238
Lorde, Audre, 153
Louisiana, dual enrollment in, 26
Lu, Min-Zhan, 225

Maasi, traditional burning practices of, 24–25
Malek, Joyce, and Laura Micciche, 21, 22, 27
Malenczyk, Rita, 148
Mamrick, Marla, 202
management (of people), 4, 8, 11, 20–21, 53, 83, 177–178, 183, 206–207; emotional, 126–127, 134; fire, 24–25, 28; land, 23–24; time, 172
manager, fire, 10, 20–24, 27–31. *See also* firefighter, firefighting
Managerial Unconscious, The (Strickland), 238
managerial, merely, 29, 45, 238
maps, forest fire, 31; institutional, 11, 57, 97–98, 100, 102, 105, 106, 108–113, 116–119
mapping, postmodern, 99, 102
market, farmers, 178, 187, 188–190
Marshall, Monet, 230
Martin, Wanda, 146
Marvin, Carolyn, 228
materiality, 53
McBeth, Mark, and Tim McCormack, 93
McConnell, Karen, 213*n*3
McGlaun, Sandee K., 66
McKenney, Rose, 209
mediation, 11, 68, 74, 76–78
Meeting the Universe Halfway (Barad), 57
metaphors: artisanal, 13, 178, 179, 180, 182–183, 185–186, 188, 190–193, 194–196; classical, 54, 56, 58, 60; conceptual,

145–146, 149–150, 152; more sustainable, vii, 5, 6–7, 9–10, 11, 20, 36, 61, 216; sustainable quantum, 60, 63
"Metaphors Matter: Transcultural Literacy" (Lu), 215
Metaphors We Live By (Lakoff and Johnson), 143n2, 149
microaggressions, 5, 39, 139–140
microresistance, 136, 138, 140, 142
Miller, Susan, 147, 235
Miller-Cochran, Susan, viii, 7, 22, 47, 153
mindfulness, 11, 86, 123–125, 128, 130–134, 139–143. *See also ahimsa*
mindlessness, 127–128, 133–134, 143
missionaries, 4
Mochrie, Colin, 217, 221
model, artisanal, 177–178, 181, 183, 186–187, 188, 196. *See also* artisan
Monae, Janelle, 216
Morrison, Toni, 239
Moustakas, Clark, 67
multiplicity, 61
Murray, Bill, 236

namaste, 130
Napier, Mick, 216
National Census of Writing, 6, 36, 37, 40, 46, 47n2, 51
NEH Consultancy Grant, 203
networks, 130, 221; complex, 20; local, 223; rhizomatic, 6, 39, 46; support, 202
Newton, Isaac, 49
nonviolence, 123–124, 131–133, 140
North, Stephen, 148

Ohio, dual enrollment in, 22
Omnivore's Dilemma, The (Pollan), 177
Opening the Front Door, 140
Ortmeier-Hooper, Christina, 102, 119
Oui Be Negroes, 230
oxymoron, 7

paradox, 7, 10, 11, 51–52, 53, 228; experience, 229; orientations, 11, 83; role, 87–88
particles (physics), 49–50, 52–53, 61–62, 235
Patanjali, Sri, 123
Peace Corps, 4
pedagogy, 4, 205, 239; best practices in, 166–168; diversity-oriented, 211; feminist, 161; restorative composition, 139, 160–165; vision of, 166; writing, 43–44, 53, 201–202, 207
Pedagogy (journal), 26
Pedagogy of the Oppressed (Freire), 94n7
Peeples, Tim, 57, 99, 102, 117, 119

penthouse, 147, 154
performance, 4, 5, 10, 12–13, 29, 126, 127, 141, 217–218, 220–228, 231–233
Performing Feminism and Administration in Rhetoric and Composition (Ratcliffe and Rickly), 7
Peters, Bradley, 100
Petroski, Henry, 199
Phelps, Louise, 117
phenomenology, 66, 67–69
Phillips, John R., 38
Phillips, Talinn, Paul Shovlin, and Megan Titus, 66
photons, 50
physics: classical, 10, 52–53; quantum, 10, 53–54, 61, 160
Pinard, Mary, 28, 29
plagiarism, 163, 171
Planck, Max, 50
plane. *See* airplane
PMLA, 147
Pollan, Michael, 12, 177, 181, 188, 189
Porter, James E., 146; and Patricia Sullivan, 99
Portland Resolution, The, 83, 110, 236, 239
positionality, 50, 97, 100, 118
Post-It notes, 102–103, 105–108, 119–120
practices: best, 71, 137, 161, 164, 166, 170, 219, 224; contemplative, 124; restorative, 157–160, 161, 168–169, 171–172
pragmatism, 11, 88, 238
Pratchett, Terry, 152
Pritchard, Eric Darnell, 230
production, artisanal, 12, 167, 177–178, 181–184, 188, 191–193. *See also* artisan
Professor X, 147
Program, First-Year Experience (Pacific Lutheran University), 199
Providence Journal, The, 153
punishment, 158, 160, 163
Pusey Library, 148
"Putting Nonfiction in Its Place" (Root), 148

Queens City College Freshman Year Initiative, 153

racism, 5, 9, 30, 86, 139; anti-Black, vii, 5
Ramis, Harold, 236
Ratcliffe, Krista, 56, 224, 225, 230; and Rebecca Rickly, 7
Ratliff, Clancy, 26
Reagan, Ronald, 77
reflection, 28, 72, 74, 105, 106, 107, 116, 145, 146, 147, 163, 185
reflection, self-, 11, 124–125, 130, 185

refraction, 49
relational accountability. *See* accountability, relational
representationalism, 53, 57, 64*n3*
Research is Ceremony (Wilson), 23
resilience, ecological, 25–26
resolution, conflict, 158
respect, 163–164; respect, mutual, 165
response/ability, 62–63, 64*n6*. *See also* Barad, Karen; Davis, Diane
responsibility, mutual, 23–24, 169, 220
Restorative Circles in Schools (Costello, Wachtel, and Wachtel), 158
rhizome, 62; rhizomatic metaphor, 35–36, 47; rhizomatic networks, 6, 39; rhizomatic relationships, 10, 37, 40, 44, 46
Rickly, Rebecca, 184
Rider, Janine, and Ester Broughton, 147
Riedner, Rachel, and Kevin Mahoney, 89, 90
Riley-Mukavetz, Andrea, 23
Rings, Mike, 213
risk, 7, 12, 21–22, 99–100, 127, 177, 191–193, 195, 199, 213, 222
Ritchie, Joy, and Kathleen Boardman, 146
Roach, Stephanie, 3, 7, 35
Root, Robert, 148
roots, 10, 11, 37, 44, 84
Rose, Shirley, and Bud Weiser, 237
Ross, Bob, 47
Royster, Jacqueline Jones, 225, 227, 229, 230
Ryan, Kathleen J., 9, 36, 158, 159

Safeway, 189
Sartre, Jean-Paul, 68
Schell, Eileen, 127
Schmidt, Erick, 218, 225
Schonberg, Eliana, 238
Schumacher, Julie, 147
Schuster, Chuck, 236
Scott, Tony, 147; and Nancy Welch, 4
screens, terministic, 35, 227
Second City, 217, 228
security, job, 26, 113, 164
"'Seeing' the WPA With/Through Postmodern Mapping" (Peeples), 99
settler colonialism, 4, 21
Shaughnessy, Mina, 160
Shire, 153
Shrewsbury, Carolyn, 161
Silence and Listening as Rhetorical Arts (Glenn and Ratcliffe), 224
Skinnell, Ryan, 207–208
Smith, Dorothy E., 101
social justice, 9, 29, 142, 212

Social Transformation of American Medicine, The (Starr), 238
solidarity, 3, 85, 86, 89, 94*n1*, 233
Sommers, Nancy, 164
Southern Utah University, 90
space, subterranean, 146, 148–150, 152–154. *See also* basement
stakeholders, 3, 12, 60, 73, 76, 78, 99, 100, 111, 113, 118, 154, 159–161, 164–166, 170–171, 177, 180, 191, 208
Standard Edited American Academic English. *See* English, Standard Edited American Academic
Starr, Paul, 238
State Board of Education, Idaho, 27
Statement on Working Conditions, CCCC, 192
steward, 126, 239
Stiles, Ryan, 217, 221
Stolley, Amy, 66
strategies, feminist, 158
Strickland, Donna, 3, 49, 178, 181, 186, 193, 200, 206–207, 215, 238; *Managerial Unconscious, The*, 238. *See also* unconscious, managerial
Stripes, 236
students, first-generation, 211–212
Stygall, Gail, 146
subordination, 121*n2*, 145, 150
Summerfield, Judith, 153, 154
sustainability, 5, 8–9, 24, 52, 59, 130, 152, 155, 181, 182–183, 186–188, 208, 240; and accountability, 9; and artisanal tutoring, 181–183, 188; ecological/environmental, 8–9, 24, 129–130, 181; emotional, 142; feminist framework of, 129; identity and role for WPAs, 5–6, 13; programmatic, 8–9, 12, 13, 59, 182, 186–188, 240; and resources, 181–182, 186–187; and responsibility, 24; trope, 8; as a value, 146, 152, 155, 183, 208; various kinds of, 5, 52; and WAC/WID, 13; of writing and writers, 13, 238–240

tagmemics, 235
Takla, Jes, 210, 212
Taylor, Breonna, vii
teaching assistants (TAs), 44, 69, 73, 78*n1*, 101
theory, grounded, 67, 69
Thorsborne, Margaret, and Peta Blood, 159, 162, 164, 165, 172
Thud! (Pratchett), 152
Tolkien, J.R.R., 151, 152
Total Quality Management, 186
training, tutor, 43

trees, 10, 20, 29, 35, 43, 46–47, 116, 119, 159
trust, 11, 36, 68, 74, 75–77, 78
"Turtles All the Way Down" (Phelps), 117
tutoring, artisanal, 179, 181, 184. *See also* artisan
tutors, writing, 115, 181

uncertainty, 11, 68, 74–78, 95, 137, 200, 206, 233
unconscious, managerial, 3–4, 49, 51, 56, 67, 238. *See also* Strickland, Donna
uniformity, 177–178, 188
union, industrial, 83–84, 94*n*2; trade, 83–86
United States Forest Service, 24
United States Postal Service, 194
universities, land-grant, 30, 31*n*2
University of Denver, 91, 239
University of Wisconsin–Eau Claire, 6
Upright Citizens Brigade, 217

Van Manen, Max, 67–69
variation (as a value), 177–180, 183, 186, 191, 213*n*2
Vidali, Amy, 39, 86
violence, 123–124, 131–133, 136, 138, 140; emotional, 136, 143
visibility, 75
vision, 39, 42, 58, 70, 75–76, 166, 174, 207, 210

Walmart, 189
warming, global, 24
Watson, Shevaun, 6
waves, 50, 52–53, 57–58, 62–63, 235
Welch, Nancy, and Tony Scott, 4
well-being, emotional, 124–125, 127, 131, 133–134, 136–138, 140
Wenger, Christy, 86
"When the First Voice You Hear Is Not Your Own" (Royster), 227
"White Lies of Craft Culture, The" (Jackson), 193
white supremacy, vii, 4, 31*n*2
Whose Line Is It Anyway?, 217, 221, 228
Williams, Robin, 217

Wilson, Shawn, 23
Wittgenstein, Ludwig, 201
women of color, 229
Wonderland, 152
word of mouth, 177, 186; and advertising, 188–190
workers, service, 127
WPA Outcomes Statement for First-Year Composition, 167
WPA: Writing Program Administration, WPA journal, 3, 35, 46, 86
writer, WPA as, 238–240
Writing Across the Curriculum (WAC), 37, 47*n*2, 201, 203
Writing Program Administrator as Researcher, The (Rose and Weiser), 237
writing program administrators (WPAs): graduate (gWPA), 11, 67, 101, 223; feminist, 7, 9, 24, 29; junior (jWPA), 10–11, 67, 84, 86, 90, 98, 223; liminal, 11, 66–69, 71, 74, 77–78; student, 67; untenured, 66; as writer, 238–240. *See also* cartographer, fire manager, light, improvisational comedy, trees
Writing Program Architecture (White-Farnham and Finer), 6
writing, second language (L2), 101, 105–108, 121*n1*

"yes, and" (improv comedy), 218, 227. *See also* blocking
yoga, 123–124, 128, 130, 132, 141, 143*n1*, 143*n*2
yogi, 123–124, 130, 132, 133, 134, 142
Young, Richard E., Alton L. Becker, and Kenneth Pike, 235
Young, Thomas, 49–50

Zaunbrecher, Nicolas J., 216, 221–222, 228, 231–232
Zawacki, Terry Myers, and Ashley Taliaferro Williams, 202
Zehr, Howard, 158; and Ted Wachtel, 157
"Zero-Sum Game of Faculty Productivity, The" (Harris), 133
zone, contact, 222

CONTRIBUTORS

Jacob Babb is an Associate Professor of English at Appalachian State University. He publishes on composition theory and pedagogy, writing program administration, and rhetoric. He has published articles in *Composition Forum, Composition Studies, Harlot,* and *WPA: Writing Program Administration* and chapters in several edited collections. He is the coeditor of *WPAs in Transition: Navigating Educational Leadership Positions* (Utah State UP, 2018) and *The Things We Carry: Strategies for Recognizing and Negotiating Emotional Labor in Writing Program Administration* (Utah State UP, 2020).

John Belk is an Associate Professor of English at Southern Utah University where he directs the Writing Program. His professional interests include histories and historiography of rhetoric, intersections of rhetoric and poetics, writing across the curriculum / in the disciplines, composition and creative writing pedagogy, and writing program administration. His work has appeared in a variety of creative and scholarly venues, including *Rhetoric Review, Rhetoric Society Quarterly, Composition Forum,* and edited anthologies. He has taught courses in first-year and intermediate writing, business writing, intermediate and advanced technical writing, multi-genre creative writing, writing poetry, and advanced courses in the history and theory of rhetoric.

Ryan J. Dippre is an Associate Professor of English and the Director of College Composition at the University of Maine. His research interests include writing through the lifespan and writing program administration. He is the co-chair, with Talinn Phillips, of the Writing through the Lifespan Collaboration, and chair of the Writing through the Lifespan Special Interest Group at CCCC. He lives with his wife and son in Maine.

Kim Gunter is an Associate Professor of English and the Director of Core Writing and the WAC/WID Signature Element at Fairfield University. She publishes on queer rhetorics, writing program administration, and composition theory and pedagogy. Her publications have appeared in *WPA: Writing Program Administration, Enculturation,* the *Journal of Basic Writing,* and elsewhere. She lives in Connecticut with one partner, two parents, and a three-legged dog.

Douglas Hesse is Professor of Writing/English at the University of Denver, where he was Founding Executive Director of Writing and where he has been named University Distinguished Scholar. He is a past president of NCTE, a past chair of CCCC, a past president of CWPA, and a past editor of *WPA: Writing Program Administration,* among other national roles. His four coauthored books and eighty-plus articles and chapters focus on creative nonfiction, writing program development and leadership, pedagogy, and professional issues in writing and English studies. *Nonfiction, the Teaching of Writing, and the Influence of Richard Lloyd-Jones* (coedited with Laura Julier) is forthcoming in 2023. He sings semi-professionally.

Andrew Hollinger is coordinator of First Year Writing at the University of Texas Rio Grande Valley. He is a recipient of the University of Texas System's Regents Outstanding Teaching Award. His work focuses on first-year writing and curriculum, WPA work and definitions, as well as materiality, publics and circulation, and genre. In addition to his teaching, scholarship, and published work, he is interested in maker rhetorics and is a practicing bookbinder and linocut artist.

Rona Kaufman is an Associate Professor of English at Pacific Lutheran University, where she teaches composition, creative nonfiction, and the English language and directs the First-Year Experience Program. Her work has appeared in *ISLE*, *JAC*, and other publications. She is the coeditor of *Placing the Academy: Essays on Landscape, Work, and Academic Identity*.

Lilian W. Mina is Associate Professor of English and the Director of Freshman English at University of Alabama at Birmingham. She is Vice President/President Elect of Council of Writing Program Administrators (CWPA). She researches digital rhetoric with a focus on multimodal composing and writing teachers' use of digital technologies. She researches WPA work, especially (technology) professional development of writing teachers, program assessment, and curriculum development. Her work has appeared in multiple journals and edited collections.

Cynthia D. Mwenja, Assistant Professor of English at the University of Montevallo, serves as both First-Year Composition Program Administrator and Harbert Writing Center Director. In addition to first-year composition, she teaches rhetoric, technical writing, composition theory, and style and grammar. Her interests include restorative composition pedagogy, writing program administration, and kinesthetic learning.

Katherine Daily O'Meara is Director of Writing Across the Curriculum (WAC) and Assistant Professor of English at St. Norbert College, a small liberal arts college in De Pere, WI, USA. She teaches courses in college writing, rhetoric and composition / writing studies, linguistics, and professional writing. Kat is an institutional ethnographer whose research comprises writing program administration, WAC/WID, accessible assessment, teacher professional development, online writing instruction (OWI), and second-language writing/writers.

Manny Piña is an Assistant Professor of English at Texas A&M University—Corpus Christi; he was previously the Associate Writing Program Administrator at St. Edward's University. His research interests include material rhetorics, digital rhetorics, critical theory and pedagogy, and transfer theory. Never one to have idle hands, when Manny isn't writing or teaching, he enjoys playing piano, guitar, and photography.

Patti Poblete (poh-BLEH-teh) is English faculty at South Puget Sound Community College. In the past, Patti has worked as an Assistant Professor and Writing Program Administrator at Henderson State University and served as Assistant Director of Iowa State University's Writing and Media Center. Patti has also acted as the Assistant Registrar of La Sierra University, where she took a deep dive into the bureaucratic side of university administration. She has been teaching at the college level for over fifteen years. Her research focuses on composition pedagogy, writing program administration, and institutional rhetoric as mediated through social media.

Scott Rogers is an Associate Professor of English at Pacific Lutheran University in Tacoma, WA, where he also serves as Dean of Assessment and Core Curriculum. He received his doctorate in Rhetoric and Composition from the University of Louisville in 2011. His research explores intersections of written communication and public memory, as well as writing program operation and assessment.

Contributors   253

Robyn Tasaka is Tutor Coordinator in the No'eau Center for Writing, Math, and Academic Success at the University of Hawai'i—West O'ahu, where her colleagues Lokelani Kenolio and Kaiulani Akamine have greatly influenced her views on student support, assessment, and navigating the university as a program administrator. She has previously taught developmental, first-year, and research writing at the University of Hawai'i—Maui College and Leeward Community College in Pearl City, Hawai'i.

Alexis Teagarden is an Associate Professor of English and Communication at the University of Massachusetts Dartmouth, where she also directs the First-Year English program. Her research interests include writing pedagogy and its intersections with web literacy and intellectual risk-taking as well as faculty development and evaluation practices. Her work can be found in *WPA: Writing Program Administration, Composition Studies, Forum: Issues about Part-Time and Contingent Faculty,* and *Kairos: A Journal of Rhetoric, Technology, and Pedagogy.*

Christy I. Wenger is the Dean of the College of Education and Liberal Arts and Professor of English, Writing and Rhetoric at Lake Superior State University. She was an Associate Professor of English, Writing and Rhetoric at Shepherd University in Shepherdstown, WV, where she serves as the Director of Writing and Rhetoric and Director of Academic Innovation. She is the author of *Yoga Minds, Writing Bodies: Contemplative Writing Pedagogy* and her articles have appeared in *Pedagogy, JAEPL,* and *WPA: Writing Program Administration.* She has also published chapters in collections such as *Women's Ethos: Intersections of Rhetorics and Feminisms,* and *Next Steps: New Directions for/in Writing about Writing.* She serves on the board of the Assembly for Expanded Perspectives on Learning and is "Connecting" Editor for the *Journal for the Assembly for Expanded Perspectives on Learning.*

Lydia Wilkes is an Assistant Professor and Writing Program Administrator in the English Department at Auburn University on the traditional land of the Upper Mvskoke/Muscogee Confederation (Creek). She was previously an Assistant Professor of English and the Director of Composition at Idaho State University in Pocatello, Idaho, where she had the opportunity to study Newe (Northern Shoshoni) language and culture with elder Drusilla Gould. *Ai'sheN gagu'.* She studies cultural rhetorics, writing program administration, and rhetorics of violence, with the goal of enacting antiracist and decolonial theories in the everyday spaces of higher education and beyond. Her publications include *Rhetoric and Guns,* which she coedited with Nate Kreuter and Ryan Skinnell.

www.ingramcontent.com/pod-product-compliance
Lightning Source LLC
Chambersburg PA
CBHW020522080526
44583CB00013B/705